D1142022

THE ENGLISH CHURCH, 940–1154

0 8 JAN

.6 JAN 2004

Please renew/return this

So that your telephone
please call the numbe

      From Are
      01923 or
Renewals: 01923 4
Enquiries: 01923 4
Minicom: 01923 4

L32   W\

THE MEDIEVAL WORLD

Editor: David Bates

THE ENGLISH CHURCH, 940–1154

H.R. LOYN

An imprint of **Pearson Education**

Harlow, England · London · New York · Reading, Massachusetts · San Francisco
Toronto · Don Mills, Ontario · Sydney · Tokyo · Singapore · Hong Kong · Seoul
Taipei · Cape Town · Madrid · Mexico City · Amsterdam · Munich · Paris · Milan

COMMUNITY INFORMATION:
LIBRARIES

H50 600 858 4

BC   05/01

274. 2'03   £ 15.99

Pearson Education Limited
Edinburgh Gate
Harlow
Essex CM20 2JE
England
and Associated Companies throughout the world

Visit us on the world wide web at:
http://www.pearsoneduc.com

First published 2000

© Pearson Education Limited 2000

The right of H.R. Loyn to be identified as author of
this Work has been asserted by him in accordance with
the Copyright, Designs and Patents Act 1988.

All rights reserved; no part of this publication may be reproduced,
stored in a retrieval system, or transmitted in any form or by any
means, electronic, mechanical, photocopying, recording, or otherwise
without either the prior written permission of the Publishers or a
licence permitting restricted copying in the United Kingdom issued by
the Copyright Licensing Agency Ltd., 90 Tottenham Court Road,
London W1P 0LP.

ISBN 0 582 30288 9 CSD
ISBN 0 582 30303 6 PPR

British Library Cataloguing-in-Publication Data
A catalogue record for this book is available from the British
Library

Library of Congress Cataloging-in-Publication Data
Loyn, H.R. (Henry Royston)
    The English church, 940–1154 / H.R. Loyn.
        p. cm. — (The medieval world)
    Includes bibliographical references and index.
    ISBN 0–582–30288–9 (alk. paper) — ISBN 0–582–30303–6 (pbk.: alk. paper)
    1. England—Church history—449–1066.   2. England—Church history
    —1066–1485.   I. Title.   II. Series.

    BR746.L69   2000
    274.2'03—dc21   00–021676

Typeset by 35 in 11/13pt Baskerville MT
Produced by Pearson Education Asia Pte Ltd
Printed in Singapore (KKP)

CONTENTS

EDITOR'S PREFACE

The history of the Church in England between the early tenth century and the middle of the twelfth, like the history of the Western European Church, forms a definable unit of study. At the beginning of the period it was emerging from the most severe phase of the Viking attacks, an episode which had been particularly damaging in England, towards an organisational structure which created much of the ecclesiastical landscape of the rest of the Middle Ages. At the end, it was moving towards the more predominantly bureaucratic and legalistic institution which was characteristic of the later Middle Ages. While the extent of the physical and intellectual capital which had survived through the Viking attacks should not be under-estimated, the most important force which drove the English Church forward in the tenth century was a monastic reform which drew its inspiration from France and the Low Countries. This drive for reform was harnessed to royal power, an alliance which reached its apogee during the reign of King Edgar (959–75). The greatest subsequent force for change was the late eleventh-century movement known as Gregorian Reform, with its accent on the distinctiveness and superiority of spiritual power and its quest for legal and theological authority, which played such a large part in unleashing the great movement known as the Twelfth Century Renaissance. Here, however, as throughout the period, it is as important to focus on the continuities as well as on the changes.

A distinguished authority on Anglo-Saxon England and the Norman Conquest who has written extensively on the history of the early medieval Church in England, Professor Henry Loyn brings to bear all his formidable range of knowledge on this important topic. Emphasising from the beginning that his subject can only be understood within the social and political context of the times, he sets out a story of evolutionary development, with the Church responding regularly to outside stimuli from the papacy and reform movements in Germany and France. The great political crises, the Danish conquest of Sweyn Forkbeard and Cnut and the Norman Conquest are seen as disruptive episodes, but as ultimately having relatively little effect on a history whose mainsprings were native and ecclesiastical. The office of bishop and its exercise by a large number of talented individuals is throughout placed at the centre of the story, with the bishop seen as the chief source of authority and the link between the political world of the royal court and the pastoral responsibilities of the parish priest. While giving due weight to matters of royal and clerical collaboration, Professor Loyn is also profoundly sensitive to the importance both of the Church's life in the localities and to its inner spiritual purpose. The great figures, such as Æthelwold, Dunstan, Oswald, Lanfranc and Anselm have their place in the book, but it also gives due attention to the parish, pastoral work and matters of belief. The chapters on the Anglo-Norman Church convey very well a sense of the changing times and the evolving climate which led on to the Becket dispute and the stronger authoritarian papacy.

This book is a particularly welcome addition to the *Medieval World* series since it supplies an authoritative survey of one of the important formative periods in the history of England. Vigorously, yet sensitively written, it conveys admirably a sense of the general, of the importance of the individual to the full story, and of the place of the Church as an organisation seeking both to maintain a pastoral and spiritual role and to make sense of turbulent times. The result provides not just a history of the Church itself, but a valuable commentary on the general history of England through a period of two and a half centuries.

David Bates

ACKNOWLEDGEMENTS

My chief personal acknowledgement to be made in connection with this book is to my friend and former colleague, Professor David Bates, who first suggested that I might attempt a short general book on the fortunes of the Church over the crisis of the Norman Conquest, and for his helpful, positive editorial support. Problems, as always, proved even more complicated than expected, but it was indeed rewarding to examine the old themes of continuity and change in relation to an institution which provided plentiful evidence of change in apparent wealth and building techniques and personnel, yet maintained many powerful elements of continuity. The English Church was involved more centrally in the Latin- and Romance-speaking culture of Europe in 1154; it still remained a distinctive English Church, an *ecclesia anglicana*.

My debt to fellow historians will be obvious. The work of scholars of the calibre of Dom David Knowles, Sir Frank Stenton, Sir Richard Southern and Frank Barlow give an essential general base for knowledge, just as specialist studies mentioned in the bibliography such as those of Dorothy Whitelock on Wulfstan, archbishop of York (1002–23), or Martin Brett of the Church in the reign of Henry I help us to understand better in detail the role of the Church in society. Special mention should be made of two publications referred to in the bibliography: *Anglo-Saxon England* (1972ff.) and the *Battle Abbey Conference* papers, now known as *Anglo-Norman Studies* (1978ff.). Without their help it would be increasingly difficult to keep up with the vast amount of contemporary research and thought put into this period.

My personal thanks go to Mrs Attley and to Mrs Venables, who produced a clear typescript out of a complicated manuscript, and to the editorial staff and copy-editor, Justin Dyer, at Pearson Education for the great care they have shown in the production of the book. To my wife, as always, my heartfelt thanks for support without which books could not be written, and for preparing the index.

ABBREVIATIONS

Generally accepted abbreviations such as J. for Journal, Proc. for Proceedings, Trans. for Transactions are not listed below.

Aelfric, *Catholic Homilies*	*The Homilies of the Anglo-Saxon Church*, part 1, *Catholic Homilies*, ed. B. Thorpe, 1844.
Anglo-Saxon Chronicle	*The Anglo-Saxon Chronicle*, ed. and trs. Dorothy Whitelock, 1961. Also in *EHD* i and ii.
BAR	*British Archaeological Reports.*
BIHR	*Bulletin of the Institute of Historical Research.*
Councils and Synods, 871–1204	*Councils and Synods with Other Documents Relevant to the English Church, AD 871–1204*, ed. Dorothy Whitelock, Martin Brett and C.N.L. Brooke, 1981.
DB i and *DB* ii	*Domesday Book* vols i and ii. Referred to in the Phillimore edition, 1975–86, general ed. John Morris to 1977, thereafter under the supervision of John Dodgson and Alison Hawkins under the names of the appropriate counties.
EETF	Early English Texts in Facsimile.
EETS	Early English Text Society.
EHD i	*English Historical Documents* i, *c*.500–1042, ed. Dorothy Whitelock, 2nd edn, 1979. Cited by number of document and at times by page.
EHD ii	*English Historical Documents* ii, 1042–1189, ed. D.C. Douglas and G.W. Greenaway, 2nd edn, 1981. Cited by number of document and at times by page.
EHR	*English Historical Review.*
Harmer, *Select English Historical Documents*	*Select English Historical Documents of the Ninth and Tenth Centuries*, ed. F.E. Harmer, 1914.

F. Liebermann,	Felix Liebermann, *Die Gesetze der Angelsachsen*, 3 vols, Halle, 1903–16, vol. i, 1903.
Proc. Brit. Acad.	*Proceedings of the British Academy.*
s.a.	*sub anno.*
Sawyer, *Anglo-Saxon Charters*	P.H. Sawyer, *Anglo-Saxon Charters: An Annotated List and Bibliography*, Royal Historical Society, 1968.
TRHS	*Transactions of the Royal Historical Society.*
Wulfstan's Homilies	*The Homilies of Wulfstan*, ed. Dorothy Bethurum, 1957.
Wulfstan's Institutes of Polity	*Die 'Institutes of Polity, Civil and Ecclesiastical': ein Werk Erzbischof Wulfstans von York*, ed. Karl Jost, Bern, 1959.

CHAPTER ONE

The English Church:
Monastic Reform in the Tenth Century

We start with a comment on one special feature of church life which is vital to understanding. It must be recognised that evidence for the state of the Church in England in 940 is patchy and hard to assess, and yet in one respect is reasonably straightforward. Thanks to King Alfred and his immediate successors, it had survived with one at least of its essential attributes unharmed. Episcopal government still existed, substantially intact. This is vastly important for the health of the Church and also provides justification for our initial chapter on the monastic revolution. For the tenth-century reformation owed its essential strength to the support of the kings, Edmund and then Edgar primarily, and to the active support of the bishops. To historians accustomed to ecclesiastical history at a later period in the Middle Ages this sometimes comes as a surprise. Only too often the records speak of quarrels, sometimes violent, between monks and bishops, of great abbeys such as St Albans, for example, or Westminster, or St Augustine's, Canterbury, struggling to release themselves from episcopal jurisdiction or at the least to relax the pressure. In the tenth century this was not so. The monastic revival depended upon active positive support from the bishops. Without Dunstan at Canterbury, Aethelwold at Winchester and Oswald at Worcester it would not have taken the dramatic shape it achieved.

The succession to the archbishopric of Canterbury was unbroken, and in 940 that prestigious office was held by the long-serving bishop, Wulfhelm, who had been translated to Canterbury from Wells in 923. York was in a more perilous state. Wulfstan I had been archbishop since 931, and continued in possession of the see until his death on 26 December 956, but the need to come to terms with resurgent Scandinavian power caused him to make many apparent compromises and clouded his later reputation. The southern bishoprics had been reorganised after the Danish wars of his father's reign by King Edward the Elder (899–924) in the first decade of the tenth century so as to provide one bishopric for each shire; and succession turned out to be continuous for Wells (909) for Somerset, and for Crediton (909) for Devon (initially with Cornwall), though complications arose with the later presence of bishops who acted independently for a Cornish see. Winchester (Hampshire), Ramsbury (Wiltshire), Sherborne (Dorset) and Selsey (Sussex) conformed to the general pattern. Canterbury and Rochester looked after the spiritual needs of Kent, while London cast its jurisdictional shadow not only over Middlesex, but also over tracts of what we later came to know as the Home Counties, in Essex, Hertfordshire, and even south of the river Thames into Surrey. Elsewhere north of the Thames in territory still under English control the situation was complicated. In Western Mercia, Hereford and Worcester survived, Worcester as a comparatively wealthy, powerful see. A measure of its importance can be judged by the fact that Coenwald, who was bishop there for nearly thirty years (929–56), was succeeded by two of the most prominent men in early English church history, by St Dunstan (957–59) and then by St Oswald (961–92). Dorchester-on-Thames was a special case. Originally a West Saxon see, by the reign of King Alfred it was regarded as the centre of a Mercian see. A somewhat shadowy though important bishop exercised authority there in the 940s and early 950s, Oskytel (or Osketel), a man of Danish origins who was translated to the archbishopric of York, probably late in 956. Further north, as one might expect, episcopal succession becomes obscure because of the political turmoil of the age. Interpretation of the available evidence depends largely on the view taken of the nature of Danish settlement in northern and eastern England.

The political story underlying such settlement is clear enough. Scandinavian princes, supported by Danish armies and by fresh groups of immigrants, mostly Danish with a strong Norwegian presence in some areas, continued in command of territories north and east of Watling Street from 878 (the date of the treaty of Wedmore between King Alfred and Guthrum) until the end of the second decade of the tenth century. Initially pagan, they were for the most part quickly converted to Christianity. Even so, severe dislocation took place in church government during those critical generations, accompanied naturally by heavy losses in wealth. Such dislocation had a permanent effect on the ecclesiastical geography of England. After 918 (some would say 912 or 914) the political initiative passes into English hands. The story then becomes one of steady West Saxon success, a virtual reabsorption of the Danelaw with sporadic eruption of renewed Scandinavian attack and temporary Scandinavian success. Eastern Mercia and East Anglia appeared to be securely back in English hands by 940. Northumbria was more volatile and Scandinavian kings ruled at York until the defeat of Eric Bloodaxe in 954. Socially and legally the effects of the invasions proved permanent and there is every justification for referring to the whole area in the east and north of England as the Danelaw. Twelfth-century law books recognised that England was subject to three laws, those of the West Saxons, the Mercians, and the Danes.

Within the Danelaw the episcopal pattern was permanently altered. In East Anglia, Dunwich and Elmham had been the respective centres for Suffolk and for Norfolk. From about 870 there is a break in episcopal lists not to be repaired until the middle of the tenth century. Theodred, bishop of London 909/21–55, at one stage late in his period of office, was in charge of Suffolk with a cathedral at Hoxne. It is possible that Norfolk also lay under his jurisdiction. Later in the tenth century a new cathedral was built at North Elmham, of relatively modest size, a centre for an unbroken succession of bishops whose diocese covered the whole of East Anglia. After the Conquest the diocesan centre moved first to Thetford (1072) and then to Norwich (1095). Changes in Eastern Mercia were more dramatic. At the onset of the Danish invasions there were two bishoprics, at Leicester and in Lindsey. Danish success, initially pagan, and the setting up of army head-quarters in the area later to be known as the Five Boroughs (Leicester, Nottingham, Derby, Lincoln and Stamford), entailed a withdrawal of epis-copal activity to the south, to Dorchester-on-Thames. There were attempts in the tenth century, as the Danes were converted, to set up a bishop with special responsibility for Lindsey, but in practice the bishop of Dorchester in Oxfordshire remained in control from the Middle Thames to the Humber, a huge diocese for its age. This arrangement was confirmed in its peculi-arities after the Norman Conquest, when the Normans moved the bishop back to Lincoln from Dorchester *c.*1072 without any attempt to partition the diocese. Further north there was even more simplification. York sur-vived as an archbishopric, though impoverished. In the middle of the cen-tury there was some revival in both its political and financial standing. Nottinghamshire was added to its sphere of control, and endowments granted which included a massive estate based on Southwell in Nottinghamshire and other property at Satter and Scrooby near the Yorkshire border. From 972 an imaginative effort was made to combine the wealthy West Mercian see of Worcester with the archbishopric of York, a combination which appeared to work well until 1016. Subsequent attempts to perpetuate this uncanonical arrangement persisted until later in the Confessor's reign, though, as we shall see, direct intervention by the Pope in 1061 put an end to this combination, which from the episcopal point of view had created a complex of land and authority to rival even the Dorchester/Lincoln see. More dramatic was the fate of the historic northern see of Lindisfarne. Subject to the full fury of Viking attack, Lindisfarne became untenable during the Alfredian period. After much wandering, well chronicled with a fund of good stories, the precious relics of St Cuthbert were taken to safety at Chester-le-Street, where bishop Eardulf (883–99) set up his see. For the best part of a century this remained the episcopal centre, until it was finally transferred to the great natural fortress of Durham in 990. With knowledge of bishops at Hexham fading away into obscurity from the late ninth century and the succession to Lichfield itself doubtful until Bishop Cynesige was translated there from Berkshire in 949, it must be confessed that episcopal presence in the north of England depended almost entirely on York and the traditions of St Cuthbert for long stretches of the tenth century. It is hard to imagine how the basic episcopal functions were carried out without a degree of improvisation and disregard of some of the stricter canonical requirements concerning confirmation and general supervision of the clergy.

For there can be no doubt that the ideal of church government still depended greatly on the order of bishops. Within its limits and inevitable obscurities the surviving evidence points firmly in that direction. Episcopal lists, supported by royal charters, provide basic information about succession to sees, and there was clear expectation that formal canonical practice, as understood in its day, should be observed. Appointment rested in practice in the hands of the king and his close advisers, and bishops tended to come from aristocratic backgrounds. There appears to have been little gross scandal. Bishops were expected to be celibate during their tenure of office. The two most fruitful sources of recruitment were from the royal chaplains and, as the Benedictine Reformation took hold, from the monasteries. Once the bishop-elect was chosen, presumably normally at the royal court, the acquiescence of the clergy was achieved in the form of presentation of the candidate at a formal synod. Steps were then taken towards consecration at a ceremony well hallowed by custom and the law of the Church. The symbols of office, the ring and the crozier, were handed over by the king with the metropolitan in attendance. Two fellow bishops were expected to be present in support for the conduct of elevation to episcopal rank. All was public and theoretically well ordered. Reality was surely different, and matters were conducted in a more haphazard fashion. The consistent elements in the proper making of a bishop were royal approval and public demonstration at a recognised centre, royal court or archiepiscopal see, and also at the diocesan centre.

Election and ratification of election of an archbishop was a matter of greater complexity. This was where an European dimension had to be taken into account, and the authority of Rome brought into play. The custom was firmly established in the English Church that the archbishop of Canterbury, the successor of St Augustine, should receive his symbol of office, the cloak known as a pallium, from the Pope at Rome. No fewer than nine out of the fourteen archbishops of Canterbury who were in office between 925 and 1066 are known to have made the long, perilous journey to Rome, and one at least, Aelfsige of Winchester, designated archbishop-elect of Canterbury in 959, died of cold when crossing the Alps. St Dunstan in 960–61, soon after his highly irregular succession to Canterbury in the lifetime of Byrhthelm, his immediate predecessor, used his visit to Rome frankly for political purposes. Byrhthelm had been a monk at Glastonbury under Dunstan and gave way gracefully to Dunstan and King Edgar; and yet doubts must have been sown in many men's minds. Dunstan used the extra prestige that came from his reception of the pallium at Rome to effect a reorganisation of the episcopate, and also relied on papal support in implementing change to the composition of the cathedral clergy. Even so, the journeying was not popular. A letter has survived from the early eleventh century in which the English bishops protest against the necessity of going to Rome. It is true that their objection lay chiefly on the sums of money, Peter's Pence and other *ad hoc* payments, which accompanied visits to Rome: payments that under the zeal of reforming impulse they associated with the sin of simony. But by and large the machinery for the selection and confirmation of the metropolitan spiritual leaders of the English Church was firmly established, and ran smoothly in orthodox grooves. In this respect England was a loyal part of the Western Church, seeking and finding guidance from the Pope at Rome.[1]

The functions of the bishops, once appointed, diocesan as well as metropolitan, were laid down in many of the legal documents that have survived from the age, especially in the writings of the homilist and statesman Wulfstan, bishop of Worcester and archbishop of York (1002–23). A bishop was a great man, normally drawn from the aristocratic and learned classes. Enough interest was shown in his position by the literate to leave us what is at the very least an ideal picture of what his office entailed and how he was expected to behave.

Sources of such knowledge are three-fold. Law codes issued in the names of the later kings included much material relating to bishops, sometimes embodying the conclusions of what were virtually ecclesiastical synods. The codes known as Edgar I and Ethelred V and VI (Wulfstan's work) provide telling examples.[2] The astonishingly full and complex piece of political and social theory written by Wulfstan that we now know as the *Institutes of Polity* contains sections dealing directly with the rights and duties of a bishop.[3] A

---

1   F.M. Stenton, *Anglo-Saxon England*, 3rd edn, 1971, pp. 486–9.
2   Liebermann, *Die Gesetze der Angelsachsen*, provides the best text of Anglo-Saxon laws (vol. i, 1903 for text under king's name or other title). Ref. to *EHD* i where possible: Ethelred V in *EHD* i, pp. 442–6.
3   *Wulfstan's Institutes of Polity*.

short, compressed anonymous tract, *Episcopus*, surviving from a period late in the Anglo-Saxon age but based on Wulfstan's work and probably from his pen, treats specifically of the role of a bishop.[4]

It is the last of these sources, *Episcopus*, that probably gives the best flavour of the high theory behind episcopal office. A bishop was expected to be an active supporter of just behaviour both in spiritual and in worldly affairs. Instruction of the clergy so that they should be able to recognise justice and apply it to the secular world was placed foremost among the bishop's duties. Peace and reconciliation are his prime objectives and, to effect that aim, he is to work closely with secular judges. He was to ensure proper procedure in the taking of oaths and the conduct of the ordeal. He was not to suffer the use of false measures or unjust weights. Significantly this duty was to apply both in the countryside and in the town. These practical matters are given priority in the tract before the homiletic material which follows in the rhythmic prose associated with Archbishop Wulfstan, though full measure is then given to that material in fine pastoral style.

Bishops were to offer spiritual protection against the wiles of the Devil to the people entrusted to their care, to teach them to distinguish the false from the true, to co-operate with secular rulers in suppressing evil acts. Their example was to be followed by all priests. They were all to share the basic Christian duty of not harming fellow Christians, not the powerful the weak, not the exalted the humble, not the office-bearer (the *scirman*) the subject, not the lord his men – nor indeed his slaves. An idealised picture of a just society begins to emerge in a context where a bishop was under obligation to work positively for the creation of such a society in which even the slaves would work willingly for their lords. The tract presents a typical mishmash of theoretical and practical. It reverts to the practical by stating no measuring-rod shall be longer than the standard, and that all measures and weights shall be equal! In case of dispute the bishop had the deciding word. The homiletic element comes heavily into play at the end of the tract when the reader is reminded that we are all God's creatures (*nydpeowan*), and have a duty to be merciful to those subject to us, in the same way as we might expect mercy at the Last Judgement.

There is a great danger that an excessive weight of homiletic exhortation, evident in the apparent secular legislation of the period as well as in the more openly spiritual codes, can lull us into an attitude of mind where we dismiss it all too easily as pious platitudes. Yet behind all this insistence on the religious element lies harsh reality. The numerous surviving royal codes of law from the reign of King Edmund onwards, notably those of

---

4   Liebermann, *Die Gesetze der Angelsachsen*, vol. i, pp. 477–9.

King Ethelred, are the products of a society anxious, at times desperate, to set up a pattern of an ordered peaceful community in which the bishops would play a leading and dignified part. They were not men withdrawn from society but an integral part of it, empowered to sustain the moral order and also to ensure that the lands and property of the Church were safeguarded. They ranked among chief counsellors of the kingdom, and were expected to attend the royal councils and to give their advice. They, or their representatives, were also expected to attend the shire courts through-out their dioceses, and to play an active part there, sharing the presidency of the courts with the ealdormen. In return they were allotted a high wergeld, or blood-price, on a footing with an earl. Theirs was an authoritative role within the diocese. Of all legal procedures the formal oath and ultimate recourse to the ordeal were key matters. The clerisy supervised by the bishop played an essential part in ensuring that oaths were properly sworn or the ordeal properly conducted. Penalties such as the imposition of pen-ance or the threat of excommunication involved episcopal action either directly or through the sanction given by immediate subordinates. Anglo-Saxon bishops were busy men, massively influential in political as well as in spiritual life.

Wulfstan confirms this picture again directly in what is in its way a theoretical masterpiece, his tract that generally goes under the title of the *Institutes of Polity*. He was well qualified to speak on such matters. A native of the Danelaw, he was trained as a monk at Ely, a true product of the first generation of the Benedictine Reformation. His contact with the Danelaw gave him extra insight and extra political strength, and it was Ely which was finally chosen as his burial place, in spite of his success and active life elsewhere. As bishop of London by 996 and then as archbishop of York (1002–23), with also tenure as concurrent bishop of Worcester (1002–16), he had full and plentiful knowledge of the cares and responsibilities of episcopal office from the inside. He was also no mean scholar and theorist, relying in his own analysis of the bishop's office on the statements of earlier scholars, notably those embodied in the treatise known as the Pseudo-Egbert, which incorporated the advanced thinking characteristic of canon-ical thought during the Carolingian Renaissance. Wulfstan in person combined the knowledge of a scholar with the skill (and occasionally the pomposity) of a homilist, and the experience of a man who had found himself at the centre of political affairs during a period of exceptional turmoil. His ability and force of character ensured him an important role in public affairs as principal legal adviser first to King Ethelred over a long period, and then even more dramatically to King Cnut. How far his personal background in the Danelaw made that possible remains a matter for conjecture. What is certain is that the codes of law drawn up under his direction early in the reign of Cnut remained the standard expression of law throughout the Norman Conquest well into the twelfth century.

In the *Institutes of Polity* Wulfstan drew on his experience to set out in writing what he called the routine daily work of a bishop. He gave prominence to his prayers and to his book-work, reading and writing, teaching and learning, and to his proper observance of church ritual and services. Almsgiving and the humble washing of the feet of the poor were then mentioned. There follows something of a surprise when Wulfstan, who bears much of the character of a puritan divine of a later age, recommends useful manual work (*handcraeftas gode*) both for himself and for his household so that no one shall be too idle. A bishop was to preach God's word in assemblies, in moots, and was to avoid wild laughter and idle childish speech, was not to drink too much, nor to indulge in stupid behaviour at home, nor on his journeying, nor in any place. Wisdom and prudence were the qualities expected of the rank, and a dignified sobriety was expected from all who followed them in their households. The ideal that emerges from the rhetoric rings true to life. Wulfstan expected his bishops to be thoughtful, sober prelates, protected by their special rank, and sensible of their duties as guides, teachers and also rulers of men, loyal shepherds to their flocks.

It is here that we must pause to consider how much weight we should place on this type of evidence. Royal legislators and monkish bishops might well be expected to provide this picture of an ideal bishop. How did it square with reality? Were there not wicked bishops, time-servers, womanisers, men obsessed with power, money, land, resources? All that one can say is that, even allowing for the partisan nature of the evidence and the filter of survival, English bishops from *c.*940–1042, and to a large measure to 1066, present a substantially unblemished front, more conspicuous in its saints that its sinners. There is not an obvious bad hat among them until we reach Archbishop Stigand, and even he has things to be said for him. Frank Barlow, among recent scholars, has looked hardest at the personnel.[5] He reminds us, before we let our enthusiasms run away with us, that there are many bishops, perhaps more than half, of whom we know little more than the name. It would be unreasonable to suppose that some at least of them had not been guilty of the drunkenness, fornication, evil-doing or playing of idle games that provided matter for the fulminations of the pious literate. But of those who have left record (and some records are voluminous) there is one archbishop, Aelfheah in 1012, who received the accolade of sanctity and a martyr's crown from posterity, two other archbishops, Dunstan of

---

5 Frank Barlow, *The English Church, 1000–1066*, 1963: an indispensable guide. The bishops as persons are discussed fully, pp. 62–95.

Canterbury (d. 988) and Oswald of York (d. 992) who were recognised as saints, and other bishops, too, notably Aethelwold of Winchester (d. 984) and, later, Wulfstan of Worcester (1062–95), who were recognised widely and quickly in England as saints. Athelstan of Hereford, after a long tenure of office (1012–56), was also held by later generations to be worthy of recognition as a saint. On the positive side, Barlow found only a few who were open to serious censure. There were some monks who were more assiduous in attending to the needs of their monastic houses than to their dioceses. There were some who with royal connivance were to all intents and purposes pluralists. There were royal clerks who, after their promotion to bishoprics, spent more time at the royal court to the neglect of diocesan needs. There are examples of excessive involvement in politics. Grimketel of Selsey, a bishop in the most English of sees with a solidly Danish name, was said to have bought the office from King Cnut. Only one bishop, Aelfwine of Winchester (1032–47), a king's priest, left a reputation for scandal, and this was probably quite unfounded: he was rumoured to have enjoyed too great an intimacy with Queen Emma. Even after allowance has been made for the chance of survival of scandal, and for a degree of self-imposed censorship on the part of contemporaries, the English episcopate emerges as a model both of energy and of propriety from the evidence surviving from the late tenth and eleventh centuries.

On the simple yet vital matter of the nature of the appointments to bishoprics in the period, enough material has survived to enable us to draw some realistic patterns. The dynamic force in the first long generation, say from the appointment of Dunstan to the abbey of Glastonbury in 940 to his death in 988, comes from the revival of the monastic order of St Benedict. Historians record the phenomenon without truly explaining it. An impetus to ascetic movements, prompting large numbers of young men and women to withdraw from worldly society, is often experienced in troubled times; and the tenth century certainly ranks among the troubled times. Western Europe was still subject to barbarian attack, Muslim raids from the south from Spain and the western Mediterranean, Magyar onslaughts from the east, until halted by the Saxon dynasty in mid-century. For England it was the danger from the north that still threatened, resulting finally in the Danish conquests under Sweyn Forkbeard and his son Cnut. But the monastic revival in Europe, as in England, was no simple eremitic seeking of the desert places. It was a true revival of the Carolingian reforms, involving endowment, building, organisation and, above all, royal patronage. Early attempts by Alfred and his immediate successors had met with only limited success, though some schools had been set up, notably at Winchester, which trained a handful of men, including Dunstan and Aethelwold, who were to revolutionise the ecclesiastical history of the kingdom in the middle years of the century. More will be said of their work when we turn to discuss the monastic and cultural achievements of the age. For the moment it is important to stress one special feature of the monastic movement in its English dimension, namely the ready acceptance by all parties that it was perfectly natural for trained Benedictine monks to accept episcopal office.

The importance of this development has prompted us to place the monastic revival at the head of the substantial chapters. This prominence is justified by the dynamic element in the monastic revival, and yet it must not mask the underlying unity of religious experience, unrivalled in any discussion of the history of the Church at this age. Living as we do in a predominantly lay society, this is a fact that needs something of an imaginative leap. A devout Muslim might find it easier to understand, though he would also be quick to point to some surprising elements of difference from, say, the attitudes towards fundamentalism that he has experienced in Afghanistan or Iran or Algeria. The energies of the monks in the tenth and eleventh centuries were more inward-turned, in two senses. The first of those concerns the personal element of withdrawal from society to live a disciplined celibate life. Such an ideal appealed to a surprising number of young males who had enough of the abstract intelligence in their psychological make-up to develop into adequate scholars and good teachers. The rule of St Benedict was calculated to temper the discipline, and also to allow enough play for talent in schoolroom, library, artist's studio, or indeed estate management, as well as in honest manual work on the soil. Energies also were turned inward in another sense, to concentrate on the inner life of the Church as a whole. Right Order in the governance of the Church was high on the monastic agenda from early days, as we shall see in the establishment of monastic chapters in several of our great cathedrals. Reform of the Church so that the gospel could be better taught was a prime concern; coercive reform of society, so obvious an aim of the Muslim fundamentalists, seems to have been left to the indeterminate future.

The Church and secular society alike were both certainly in a very malleable state towards the middle of the tenth century. Uncertainties abounded in the face of external threats from pagan Scandinavia and also in the dangers of internal disruptions. Stabilisation came from an unexpected quarter in the shape of a wholesale reform of the monasteries with a resulting impact on the whole of English society. The foundation for this development was laid during the reign of King Edmund (940–46), King Eadred (946–56) and, above all, King Edgar (959–75); the three most powerful figures were Dunstan, Aethelwold and Oswald, all of whom came to be regarded soon after their deaths as saints, and all of whom made permanent impact on church organisation in England.

The earliest Life of St Dunstan, written within easy living memory of his death in 988, was revised, copied and received with interest on the Continent; a version was sent to the abbot of Fleury before 1004.[6] In it the writer, to all appearance a foreigner with some personal knowledge of the saint and yet with a degree of detachment from the political life of England, explains Dunstan's psychology in one sweeping comment. He tells how King Edmund at the very beginning of his reign, the autumn of 939, summoned Dunstan to him to take a place among the royal courtiers and chief men of the palace, and how Dunstan remained there a long time (something of an exaggeration), holding in holy governance a pair of reins, namely of the contemplative rule and of the practical life. This was a good image. It was precisely the ability of Dunstan and his key helpers to maintain a balance between their monkish discipline and their practical duties as governors of the Church that enabled them to carry church reform to a successful resolution.

Other sources, lay and ecclesiastical, fill out the picture. Dunstan enjoyed an exceptionally long and fruitful life. Born in 909 into an aristocratic Somerset family, he had connections by blood with the royal house of Wessex. The patronage of his uncle, Aethelhelm, bishop of Wells (909–14), and then archbishop of Canterbury (914–23), and of his kinsman, Aelfheah, bishop of Winchester (934–51), ensured that this able young man was well educated both at the school at Glastonbury and at the royal court. There are stories of unhappiness at this stage, of anxieties over marriage or celibacy, of unpopularity and rivalry with other young noblemen at court. It is clear that King Edmund summoned him as a potential high flyer, and it is clear also he was not a success, so much so that he was prepared to go into exile. Instead, as the dramatic story seized on by his biographers tells it, King Edmund, rescued from certain death, when his horse reared away from the cliff's edge at Cheddar Gorge, attributed his escape to Dunstan, and quickly made him abbot of Glastonbury in the summer of 940.

For the following decade and a half, with the support of King Edmund and even more so of his successor, King Eadred (946–56), Glastonbury became both powerhouse and seedbed for a religious revival, standing out as a superb example of a disciplined house of prayer, education and influence, following the use prescribed in the Rule of St Benedict. Dunstan himself remained a political figure as well as abbot, acting as one of Eadred's chief advisers. On King Eadred's death he fell into disfavour because of his

---

6 *Memorials of St Dunstan*, ed. William Stubbs, Rolls Series, 1874, pp. 3–52: *EHD* i, no. 234. Dom David Knowles provides the best account of the tenth-century reformation, *The Monastic Order in England*, 1940, pp. 31–82.

open admonition of the dissolute behaviour of the new young king Eadwig, and he went into what turned out to be a fruitful exile in Ghent. When Eadwig's brother, King Edgar, succeeded to half the kingdom in 957, Dunstan was recalled to become, first, bishop of Worcester in 957, and then bishop of London in 959. After Edgar's succession to the whole kingdom in 959, Dunstan was translated from his London see to Canterbury, where he exercised a most productive lengthy period as archbishop (960–88). He continued to be at the centre of political life throughout this period, though the active role in furthering monastic reform fell to the other two great men of the movement, Aethelwold and Oswald. A cult, and stories of miracles gathered around him in his own lifetime. By the later years of King Ethelred he was regarded as a saint: the laws of Cnut recognised 19 May, the date of his death, as a named holy day in his memory. Although to some measure forced to share the saintly honour locally with St Aelfheah (Alphege), martyred in 1012, and later overshadowed by the tremendous fame of Thomas Becket after his death in 1170, St Dunstan remained a powerful memory at Canterbury and at his own special monastery of Glastonbury.[7]

The two other outstanding figures of the movement, Aethelwold, bishop of Winchester (963–84), and Oswald, bishop of Worcester (961–92) and also archbishop of York (972–92), both provide parallels and some contrasts to St Dunstan, who probably in age and certainly in rank remained the leader of the reform movement. Both made such impact on popular opinion that they, like Dunstan, became cult figures and miracles were attributed to them. Already by the early eleventh century they were recognised as saints and days in the ecclesiastical calendar were awarded them, Aethelwold on 1 August, Oswald on 28 February.

Aethelwold had been trained and consecrated into priestly orders by Aelfheah, bishop of Winchester (934–51). He was ordained at the same time as Dunstan, when it was prophesied that both of them would in time become bishops. He accompanied Dunstan to Glastonbury but then seriously considered going overseas, an interesting indication of the attraction of the spiritual life of Western Europe at an early stage of the German political revival. King Eadred and the queen mother forbade the move, granting him instead the poorly endowed little church at Abingdon, where he set up an austere monastery on the pattern of Dunstan's Glastonbury. A little later the king increased the initial endowment of Abingdon from

---

7   In the late twelfth century the purported discovery of the bodies of King Arthur and Guinevere at Glastonbury and the resulting inflow of money and pilgrims removed some of the tension that had arisen with post-Becket Canterbury over the relics of Dunstan. R.F. Treharne, *The Glastonbury Legends*, 1967.

40 hides by adding the substantial royal estate of 100 hides to the abbey. A practical man, Aethelwold busied himself with the physical construction of the monastery, and was severely injured in an accident, recovery from which was regarded as a miracle. He had sent his pupil, Osgar, to Fleury to perfect his knowledge of the Rule and he also summoned monks from Corbie to teach the proper up-to-date methods of chanting the psalms. Indeed he should be remembered as one of the outstanding liturgists of the late Anglo-Saxon Church, encouraging commentary based on the work of the Carolingian scholar Amalarius of Metz (c.775–852/3), contributing directly to the proper ordering of the Mass. Later traditions transmitted through Benedictionals and Pontificals of the post-Conquest period indicate a solid continuity of custom leading back to the tenth-century reformation, when the habit of establishing standard ritual and attempting to explain it took root. Texts such as the Benedictine Office, associated with Archbishop Wulfstan, with its free use of the vernacular to translate or paraphrase basic texts, also show the need for precise definition of matters such as the standard canonical hours, a follow-through as it were of Aethelwold and his helpers in the first generation of reform.[8]

Aethelwold and Dunstan had both been influential teachers of the young prince, Edgar, presumably at Glastonbury, and it was natural after Edgar's succession to the throne in 959 and Dunstan's elevation to Canterbury that preferment should be found for Aethelwold. He was appointed to the see of Winchester in 963, and for the following decade emerged as a dynamic reformer, even overshadowing St Dunstan. The Anglo-Saxon Chronicle concentrates heavily on ecclesiastical affairs during the reign of King Edgar, and one version states precisely that the king chose Aethelwold and that Dunstan consecrated him on 29 November 963.[9] In the following years dramatic moves were made. The Chronicle gives the credit to the king, but it is clear that Aethelwold was the active agent. In Winchester priests were driven from the Old and New Minsters and replaced by monks. Similar actions were taken at Chertsey and at Milton. New abbots were then chosen for New Minster at Winchester, and at Chertsey and Milton. Ordberht, who was chosen for Chertsey, later became bishop of Selsey. A great council was held at Easter, 964, at which the king was reputed to have decreed the foundation of no fewer than fifty monasteries. A famous charter was issued in favour of New Minster, which was reputed to be the work of Aethelwold himself. The content of the charter revealed some of the inner thoughts concerned with the reform movement. The Rule of St Benedict was to be strictly

---

8 *The Benedictine Office: An Old English Text*, ed. James Ure, 1957.
9 *Anglo-Saxon Chronicle* (E), *s.a.* 963.

observed. The monks had a special charge to intercede for the welfare of the king, his family, and for the kingdom in general. In return, the possessions of the monasteries were to be placed under strong royal privilege and protection.[10]

Winchester indeed proved a true dynamic centre. New Minster had become a leading new foundation at this stage of the reformation, and Aethelwold appointed Aethelgar, who had been his pupil at Glastonbury, to be its abbot. He also revived the nunnery at Winchester, the Nunnaminster, appointing in that instance an elderly friend of his own family, Aethelthryth, as abbess. With three reformed monastic houses in the compass of one city, Winchester became a focal point for ecclesiastical activity. The fortunate survival of the *Liber Vitae* of New Minster (later Hyde Abbey) gives a taste in content and in the splendour of its artistry of the vigour of the spiritual and aesthetic life so generated. Its pictorial frontispiece of 1031, one of the best-known products of Anglo-Saxon art, shows King Cnut and Queen Emma placing a great cross of gold on the altar of New Minster.[11] Building activity became intense, and archaeological excavation has uncovered the scope of an ambitious tenth-century programme that successfully set out to contain the three minsters within a single monastic enclosure. Principal attention was directed to the cathedral, the Old Minster, where the cult of the obscure bishop St Swithun was revived and a vast western work constructed over the site of his grave. Aethelwold's full plans were not realised in his own lifetime (he died in 984), but in 980 a solemn service of dedication was held by St Dunstan in the presence of the king, the royal court and all the monastic bishops. More than a decade later, probably in 993 or 994, work on the Old Minster was complete, and the new archbishop, Sigeric, rededicated the church in a magnificent ceremony.[12]

Aethelwold's work for Winchester was part, but only part, of his contribution. He was also the principal begetter of the *Regularis Concordia*, a formal agreement drawn up by the English monastic houses shortly after 970, establishing the version of the Rule of St Benedict considered acceptable to them. Aethelwold appears to have drafted the detail but the inspiration and physical power behind the creation came in part at least from St Dunstan

---

10 *Councils and Synods, 871–1204*, no. 31, pp. 119–33. Possibly an expansion of the charter of 966 but certainly in Aethelwold's lifetime (d. 984). Sawyer, *Anglo-Saxon Charters*, no. 745, p. 240.

11 *The Liber Vitae of the New Minster and Hyde Abbey, Winchester*, ed. Simon Keynes, EETF, Copenhagen, 1996.

12 *Frithegodi Monachi Breviloquium Vitae Wilfredi et Wulfstani Cantoris Narratio Metrica de Sancto Swithuno*, ed. Alistair Campbell, Zurich, 1950, pp. 71–2, 270–3.

and King Edgar. Continental reforming impulses were taken fully into account. The version of the Rule drawn up by St Benedict of Aniane in 817 was held as a model, and representatives of the abbeys of Fleury and of Ghent were present at a powerful synod held at Winchester to determine the proper form. Special English features were present. Very conspicuous were the prayers that were to be offered for the king, the queen and the royal family. King Edgar and Archbishop Dunstan were clearly anxious that the fervour behind the monastic movement should not die and maximum royal effort was given to ensure continuity and also a surprising degree of national uniformity. Customs as far as possible were to be uniform throughout the kingdom, helping to cement the relationship between Church and State. The king took pains to protect the monasteries; the queen was to give active support to the nunneries. Abbots were to be elected freely, though with the consent and advice of the king. They were powerful men, often in attendance on the king, substantial landlords with all that that entailed. Much routine fell inevitably on the shoulders of their subordinates, deans or priors. There were hints that the arrangements at Winchester and at Worcester, where the bishops were also abbots, ruling a monastic chapter, were regarded as ideal. The king was seen as performing a Christian duty in preventing encroachments by lay nobles on monastic lands and rights. With proper emphasis on hospitality, humility and good works, the *Regularis Concordia* presents a splendid monument to the vitality of thought and vigour behind this tenth-century reformation.

So much for the political and social background. On the internal ordering of the monasteries the aim, successfully achieved, of the *Concordia* was to provide an up-to-date version of the Benedictine Rule for England. A simple yet austere observance was to be demanded. The life of the monks was strictly regulated around the divine offices. The timetable fitted in meals (no more than two a day), work and sleep to the sequence of services at chapel: nocturns, matins, prime, the first mass, terce, the chapter meeting, sung mass, nones, vespers and compline. Complete obedience to the abbot was mandatory. Silence was to be observed except when speech was necessary. There was to be frequent confession before the taking of the Eucharist. Among the specifically English elements to be found in the details of the *Concordia* were the recognition of provision for local saints and the ringing of bells 'as is the custom in this country'. In theory at least the discipline was strict in a thoroughly puritan fashion: psalms were to be said; there was to be no 'idle gossip'. There was a pleasing and revealing comment on education and caring for the young. It is extremely probable that it was this side of the function of the monasteries, though not overemphasised in contemporary theory, that in fact ensured continuity and full establishment support.

Monastic schools bred the most powerful clerics and administrators of the succeeding generation.[13]

Winchester under Aethelwold became one of the conspicuous centres of Christendom, politically and culturally, but it was no isolated phenomenon in England. St Dunstan was still busy at Canterbury up to the time of his death in 988, and the third member of the active leaders of reform, St Oswald, was also showing himself capable of work of permanent importance at Worcester and then also at York. On Dunstan's translation to Canterbury in 960, Oswald had been appointed to the see of Worcester. Such was his ability and prestige that in 972, after the death of his kinsman Oskytel, and the resignation of Oskytel's immediate successor, he was appointed also archbishop of York. This astonishing arrangement, effective in practice, remained in force until his death and proved a precedent for some seventy years after his death, not always followed, but clearly potent in men's minds.

Oswald's own background was complex. He was a kinsman of the Danish archbishop of Canterbury, Oda, who died in 958, and was therefore well qualified to keep a restraining hand on the Anglo-Danish city and church of York. He was more deeply and directly affected by Continental practice than many of his contemporaries, having been trained as a monk at Fleury. His most creative work was done in the south, where he was bishop at Worcester, a prosperous see, least ravaged by the Danish attacks and settlement of earlier generations. Reform was achieved at a more gentle pace than at Winchester, probably in two main phases, initially in 964–65 and then more steadily in the 970s. From his episcopal resources Oswald set up a small community of monks to service the cathedral. He brought back Germanus, a friend and possibly a former pupil, from Fleury (though previously a Winchester product) to establish a monastery at Westbury which quickly became a powerful centre for the new reform. After King Edgar's conversion to the idea of a wider spread of monasticism Oswald joined Aethelwold in spearheading the expansion not only within Wessex and the West Midlands but also in the Danelaw. While Aethelwold sponsored Ely, Oswald sponsored Ramsey, to the point where he himself became its abbot. He remained so throughout his long career, probably using it as an occasional retreat from the cares of his diocese. Within Western Mercia a spectacular expansion took place with the setting up of Winchcombe (with Germanus moved from Westbury to be its first abbot), Pershore, Evesham (perhaps jointly with Aethelwold) and Deerhurst (as a cell of Bath). Such an expansion involved endowments and caused conflict with

---

13   *Regularis Concordia*, ed. Dom Thomas Symons, 1953; specific references to the ringing or tolling of bells appear on pp. 30, 48, 50, and in connection with burial, pp. 65 and 67.

some of the existing landlords. At Worcester itself Oswald faced no easy task in establishing his community of monks. He had to confront the existing secular clergy and seems to have adopted a similar policy to that of Dunstan at Canterbury, gradually replacing the secular with the regular. The earliest Life of St Oswald, written by Byrhtferth of Ramsey, rejoiced that he caused monks to serve God where once only deacons and birds had lodged. He built a new and large church, dedicated to the Virgin, side by side with the older cathedral (dedicated to St Peter); and in time it was Oswald's church served by monks that became recognised as the cathedral. In energy and achievement Oswald equalled Aethelwold and Dunstan; and if we knew more about his tenure of the archbishopic of York we might even find that he surpassed them.[14]

Indeed it is possible that Oswald's slow but sure success may have been a prime factor in the so-called 'reaction against the monasteries' which came after the death at an early age of King Edgar on 8 July 975. Undoubtedly this created problems. Some ealdormen and wealthy thegns, not necessarily the brightest, must have felt their power or resources had been diminished by the new monasteries or monastic bishoprics such as Worcester, as more governmental responsibilities were laden on episcopal or abbatial shoulders. The earliest Life of St Oswald, in its muddled way, associated monastic troubles directly to a dispute over succession to the throne between Edward the Martyr (975–78) and his young half-brother, Ethelred (978–1016). As far as the monks were concerned, the Life established Aelfhere, the Mercian ealdorman, as the villain of the piece; and this in its Mercian setting may again be a hint at Oswald's success. The reaction may have been violent in some places, involving expulsion of abbots and monks, but it was not deep-rooted. Byrhtferth may have been weak on style but he had some facts straight, and he stressed the support given to the monks at the royal court, notably by the warlike thegn Aelfwold, brother of the East Anglian ealdorman Ethelwine, and the powerful Byrhtnoth, the ealdorman later immortalised by his heroic defeat at Maldon in 991.[15] Men close to the royal centre would know the value of the monasteries to them politically and socially, particularly as their womenfolk grew more involved. Endowment of monastic houses and nunneries did not necessarily involve loss to aristocratic kindreds.

Taking a stand in the early 990s after the deaths of the three great founding fathers of reform, Dunstan, Aethelwold and Oswald, we can see

---

14 *Vita Oswaldi archiepiscopi Eboracensis*, ed. James Raine, *The Historians of the Church of York and its Archbishops*, vol. i, Rolls Series 71, 1879, pp. 399–475. *EHD* i, no. 236, pp. 911ff.

15 *EHD* i, no. 236, p. 914.

what a profound impact their work had on the structure of the Church in England. Merely in terms of number the increase was phenomenal. When Dunstan returned from exile in 957 there were no more than two or three active monasteries as such, though these were men and women who lived austere lives of self-abnegation in rough accord with an ordered Rule. In the following half-century more than thirty monasteries were set up and five or six nunneries. Some of these, like Westminster, for example, were based on old minster churches, but many were completely new foundations. Malmesbury, Bath and Westminster owed much to the direct efforts of Dunstan himself, originating from his Glastonbury interests or from his period as bishop of London. Other, smaller houses were directly derived from Glastonbury, such as Milton and Exeter, Cerne, Tavistock, Horton, Cranborne and perhaps Buckfast. Wulfsige, who had been a monk at Glastonbury, converted Sherborne into a monastery when he became bishop there in 993. At Canterbury itself, curiously enough, there is little evidence of monastic reform. It could be that archbishop Oda (941–58) had already initiated changes that enabled Christ Church, Canterbury, to have conformed quickly to the new pattern of monastic chapter. Oda is remembered for his energetic support of reform in the secular church and also for acquiring relics of the Northumbrian saint, Wilfrid, for his cathedral. He was also responsible for intruding Canterbury interests back into the Danelaw at Ely, and by reversion ultimately of a fine Suffolk estate at Monks Eleigh. King Eadred left Oda a substantial personal bequest in gold and a further £400 in case of need to relieve the people of Kent, Surrey, Sussex and Berkshire from hunger or from the ravages of a heathen army.[16] Dunstan followed fully in this tradition, looked after the affairs of the archiepiscopal see with royal co-operation and was very well regarded there. It nevertheless remains of note that no evidence survives of the sweeping changes in the monastic interest at Canterbury of the sort experienced at Winchester and Worcester. Glastonbury, not Canterbury, remained Dunstan's personal source of inspiration and powerhouse for monastic reform.[17]

Even in the matter of the institution of new monastic houses, it is Aethelwold who emerges as the immediate dynamic figure. Abingdon remained dear to his heart, and the introduction of Abingdon monks into the Old and New Minsters at Winchester was followed in rapid succession by the creation of three of the most influential houses in English monastic history, at Peterborough (966), Ely (970) and Thorney (972). Croyland, St

16   Harmer, *Select English Historical Documents*, no. 21. *EHD* i, no. 107.
17   Douglas Dales, *Dunstan, Saint and Statesman*, 1988, p. 58, comments that it was only under Archbishop Aelfric in 997 that Christ Church became fully monastic.

Neots and Chertsey also owed their origins to this period. St Albans presents more difficult problems. The antiquity of the site, the scene of the death of St Alban, protomartyr, the long monastic history dating from the foundation of an abbey by King Offa in 793, coupled with the certainty of a sad falling-off by the early tenth century, made it a ripe target for the reformers. Aelfric, its first abbot of the new reformed generation, in 969 or 970, appears to have been a monk from Abingdon. If strong St Albans tradition can be trusted, he succeeded an energetic reformer of an earlier type, Ulsinus or Wulfrin, who laid the foundation for a well-organised borough in the 940s and 950s and established subsidiary churches which affirmed the ecclesiastical pattern of the city in the Middle Ages at St Stephens, St Michaels and St Peters. But early Lives of St Oswald give Oswald himself the main credit for reform. We should probably recognise that coincidence of aim among the Benedictines often led to a duality of initiative. Both Aethelwold and Oswald played parts in reforming, indeed virtually refounding, this powerful house, just one day's journey along Watling Street from London.[18]

Oswald's own specific foundations depended largely on his two monastic houses, first at Westbury, and then at Ramsey. Among the houses assigned to him by his biographers in Mercia were Worcester itself, Evesham, Pershore, Winchcombe and Deerhurst. Ramsey was his favoured establishment, the apple of his eye and the training ground for many of his favoured monks and helpers. Activity further north, perfectly possible when we consider Oswald's role as archbishop of York, was virtually non-existent. Only at Ripon is there a hint of some move in the direction of ascetic reform inspired by Oswald.[19] The cult of St Cuthbert was quite another matter, intense, local, old-fashioned and, as far as can be judged, outside the mainstream of Benedictine reform, though it is worth bearing in mind that the body of St Cuthbert, the central object of the cult, reached its final resting place at Durham towards the end of the tenth century, traditionally in 995.[20]

Aethelwold himself operated principally from Abingdon and Winchester Old Minster, both of which houses owed almost everything to him, Abingdon from the foundation and the Old Minster from his arrival as bishop. At Winchester he created, by what was something of a revolutionary act, a

---

18 *Vita Oswaldi*, ed. Raine, p. 427.

19 Knowles, *Monastic Order*, p. 52.

20 *St Cuthbert. His Cult and his Community to AD 1200*, eds Gerald Bonner, David Rollason and Clare Stancliffe, 1989, esp. pt 4, pp. 367–467, which deals with St Cuthbert's community at Chester-le-Street and Durham.

monastic chapter, so setting an example which was to emerge as one of the principal peculiarities of English ecclesiastical history in the following centuries, cathedrals ruled by bishops who were also abbots. His zeal in propagating the monastic message was intense. If the Ely records may be believed, that great Fenland abbey also became a focal point for spreading the monastic culture. Aethelwold's personal endowment of the abbey suggests great private wealth, some apparently inherited. He also found patrons for Ely, notably the wealthy thegn Wulfstan of Dalham (near Newmarket). At Peterborough, known as Medeshamstede until the refoundation, he bought the site, establishing Aldulf there as abbot, who afterwards succeeded Oswald as bishop of Worcester and archbishop of York. His personal gifts to Peterborough were lavish, including church ornaments, a Gospel Book, crosses, candlesticks, bells, vestments and, most interesting of all, books, which included works of St Augustine, Bede and Isidore of Seville.[21] Some estates given illustrate the wealth of Aethelwold and his skill in effecting suitable exchanges which helped him to consolidate land-holding into more efficient units. We are occasionally provided with insights into how these acquisitions were made. A charter tells us of the dramatic process by means of which Aethelwold acquired Ailsworth in Northamptonshire in exchange from a certain Wulfstan, son of Aelsi. A widow and her son had practised witchcraft on Aelsi by pin-sticking. Found guilty, the widow was drowned at London Bridge, while her son became an outlaw. Their estate at Ailsworth was forfeit to King Edgar, who gave it to Wulfstan, who then exchanged it with Aethelwold.[22] Thorney was also directly patronised by Aethelwold, and its first abbot, Godeman, was, on his own testimony, presumably when still chaplain to the bishop at Winchester, responsible for the splendid Benedictional associated with Aethelwold and the Winchester school.[23] Other houses owed much, directly or indirectly, to the active bishop of Winchester. The example of Abingdon and of Winchester itself was transmitted through Peterborough and Ely to Croyland, St Neots, Stow and Chertsey, ultimately to Bury St Edmunds and St Benet's Holme; and some of the West Country monasteries clearly had some association in the early stages with Aethelwold. Indeed to divide the foundations up into rigid groups can itself be very misleading. The impetus behind the creation of so many monasteries at this period was national, and the king, Dunstan, Aethelwold

---

21   A.J. Robertson, ed., *Anglo-Saxon Charters*, 2nd edn 1956, no. 39, pp. 72–5.
22   Ibid., no. 37. *EHD* i, no. 112.
23   Francis Wormald, *The Benedictional of St Aethelwold*, 1959; also J.J.C. Alexander, 'The Benedictional of St Aethelwold and Anglo-Saxon Illumination of the Reform Period', *Tenth-Century Studies*, ed. David Parsons, 1975, ch. 12, pp. 169–83.

and Oswald deserve jointly the credit for the creation of institutions that were to have permanent impact on English society.

There remains one important element in the revival which we have scarcely touched on, and that is the role of women in the whole movement. There is plentiful evidence of support from royal and aristocratic ladies, queens, queen mothers and the wives or widows of ealdormen. As part of his Winchester reforms, Aethelwold saw to it that the royal kinswoman Etheldreda was set up as the abbess of the Nunnaminster. King Edgar's third wife, Aelfthryth, was among the foremost of those who helped to foster and encourage the creation of monasteries. According to the preface of the *Regularis Concordia*, of which a copy was made expressly for nunneries, she had a special responsibility for all the English nunneries. Yet it does not seem from the evidence that a great deal of this support was channelled into the creation of institutions for women. Only nine nunneries as such are known in pre-Conquest days, two of which admittedly were very wealthy, Wilton and Shaftesbury.[24] Barking and Romney were also substantially endowed, but the others, Leominster, the Nunnaminster itself at Winchester, Amesbury, Wherwell and Chatteris, rank among the minor houses. Anglo-Saxon wills from time to time indicate the existence of small household communities of religious women, pledged to a celibate life, widows of great men with their servants free or unfree. In Ethelred's reign a cloistered nun was referred to as a *myncen*, but a woman living outside a nunnery under religious vows was called a *nunne*. Nunneries themselves were more aristocratic in personnel even than monasteries, as far as can be judged. But it is fair to record a strong feminine element in support of the religious revival both physically and psychologically. Encouragement was strong in endowment, in gifts, and in especial concern over spiritual and physical safeguards and in education.

Endowment of the new institutions quickly became a matter of grave social concern. The commitment of a heavy proportion of national resources to monasteries led to calculable social tension. Thirty or so virtually new institutions made a formidable impact on resources and on manpower. At a time when 300 hides was regarded as a proper endowment for a bishopric, Abingdon, an influential house, though not among the largest, ranking eighth in value at the time of Domesday Book, expected an endowment of 100 hides, that is, the equivalent of the returns from the equivalent of some twenty moderately sized villages.[25] In terms of manpower, each

---

24 Knowles, *Monastic Order*, pp. 136–7.
25 F.M. Stenton, *The Early History of the Abbey of Abingdon*, 1913. Knowles, *Monastic Order*, app. vi, p. 702 (value of £462.3.3).

reformed monastery would have at least twelve monks, and some exceeded that figure by a substantial factor, holding perhaps as many as fifty or sixty tonsured monks.

We may wonder where the men (and the women, too, for that matter) came from, prepared to dedicate their lives to prayer, liturgy and hard labour. The genuine and deep religious impulse behind the movement must not be neglected. Insistence on celibacy was strict, and the harsh regulation of daily life expressed in monastic regulations can be interpreted in modern psychological terms as a deliberate attempt to control, suppress and rechannel the sexual drive of the young oblates. The element of sacrifice involved in taking the tonsure must have been only too evident to those who finally took the decisive step.

We have a growing awareness that the tenth-century revival, following dramatic reform movements on the Continent, notably in Lorraine and Burgundy, is itself a symptom of economic recovery and growth, bearing with it the existence of some surplus population in significant age-groups. The tenth century in general, which for long has been regarded as a desperately low period in the history of Western Europe, is receiving a better press. The development of a more efficient agrarian base associated with the extension and stabilisation of a manorial economy is one factor. Increasing regular trade through the widespread establishment of towns or potential towns is another. Fear of absolute disruption at the hands of barbarians was still powerful in the first half of the century. Against that, the military and political success of the Saxon house in Germany, of some of the great princely families in France and of the West Saxon dynasty in England gave a measure of peace over significant areas. Local landlords could provide similar protection in smaller localities.

Within this more hopeful framework, reformed monasteries could play a significant role. For, as we have said before, monks were not idle. Abbots were expected to play a prominent part in the royal council. In the German empire after 962 and in King Edgar's England their wealth brought consequent and increasing responsibility. Abbots, like bishops, were also administrators, exercising legal and financial authority. Outstanding examples occur in the Danelaw, where Ely and later Bury St Edmunds enjoyed legal lordship over many hundreds of Suffolk. In Worcester the abbot-bishop held a prosperous estate stretching over three hundreds that came to be known as the Oswaldslaw, that is to say, the territory subject to the jurisdiction of St Oswald, the patron saint of Worcester. For men willing to accept celibacy and the discipline of the cloister, withdrawal from society to a life of prayer and liturgical service was an option but by no means the only option. An active life of surprising vitality was also possible in building, teaching, scholarship, illuminating manuscripts, estate management, and many other fields. All such activities, of course, would be conducted within the framework of a disciplined Rule which ordered life according to a liturgical clock of proper hours and proper devotion.

For many reasons, political and institutional as well as social, monastic reform justifies a degree of priority in a discussion of the English Church during the later tenth century. By 1000 a network of monasteries, many new and some re-founded, existed as powerful influences on the neighbourhoods in southern England, and also on the royal and national scene. They represent elements of potential stability in a country still subject to pagan attack, ravaged by Scandinavian pirates intent on booty and ultimately on political conquest. The existence of monasteries gives substance to the statements of homilists and law-givers who set out their ideals of Christian kingship. They offer hope of providing trained men who can translate these ideals into reality.

CHAPTER TWO

Reform and its Impact on the English Church: The Age of Aelfric and Wulfstan

Monastic reform has rightly been given precedence because it is there in the monasteries that the dynamic for the age can be discerned in ecclesiastical and cultural affairs. In the generation that ran from the reforms at Glastonbury in the 940s to the accession of King Ethelred in 978 political advance was made that led to a creation of a true monarchy of England under King Edgar and at the same time ecclesiastical life was revitalised, principally through the impetus provided by the sheer size and success of the monastic revival. The fruits of the activity became apparent in the succeeding generation. Political turmoil ending in Danish Conquest has obscured understandably the extraordinary achievements of administrators and scholars during the reign of King Ethelred (978–1016). The Anglo-Saxon Chronicle, in itself a fine vernacular composition, tells a sorry story of mismanagement, treachery, waste and final disaster. Not even the bravery of Ethelred's son and immediate short-lived successor, Edmund Ironside, can temper the sense of ineffectiveness and decline. Yet the substructure is surprisingly strong. In law-giving and in the means of implementing law through public courts in shires, wapentakes and hundreds, England was without equal in Western Europe. The tax system and the coinage was sophisticated. The revived monastic order provided the manpower and to some extent the ethos in consolidating these achievements.

From the beginning, careful attention was paid to education. There already existed much that the new men could build on, general awareness of the basic importance of the Bible with its storehouse of examples, and the works of the great Fathers of the early Church, St Augustine of Hippo, St Jerome and, above all in the English context, St Gregory the Great, Pope from 590 to 604 and initiator and inspirer of the Conversion of the English. The heritage from King Alfred's work was impressive, including the physical possession of the translations made at his command from Latin into Anglo-Saxon. What made the contribution of the teaching generation unique in the later tenth century was the heavy concentration on the vernacular. English prose blossomed under their ministrations into a flexible and controlled medium of communication. The use to which it was put was not as an instrument of original thought but rather as a practical means of disseminating religious, legal, and social ideas necessary for the creation of a Christian community.

The two commanding figures in this making of a true Golden Age of English Prose were Wulfstan and Aelfric. We have already mentioned Wulfstan in connection with his description of the duties of a bishop, and he does indeed seem to touch society at so many points as a statesman, a leader of the Church, and as an homilist. Both men were blessed with a long and active life. Born in the 950s, they were of a generation ready and able to benefit from the enthusiasm of the first flood of monastic reformers. Wulfstan's career took him to high episcopal office at London (996), Worcester (1002–16) and York (1002–23). Aelfric's path was quieter but also distinguished, first at Winchester (972–87), then as abbot of Cerne (987–1004), and then to Eynsham, where he remained as abbot until his death, probably in the early 1020s.

Both were, needless to say, well trained in Latin and perfectly capable of writing well in that tongue. However, they, and their fellow scholars, were more intent on moulding the English language into an effective means of communicating basic religious truths. In one sense they were in immediate descent from the powerful Alfredian scholars who attempted to make the works essential for a Christian available to an English-speaker, but they went further. Through homilies and pastoral letters they aimed to spread orthodox doctrine widely through their settled communities. They had even more of a direct missionary flavour to their work, much of it in a new Anglo-Danish society, than had been the case with the Alfredians. Local rulers and men of influence, ealdormen and thegns, asked Aelfric expressly for more work in the vernacular so that Christian teaching could reach the whole population. In practice they and other contemporary scholars, notably Byrhtferth at Ramsey, went far beyond even that brief. Tracts on science, grammar and philosophy were written, as well as lives of saints and commentaries on the Bible and on doctrine. Among surviving manuscripts, versions of the first six books of the Old Testament and the West Saxon Gospels serve to remind us that these were the only significant prose translations into English before the time of Wycliffe. As such they continued to be used well into the twelfth century.

Wulfstan, a formidable gentleman-scholar with a fine command of Latin, was fully capable of correcting his scribe's manuscripts in his own distinctive hand. Manuscripts were for the most part written in a very clear and disciplined fashion and yet often enlivened with line-drawings conspicuous for their vitality and also for their pedagogic quality. Even the most cursory examination of the prose that has survived from this period brings to mind the purposeful educational policy that lay behind the enterprise. Aelfric's Catholic Homilies, to take an outstanding example, provided a set of writings, sermons or basic material for sermons, applicable to the whole Christian year, a treasure house to draw from for any conscientious priest. Exact analysis of the grammar and vocabulary of the scholars has enabled modern historians to appreciate fully the achievements of the age in linguistic and also in educational dimensions. Aethelwold at Winchester emerges as a central figure to the whole enterprise, but substantial unnamed teachers and supporting priests and monks were soon involved. The practical skills of scholars and artists from Winchester, Canterbury, Glastonbury, Worcester and Abingdon had a cumulative impact. One can sense the underlying discipline of the Benedictine Order applied to lexicographical and grammatical problems to achieve a broader command of Latin and English in a manner not unworthy of earlier and later Academies. The polish and control of Aelfric's writings at his best provide supreme examples of its success.[1]

The high quality of Old English prose gives a solid background to religious instruction. It is altogether remarkable, given the troubled state of King Ethelred's reign, to recognise that basic religious knowledge was widely diffused. In the Danelaw as well as in the inner heart of Christian England, south and west of Watling Street, the Christian message became better known and more deeply understood. Wulfstan in particular, preacher as well as homilist, used poetic rhythms native to Anglo-Saxon to drive home the Christian message. As a teacher of Christian social discipline he was exceptionally powerful, using his high rhetoric to maximum effect. No remote scholar, he knew what the clergy needed. His constant iteration of the eight (but not seven!) deadly sins was calculated to give any local preacher full measure for his moral sermons and exhortations: covetousness, greed, lust, wrath, depression, sloth, vainglory and pride. The corresponding virtues were perhaps a shade less attractive to the preacher but are still naturally

---

1 Milton McC. Gatch, *Preaching and Theology in Anglo-Saxon England: Aelfric and Wulfstan*, 1997. Good guides to bibliography are given in the relevant sections of *EHD* i, 1979 and in Simon Keynes, *Anglo-Saxon History: A Select Bibliography*, 3rd rev. edn, *Old English Newsletter: Subsidia*, 13, Western Michigan University, 1998. A perceptive general discussion is given by Joyce Hill, 'Monastic Reform and the Secular Church: Aelfric's Pastoral Letters in Context', *England in the Eleventh Century*, ed. Carola Hicks, 1992, pp. 103–18.

prominent in the works transmitted by the homilists. In one of his finest sermons, written carefully for use and also for transmission to posterity, Wulfstan conflated the two in a set of oppositions, any one of which would provide matter for a sermon:

> Dear people, earnestly I betreat you, turn from evil and from unrighteousness, and turn to good works, ever the longer so the greater. Consider carefully God's law and hold fast to it, and often in the course of the year prepare yourself for your communion. Alas, dear people, do not delay, in no wise delay, but hasten often and turn to God. And he who was covetous of other men's things and possessions, let him be generous of his own things and eager in almsgiving. He who was greedy, let him be temperate; and he who was lustful in foul adultery, let him be cleaner in his own soul. He who was full of wrath, let him be mild and gentle. He who was depressed, let him be joyful. He who was slothful, let him be diligent. He who in vainglory sought empty honours, let him take anxious thought how he might best please his Creator. He who was proud, let him be humble.[2]

In typical fashion Wulfstan, having faithfully worked through the eight sins, finds that he cannot check his rhetoric and in the same style adds what can best be called illustrative embroidery, further parsonical ammunition with which to discipline a congregation:

> He who was a thief, let him work for good with righteous toil. He who was lazy, let him be truly wakeful. He who was tardy, let him be punctual, often in church for his own needs. He who was a liar, let him turn to the truth. He who was a backbiter, let him be guarded in his speech. He who was foolish in talk, let him be wise in his words. And he who had been active in evil-doing, let him busy himself with holy prayers. And he who lacked belief in the true faith, let him believe in righteous godliness. Thus man shall make amends with right from each wrong, and weed out the weeds, and cultivate the good seed.

Wulfstan could also use his talents to political ends. In his most impassioned sermon, delivered at a moment of political crisis when it seemed that not only the Danish armies under King Sweyn would triumph but also heathenism, he attributed the disaster to the sins of the people. He expressed his view vigorously in a magniloquent purple passage in his *Sermo Lupi ad Anglos*, the Sermon of the Wolf to the English:

---

2 *Wulfstan's Homilies*, no. Xc, pp. 206–7.

Here in this land, as is plain to see, too many are grievously injured through the afflictions of sin. Here are killers of men and killers of kinsfolk and slayers of priests and persecutors of monasteries, and here are perjurers and murderers, and here are prostitutes and murderers of children and many foul perjured fornicators, and here are witches and sorcerers, and here are thieves and robbers and plunderers, and, in short, countless crimes and wicked acts of every kind. And we are not ashamed of them at all, but we are ashamed of beginning atonement as books teach, and that is plain to see in this wretched people corrupted by sin.[3]

The new mastery of English and confidence in the vernacular proved to be one of the most effective and slightly surprising outcomes of the Benedictine revival.

Necessary emphasis on this revival must not blind us to coincidental developments in the secular church. Bishops (some of whom were also abbots), cathedrals, abbots and monasteries provided the dynamic focus for religious activity, but all this could only too easily prove to be remote from the villages and rudimentary manors of a still overwhelmingly agrarian England. Aelfric himself was fully aware of what had been achieved and also of where the dangers lay. In his grammar and glossary he asked in his introduction where wise teachers were to come from among God's folk unless they were well instructed in their youth. He warned against possible cooling off and decay in England, even as had occurred some few years before when no English priest could so much as understand even a single letter in Latin until Dunstan and Aethelwold had revived learning among the monks. He looked back, in common with the literate of his age and generation, to King Edgar's reign as a true Golden Age when the king fostered what he referred to as *Christendom*, helped by Dunstan the steadfast (*se anraeda*) and Aethelwold the man of honour (*se arwista*). There can be no doubt that an ideal picture of a Christian community, a theocracy, existed in full vigour with the higher clergy.[4]

These theoretical notions seem for once to have been properly mirrored by activity on the ground. Monasteries were sure enough the spearhead of reform, but the recipients were immediately the villages, hamlets, and also the towns and townships of tenth-century England, markedly so south of the Humber, and even in the Anglo-Scandinavian regions of the territory of the Five Boroughs and East Anglia. Pastoral care throughout the early

---

3   Ibid., no. 20, pp. 271–2. Wulfstan, *Sermo Lupi ad Anglos*, ed. Dorothy Whitelock, 3rd edn, 1965 – also translated *EHD* i, no. 240, p. 933.

4   *Aelfrics Grammatik und Glossar*, ed. Julius von Zupitza, Berlin, 1880, p. 3: Aelfric, *Lives of Three English Saints*, ed. G.I. Needham, revi. edn, 1976, pp. 80–1.

Anglo-Saxon period had depended greatly on episcopal initiative exercised through churches confusingly called *monasteria*, minster churches as we translate the term, occupying central sites. Such minsters would be served by groups of priests and helpers, not normally bound by the discipline of a formal Rule. By 800 it has been estimated that there were few settlements in lowland England that were more than five or six miles from a minster. The term 'minster' itself covered a variety of establishments, but normally involved a group of clergy, some priests, many deacons, responsible for the routine everyday religious life of the community: baptism, marriage, provision of regular services, especially the mass, and burial of the dead. The enactments of church councils in the eighth and ninth centuries make it clear that bishops tightened their control over minsters to the point where in theory at least they supplied their communities with an effective pastoral structure.

One must not imagine too ordered a structure. Buildings were often rudimentary. Use of holy places and customs even from pagan days was to be expected: holy wells, rough crosses at a central point or odd topographical feature, hill or grove. King Alfred had tried to bring more system into the organisation. Clear provision was made for sanctuary at churches, with care taken that the church building itself should not be out of use during the period in which the criminal or suspected criminal or fugitive was being held.[5] Legal evidence, reflecting the practice of a violent age, was confused and episodic until, in the full flood of the early days of monastic reform, King Edgar issued a code of laws at Andover, making a firm bid to clarify essential financial points about ecclesiastical rights and dues, and in so doing to clarify the nature and status of various types of church.[6]

The importance of this code has long been recognised. It is the first royal enactment to declare legal penalties for the non-payment of tithes. Tithes were to be paid to the old minsters, that is, to the long-established minster churches of the kingdom. They were to be paid from all land that had been brought under the plough, both from the thegn's demesne and from the land of his tenants. A thegn who had a church with a graveyard on his own estate, or on his bookland, was allowed to pay a third of his tithes into that church; if there was no graveyard, his priest was to have a degree of choice from the remaining nine tenths. Traditional dues known as church-scot and plough-alms were to be rendered to the old minster from every free hearth. Payments were to be made according to the rhythm of the liturgical year: plough-alms fifteen days after Easter, the tithe of all young stock by

---

5   Alfred, 5, 5.1. *EHD* i, p. 410.
6   Edgar, 1–5. *EHD* i, pp. 431–2.

Pentecost, the fruits of the earth by the equinox, and all church-scot by Martinmas. Failure to pay the tithes involved royal and episcopal discipline and severe penalties. The king's reeve, the bishop's reeve and the mass-priest were empowered to seize the minster's tithe without the consent of the offender and to leave him with one tithe only. The remaining eight parts of the yield were to be divided into two, half for the lord of the estate, half for the bishop. This harsh rule was to apply whether the offender was a king's man or a thegn's. Presumably the possibility that a thegn himself should withhold tithes was unthinkable. On top of all this, Peter's Pence was rigorously defined. Every hearth-penny had to be paid by St Peter's Day, 29 June. Failure to pay incurred penalties of almost unbelievable severity. If not paid by the appointed day, a further 30 pence had to be found in addition; and the culprit was to take it to Rome himself and bring back a document of receipt to prove that he had paid it. On his return a further 120 shillings was to be handed to the king, enough to bankrupt the poor man. The payment to the king was increased to 200 shillings on a second offence, and a third failure was to be followed by forfeiture of all his property.[7] It is hard to see how such draconian decrees could possibly have been implemented. Threats rather than reality is the likely answer, threats enough to increase the pressure on the poor man until his subservience to his lord who could afford to pay for him was complete. The code was rounded off by regulation for Sunday observance (from Saturday noon to Monday) and other festivals, Friday fasting, payments for every Christian soul, and right of sanctuary.

For insight into the workings of what was virtually in theory a theocracy, the code is illuminating. Minsters emerge clearly as important disciplinary and financial institutions in such a set-up. But side by side with the old minsters there also existed a multiplicity of lesser churches, some with grave-yards, some without, that had been founded by thegns on their own land. We have been less free than historians of corresponding institutions in Germany in attributing generalised names to them, and yet there is much evidence to support the existence in Anglo-Saxon England as much as in Old Saxony of so-called 'territorial churches' and principles of 'landlord control'. Tenth-century English thegns, and especially those designated king's thegns, were developing fast into what can be called for all practical purposes a landed class. For understandable reasons, the term 'feudal' has gone into disrepute among historians, possibly temporarily only. And yet when a clear distinction is made, as among the best of French historians, between

---

7   Edgar, 41–3. *EHD* i, p. 432. H.R. Loyn, 'Peter's Pence', *Lambeth Palace Library Annual Report*, 1984, pp. 10–20.

feudalism and manorialism, feudal terminology is useful and helpful. In England, in common with much of the Western world, the tenth century was the period when much of the organisation of a great part of our agrarian life fell into a shape corresponding to that of our picture of a medieval manor; rudimentary perhaps, but fully recognisable. The result in ecclesiastical terms was a proliferation of territorial churches, mostly small, attached to the manors, sometimes newly created and freshly endowed.

The legal concern of the royal law codes over basic financial matters then becomes intelligible, and is echoed and re-echoed throughout the elaborate codifications that are a feature of the reign of King Ethelred. The consequences of the monastic reform were now evident, and so was its deep penetration into the secular church. Elaborate rules were formulated, and a systematic division of churches into their various categories. As we have already stated, it was Wulfstan, archbishop of York (1002–23), who was the chief inspiration behind this legislative activity. His characteristic style can be identified throughout King Ethelred's reign and further in the authentic law-codes of King Cnut, Ethelred's effective successor. Late in Ethelred's reign, in 1014, Wulfstan was responsible for an elaborate statement of ecclesiastical law, known to historians as Ethelred VIII.[8] It has a special importance, among other things, because it hints at the practical world that underlay these solemn statements with their emphasis on Christian kingship and disciplined theocracy. The year 1014 was one of utmost political turbulence and physical violence. The homilist and realist in Wulfstan overcame the theorist as he lamented how the laws of Christ had been neglected and the laws of the king had been belittled, in spite of their intrinsic wisdom and despite the fact that they had been the product of councils held in places of note since King Edgar's day. Dues from civil penalties previously shared between Christ and the king had been separated, and things had gone from bad to worse. He prayed God for improvement, but added weakly that improvement could only come if there were zealous desire to begin it in earnest. Yet the actual code itself was an admirable treatise bringing together a wealth of statements over the rights and duties of the Church. In many ways it represents Wulfstan's mature personal views, preparatory to his final legal achievement in the laws of Cnut. By a curious trick of fate the improvement for which he prayed came with the Danish Conquest which gave Wulfstan the opportunity to frame a set of legal enactments in the laws attributed to King Cnut that were to endure for more than a century, through the crisis of the Norman Conquest, as an authoritative account of both ecclesiastical law (Cnut I) and secular law (Cnut II) in England.

---

8   Ethelred VIII. *EHD* i, no. 46, pp. 448–51.

The Ethelred code laid the foundation for such an achievement. Wulfstan started with a statement concerning matters that must have occasioned dispute and serious trouble. Churches were assured that their right to offer sanctuary was to be protected with the full force of law. A homicide was to be pursued until he reached an inviolable sanctuary, after which the king could offer him his life, although only on condition that full amends were made to God and to man. His wergeld, a substantial payment in its own right, had to be offered to the king in order that he should obtain the legal right to offer compensation. The penalty for breaking the king's *mund* (his protection – for all men were in some sense and to some degree in the royal *mund*) would go to the church, while the full agreed compensation price went to the kin of the dead man and to his lord. For lesser offences, penalties were to be paid in accord with the nature of the offence, the status of the offender, and also the status of the church. Such legal niceties give us precious insight into the way churches were seen and their status assessed.

We are told that there were four types of church, all equal in terms of their religious sanctity, but varying dramatically in accord with their secular status. The differences are expressed in terms of the penalties imposed for breaking their special peace, their *grith*, as it is called in Anglo-Saxon. Violation of a chief minster, a Christ Church, Canterbury, a Winchester Old Minster, a Glastonbury or a St Albans, was to suffer the heavy penalty of £5, the equivalent of the penalty for infringement of the king's own *grith*. A middle-ranking minster, say of the order of Hitchin, Welwyn, Braughing or probably Ashwell in Hertfordshire, or King's Sutton or Brixworth in Northamptonshire, was placed in the 120 shilling category, the equivalent of a standard royal fine. A still lesser church with a burial place possessed a *grith*-price of 60 shillings, and a mere field church, presumably with no burial rights, only 30 shillings. The code is carefully drafted. Echoes of earlier legislation abound and proper homage is paid to the laws of King Edgar. In the face of secular disaster, Wulfstan reflected public opinion in looking back to Edgar's reign as a true Golden Age in the Past. He also showed implicitly how the pouring of resources into the monastic revival demanded sharper differentiation. Any violation of ecclesiastical right was a serious matter, but the existence now in the early eleventh century of a significant number of great buildings in stone made it essential to signal substantial differences in penalties in money terms. Our territorial churches, some newly founded, some upgraded from dependent chapels, fell into the last two categories, with the dividing line both in reputation and in financial return resting possibly principally on the division between the churches with graveyards and those without. The churches themselves, all of them, were to be safeguarded and preserved. Tithes were now treated as a major element in financial provision, and we are told that a third of the tithes should be used for the repair of the church, a third for maintenance of the clergy, and a third for provision of charity for God's poor. One is conscious from such an enactment that a strong element of flexibility in the use of coinage would be part and parcel of such transactions; and the reforms of Edgar's reign implemented in the issue of an ordered, controlled coinage of silver pence throughout Ethelred's reign become more intelligible.

Special interest attaches itself to an analysis of the clerical order, made in the interest of bringing them into line with the laity in matters concerning accusations made against them. The two main elements of proof involved inevitably a strong clerical presence, that is to say, ordeal and compurgation, but, out of the sheer inevitable happenings of everyday life, clerics were sometimes bound to be accused, and the general problem then arose of how they were to respond to such accusations. Accusations themselves were of different intensity depending on the number of men prepared to take oaths that the accused had indeed committed the offence, and the law recognised the two categories of simple accusation and three-fold accusation. Attention was given first to the monks. A mass-priest who lived according to a Rule could clear himself simply by saying mass (if he dared) if he faced a simple accusation; for a three-fold he needed the support of two of his brethren. A deacon living to a Rule needed the two supports even for a simple accusation and six if the charge were three-fold. In descending order, a secular mass priest was to clear himself on the same terms as a monkish deacon. A minister of the altar without friends or oathhelpers was to go to the ordeal of consecrated bread, although the reservation was made that he could be allowed to clear himself on the host, that is to say, to dare to celebrate mass. We are reminded cogently of the violence that lay under the surface in Ethelred's time when we read that a man in orders, if charged with being either the actual slayer or instigator of a blood-feud, was to clear himself in the same manner as any layman by the oaths of his kinsmen. Only if he is without kin is he allowed to clear himself with his companions or associates (*geferan*), perhaps his fellow priests, or by the ordeal of the consecrated bread taken after fasting. A sharp distinction is made here, fully in tune with the Benedictine revival, between priests and monks, even if the monks should be priest-monks. A priest remained within his kin, a monk did not. In gnomic fashion, the legislator summed up the situation by stating that a man left his kin-law when he bowed down to his Rule-law (*he gæð of his mæglage, þonne he gebihð to regollage*).[9] As for punishments,

---

9   Ethelred VIII, 25, *EHD* i, p. 450.

these could be severe. A priest committing homicide or any grave crime was to forfeit both his priestly status and his country and to be exiled in pilgrimage as far as the Pope might prescribe for him. For lesser offences, atonement was called for to man and to God even as the bishops would instruct him. He was also to find a protector who would stand surety for his good behaviour. Worldly advantage could come to the priest who behaved himself. If he ordered his life properly according to the instructions laid down in books of ecclesiastical law, he was entitled to the full wergeld of a thegn both in life and death. Priests were instructed to observe celibacy and to avoid participation in warfare.

The law code ends with a whole series of edicts directed to the end that men in every order should lead the life according to Rule and the king's reeves were to support them. Indeed the king was to act as a protector to all in Holy Orders (as to foreigners). Excommunication was to be imposed as an ultimate penalty. In a set of short sharp sentences after invoking the precedents of Athelstan, Edmund and Edgar, expression is given to the political dogma of Church and State when men are ordered zealously to honour the true Christian religion and utterly despise heathen practice and also loyally to obey one royal lord in a community where each would love and support one another in true fidelity.

The substance of Ethelred's 1014 code provided the basis for King Cnut's first code; and with refinements and embellishments, Cnut's laws, the work of archbishop Wulfstan, remained, as we have suggested, authoritative for well over a century. Wulfstan himself appears to have been a complicated character, torn between two personae: in one, warring against the iniquities of the time in splendid homilies, and in the other, a successful statesman and ecclesiastical prince. Some of this tension is openly apparent in his most powerful work, to which we have already referred, the 'Sermon of the Wolf [*Sermo Lupi*] to the English', significantly also a product of the *annus horribilis*, 1014. In it he arraigns his countrymen as worse than the heathen. The rights of freemen have been withdrawn and the rights of slaves (they are recognised as *having* rights) have been restricted. With the immediate troubles of Ethelred's reign in mind, he blames English defeats on widespread disloyalty: slaves had been running away to become Vikings, and all sense of rank and status shamefully neglected or destroyed. Breaking of church laws, failure to pay church dues and reliance on wizards and sorceresses incurred Wulfstan's special wrath. Comparison was made with the Britons at the time of Gildas, when they had angered God so excessively with their sins that the English were allowed to conquer their land. This is fine rhetoric and fine prose. The ideal of an ordered Christian kingdom in the past under King Edgar is heavily in Wulfstan's mind. By his legal work he struggled to show in detail how such a Christendom could be sustained.[10]

A fortunate by-product of his struggles is that we are able to reconstruct the basic structures of the Church in the early eleventh century into the great churches, minsters, and lesser churches of various types and sizes. Archaeologists and architectural historians are giving us more vivid visual images to put side by side with the theoretical concepts. The sheer success, energy and vitality of the Norman settlement has inevitably distorted the picture. The Normans were mostly prepared to preserve the sites of great churches but not the fabric. There is no great Norman church – and there are many of them – which preserves anything significant of the Anglo-Saxon church above ground. To take one prime example, the huge Norman abbey at St Albans preserves some Anglo-Saxon work, re-used from an ancient church, at triforium level in the south transept. We are still looking for certain traces of the Anglo-Saxon predecessor, possibly under the nave of the Norman abbey, possibly on a green site to the south of the present church. Up till recently the comparatively modest remains of the abandoned cathedral at North Elmham and bits and pieces deduced from surviving ruins such as those of St Augustine's Abbey, Canterbury, were the most we had to go on. Discovery of exciting foundation plans at Christ Church, Canterbury, by archaeologists in the early 1990s gives better hope of appreciation of the achievement of later Anglo-Saxon architects, and the solid and sensational work of reconstruction that has now been possible at the Old Minster, Winchester, has given substance for the first time to the literary evidence which tells of great buildings at Abingdon, Worcester, Ely, Ramsey, Thorney, Peterborough and Durham, as well as Glastonbury, Winchester and Canterbury. Archaeologists, led by Martin and Birthe Biddle, enable us to trace the development of the Old Minster, Winchester, in the second half of the tenth century.[11] Under the impetus of the Reform movement it was subject to rebuilding in two stages. Between 971 and 980 it was extended westwards over the grave of St Swithun and a solemn service of rededication was held. The core of the Old Minster was then extended eastwards and the east part was remodelled to form the crossing and high

---

10 *Sermo Lupi, EHD* i, p. 933.
11 *The Anglo-Saxon Minsters at Winchester*, ed. Martin Biddle, Winchester Studies iv, forthcoming, 2000; *Winchester in the Early Middle Ages*, ed. Martin Biddle, *Winchester Studies* i, 1976; Birthe Kjølbye-Biddle, 'Old Minster, St Swithun's Day, 1093', *Winchester Cathedral: Nine Hundred Years, 1093–1993*, ed. John Mordaunt Crook, 1993; also Lawrence Hoey, 'New Studies in Canterbury Cathedral', *Avista Forum* 9, 1995, pp. 6–9 and *The Liber Vitae of the New Minster and Hyde Abbey, Winchester*, ed. Simon Keynes, EETF, Copenhagen, 1996.

altar of the new monastic cathedral. A second dedication took place in the episcopacy of bishop Aelfheah in 993–94. When complete, the church was nearly 250 feet in length (76 metres). The westwork was built on a square foundation of 25 metres and is calculated to have been as much as 40, perhaps even 50, metres in height. The royal palace lay near and the Biddles have suggested that the westwork may have resembled the building at Corvey on the Weser, where provision was made for the local ruler to sit in splendour, wearing his crown on the great ceremonial occasions. Early eleventh-century Winchester became a natural centre for government with its royal palace, its huge new buildings and monastic complex. King Cnut, the Danish conqueror, showed shrewd political sense when he made it his favoured home. It became very much his adopted city; and it was altogether fitting that it should be chosen as his burial place.[12]

What, then, of the churches in the next rungs down? Where do we find minsters or moderately sized minsters, substantial churches with grave-yards? Surviving churches are few in number and their status often uncertain. Fragments, sometimes considerable fragments, are more frequent, and with the help of the best modern guides it is possible to gain some sound impression of the size and nature of the physical shape of the buildings. Among the best to arouse the imagination in this way are Earl's Barton and Brixworth (in all its complexities) in Northamptonshire.[13] Others that are effective in this way include Sompting and Reculver in the South-East, Wing in Buckinghamshire, Breamore in Hampshire (with an Anglo-Saxon inscription surviving over the arch leading to the south porticus), St Mary's, Deerhurst in Gloucestershire, and, further north, Barton-on-Humber in Humberside.[14] The mysterious site at Much Wenlock in Shropshire, although preserving little of the Anglo-Saxon masonry, also gives the right impression. In some respects Wing provides the finest example of a church which enables us to imagine what a minster looked like in late Anglo-Saxon England. An aisled church, its seven-sided apse and elaborate crypt is still there to see; and the enjoyment is heightened when we learn from written evidence that the Lady Aelfgifu, probably the widow of King Eadwig, left

12   *Winchester in the Early Middle Ages*, ed. Biddle, pp. 449–69, gives the best account of the late Saxon burh. *Winchester Cathedral: Nine Hundred Years, 1093–1993*, ed. Crook.

13   Harold M. and Joan Taylor, *Anglo-Saxon Architecture*, 3 vols, 1965–78, provides the indispensable guide to the study of Anglo-Saxon churches. A perceptive review of the implications of the appearance of this great work appeared in *Anglo-Saxon England* 14, 1981, pp. 293–317 by Martin Biddle, Rosemary Cramp, Milton McC. Gatch and Birthe Kjølbye-Biddle. David Parsons gives good insight into the Brixworth problems in 'Brixworth and its Monastery Church', *Mercian Studies*, ed. Ann Dornier, 1977.

14   Taylor and Taylor, *Anglo-Saxon Architecture*, *passim*.

the church at some time just before 975 to her brother-in-law, King Edgar himself.[15]

Hopes of recovery of the picture of minsters and territorial churches developing into parishes depend partly on the archaeologist. As archaeological techniques grow more sophisticated, it is becoming possible to interpret successfully even the smallest of surviving fragments and foundations. Sometimes later medieval records can be brought into play, and we are able, thanks in particular to the labours of John Blair, to have a much better idea of the nature and spread of minster churches.[16] One tentative and yet not altogether surprising conclusion from modern investigation is that minster organisation survived more vigorously in the Danelaw and the North into the twelfth century than elsewhere. Much depended on endowment. Analysis based on the statistics of Domesday Book shows that whereas a proportion of landed wealth amounting to something of the order of a quarter lay in the hands of the Church in English England, south and west of Watling Street, the proportion in the Danelaw (apart from the exceptional case of the Fenland abbeys) was more like a tenth. Where the West Saxon dynasty was in firmest control, grants of monastic or ecclesiastical land to royal officers was common, leading to something on the scale of a technical advocacy parallel to developments in Germany and ripe for further exploitation after the Norman Conquest. These were also the areas where manorial lordship was most precisely defined and also where something akin to a predominantly parochial system was developing.

In the Danelaw, where the sites of middle-Saxon monasteries often coincided with the location of later mother-churches serving large parishes, the full minster model survived in greater strength. Rapid conversion of the Scandinavian settlers meant that the new predominantly Danish landlords had a vested interest in preserving the familiar pattern as a guarantee of the stability they needed if they were to gain full advantage from their new acquisitions. Examples to which attention should be drawn include Repton, Wirksworth, Bakewell and Derby in Derbyshire, Gillon, Ripon, Howden, Otley and Beverley in Yorkshire, and Southwell in Nottinghamshire. Repton, Ripon, Beverley and Southwell had a special importance, as we saw earlier, in reviving the fortunes of the archbishopric of York. Southwell is unusual in the wealth of its documentary evidence. A charter of 956 survives which

15 Ibid., vol. ii, pp. 665–72. Aelfgifu's will published by Dorothy Whitelock, *Anglo-Saxon Wills*, 1930, no. VIII.

16 John Blair, 'Secular Minster Churches in Domesday Book', *Domesday Book: A Reassessment*, ed. Peter Sawyer, 1985, pp. 104–42; *Minsters and Parish Churches: The Local Church in Transition 950–1200*, ed. John Blair, 1988; and especially *Pastoral Care before the Parish*, ed. John Blair and Richard Sharpe 1992.

gives the name of eleven dependencies. In Domesday Book Southwell enjoys proceeds from twelve berewicks, unnamed, with the implication that their relationship with their mother-church at Southwell was common knowledge.[17] Similar information about other substantial churches such as Howden and Sherburn-in-Elmet suggests a vitality in the life of northern minsters served by a number of priests. Repton also presents a picture of continuity and complexity. Used in the eighth century as a royal mausoleum, the site became the location for wholesale Viking burial in the 870s, only to revert later when the pagan mound became a focal point in a tenth-century Christian graveyard.[18] The greater minsters in turn became models for many foundations associated with medium-sized estates for which no good evidence for early origins can be found: Osmotherly, Upper Poppleton, Topcliffe, Silbstone and Bamborough fall into this category, some with communities of priests to serve them. In the northern Danelaw the absence of reformed Benedictine monasteries made a vital difference to the ecclesiastical polity. Lincolnshire, now that the evidence relating to religious sculpture has been examined, gives us a puzzling case-study where the fragmented tenurial situation led to a proliferation of local churches, many quite well endowed.[19]

Urban churches should not be neglected. Some towns flourished in later Anglo-Saxon England and by 1066 there were as many as thirty-seven churches in Lincoln and forty-six in Norwich. Such, however, provide something of an antithesis to our minsters, which flourish best in prosperous agrarian surroundings. Northamptonshire, for example, has been subject to intense study and has been shown to possess many minsters fated to enjoy a long life at the head of substantial parishes deep into the Middle Ages and beyond. King's Sutton, on the extreme west of the shire, is a conspicuous example. All who know its commanding topographical position will not be surprised to hear that its jurisdiction and influence, its *parochia*, extended far and wide, at one time reaching Watling Street some fifteen miles to the north-east, and possibly as far as Buckingham in the other direction.[20]

---

17 *DB* i, 283a, Notts. Land of the Archbishop of York: 'In Sudwelle numerantur XII berewickes'; *Southwell and Nottinghamshire: Medieval Art, Architecture and Industry*, ed. Jennifer Alexander, Brit. Arch. Ass. Conference Transactions xxi, 1998.

18 H.M. Taylor, 'St Wystan's Church, Repton, Derbyshire: A Reconstruction Essay', *Arch. J.* 144, 1987, pp. 205–45; Martin Biddle, 'Repton and the Vikings', *Antiquity* 66, no. 250, 1992, pp. 36–51.

19 *Corpus of Anglo-Saxon Sculpture, vol. V, Lincolnshire*, ed. Paul Everson and David Stocker, British Academy, 1998.

20 The Domesday Book entries for Northamptonshire indicate the persistent strength of the soke of King's Sutton: *DB*; 219c (royal land); 220b (Odo of Bayeux's); 222b (King's Almsmen); 223c and d (Robert of Mortain's); 224d (Earl Hugh's); and also probably 224c (Hugh of Grandmesnil's).

Brigstock, Nassington and Chipping Warden are other likely minsters, while in Oxfordshire Bampton is emerging as an important minster as archaeologists and historians discover its long continuity and significant control of an extensive and prosperous parish.

Similar evidence pointing to continued importance of minsters at what were true topographical central sites may be found throughout England, melding institutionally into similar *clas* churches on the Celtic fringes. When it comes to the question of lesser churches, we confront different problems. Just as the tenth century proved a critical period for the growth of manorial lordship and the development of what amounted to a complex thegnly class, so, complementary to both of these social phenomena, came the growth of proprietary churches. Some of these churches, owing foundation and endowment to great men or to local landlords, were to have long lives in front of them as centres of prosperous parishes; others never grew beyond the status of dominical chapel. Where they flourished, rebuilding under new Norman lords expunged traces of earlier work. Of the four hundred or so churches which still contain significant features of Anglo-Saxon work, only a handful survive in a sufficiently complete and relatively unaltered form to give us an impression of what a lesser church truly looked like in the later Anglo-Saxon period. Escomb in County Durham is of an even earlier date, probably eighth century, but remained in use throughout the period and indeed virtually continuously until present times. St Laurence's Church at Bradford-on-Avon is also of eighth century foundation but its elaborate arcading and plaster work mark a careful reconstruction in the later tenth century. Greensted in Essex is of special interest as the only surviving example of what must have been extensive wooden building in the Saxon and Anglo-Scandinavian worlds. The addition of a Tudor brick chancel and reconstruction in 1848 makes it difficult to envisage the church as it stood in Anglo-Saxon days, though the solidity of the surviving oak tree trunks of the nave remind us of the skills and enduring qualities of so many English churches which are now lost.[21] Perhaps the two most striking examples of late Saxon church building on a small scale came from very different parts of the country. A cluster of Anglo-Saxon buildings still exists in the Vale of Pickering in the North Riding of Yorkshire. Among them is the church at Kirkdale dedicated to St Gregory and well known for its preservation of sculpture and grave-slabs. There is an Anglo-Saxon inscription on the sundial, built into the wall over the south door, which gives us the time of the rebuilding with almost unique accuracy to 1055–65, the

---

21 Taylor and Taylor, *Anglo-Saxon Architecture*, vol. i, pp. 262–4: and *passim* vols i–iii for most Anglo-Saxon survivals.

period when Tostig, Harold's brother, was earl of Northumbria. It also provides a telling example of how the landlord class was busying itself with church building or restoration:

> Orm, the son of Gamal, bought St Gregory's church when it was all broken and destroyed, and had it rebuilt from the ground in honour of Christ and St Gregory, in the days of Edward the king and Tostig the earl.[22]

Our other example comes from Gloucestershire. At Deerhurst, only a few hundred yards from the great church of St Mary's, alterations to what was then regarded as an ordinary house revealed in 1885 the existence of a chapel consisting of a nave and chancel. Some two centuries earlier a Latin inscription had been discovered which now made sense in relation to the newly discovered chapel. Again by extraordinary chance it gives us precision in dating. Earl Odda, referred to in the inscription, died in August 1056 and his brother Aelfric in December 1053, both at Deerhurst. The inscription reads in translation:

> Earl Odda had this royal hall built and dedicated in honour of the Holy Trinity for the soul of his brother Aelfric whose body rests in this place. Bishop Ealdred dedicated it the second of the Ides of April in the fourteenth year of the reign of Edward, king of the English [i.e. 12 April 1056].[23]

Chance has left us with evidence of church building and local ecclesiastical patronage, but conscious design tells occasionally of the massive efforts made on behalf of great churches such as those at Canterbury, Winchester, York, Abingdon, Peterborough and the like. One foundation of enormous importance in northern history to leave dramatic record of its history during this period is Durham, and it would be wrong not to give it special mention in any discussion of foundation and patronage. Its story is not a simple account of personal patronage by kings or magnates, but rather an unusual concentration of regional patronage over a long period. Possession of the body and relics of St Cuthbert was the reason of being for the greatness of Durham. In 875, under heavy Viking pressure, Lindisfarne was abandoned by its monks, who for seven years wandered through the North, even

---

22 P. Hunter Blair, *An Introduction to Anglo-Saxon England*, 1956, pp. 191–2 and plate XII, a good photograph of the sundial.

23 H.M. Taylor, *Deerhurst Studies: The Anglo-Saxon Fabric*, 1977; *St. Mary's Church, Deerhurst*, ed. Philip Rahtz and Lorna Watts with others, *Society of Antiquaries Research Committee Report* (2nd on Deerhurst), 1997.

contemplating exile in Ireland, until they settled in Chester-le-Street. The strength of the cult of St Cuthbert brought them wealth and possessions. They had taken with them other treasures, including the Book of Lindisfarne, and their possession of St Cuthbert's body made them a focal point of veneration in the North. Under further Scandinavian pressure they made their final move to the splendid safe site at Durham in 995. Bishop Ealdhun began to build his new cathedral on this rocky outcrop, enjoying the fruits of grants of land which formed the nucleus of the county of Durham and the later Palatinate. Concentration of patronage on Durham has some features of the spectacular to it, partly because of the continued fear in the region of renewed pagan attack, but it is well to remember that side by side with the creation of this new episcopal centre there persisted small churches of the nature of Escomb to remind us of the range of ecclesiastical institutions that emerged into the more settled years of the mid-eleventh century.[24]

Concentration of the material manifestations of church life in the buildings and foundations is all well and good, but serves directly to prompt other and deeper questions. How were these churches in all their variety serviced? What sort of men were the clergy, and how did they face up to their social and pastoral duties? There are further and even deeper underlying problems to which surviving evidence provides only partial answers at best. How was the whole apparatus of ecclesiastical authority articulated? Were the theoretical clear-cut statements about episcopal functions no more than a pale reflection of reality? Was celibacy the norm, and to what degree and for whom? Reformers looked back to the works of the four great Fathers of the early Church for their inspiration, to St Ambrose and St Jerome, more so to St Augustine of Hippo, and especially to St Gregory the Great, Pope and master figure in initiating the Conversion of the English. They also looked more immediately to the work of their Carolingian predecessors, Smaragdus and Haymo (and before them Pirmin), and to earlier Anglo-Saxon books of canon law and penitentials. Favoured canonical decrees from a surprising wealth of source led them to formulate disciplined theoretical structures. For example, they framed a logical pattern to describe the basic division of clerical grades into seven (sometimes eight) categories. These grades were all, according to the homilists, drawing on the ancient traditions of the Church, associated in one way or another with major biblical events and the Life of Christ. The *hostiarius*, or gatekeeper,

---

24 David Rollason, 'Symeon of Durham and the Community of Durham in the Eleventh Century', *England in the Eleventh Century*, ed. Carola Hicks, 1992, pp. 183–98, makes the shrewd point (p. 198) that the replacement of a secular community at Durham by a monastery may have been as much a part of the advancement of Norman control in the North as of a process of ecclesiastical reform.

was related to the locking and unlocking of Noah's Ark before and after the Flood; the *lector* to Isaiah's prophecy of the Holy Spirit; the exorcist to Christ's driving out of the seven demons from Mary Magdalene; the acolyte to the reception of candlestick and taper from the archdeacon at ordination, as symbol of Christ bringing light to the world; the sub-deacon to the miracle of the water and wine at the marriage feast at Canaan in Galilee; the deacon to the miracle of the loaves and fishes; and the priesthood to the mystery of the mass itself. As to the bishop, we are told that Christ was a bishop when he lifted his hands and blessed the apostles before he ascended into heaven. Clerical grades are thus woven mystically into the inner beliefs and liturgy of the Church.[25]

Such is the theoretical basis. There remains a strong suspicion that the main division in practice came between priests and deacons, on the one hand, and the lower orders, on the other, still *clerici* or clerks, but bundled together in a sub-diaconate medley. The regular use of the term 'mass-priest' is in itself quite suggestive. When a clerk, whether a monk or monk-trained or not, reached the age of thirty, he was eligible to receive the rank of priest at the hand of a bishop. The procedure was described in detail. A month before the time for ordination he was to present himself to the bishop, properly equipped with food for himself and fodder for his horse (so that he should not be a burden to the bishop), and submit himself to an examination. Subject then to his willingness to receive the bishop's instructions, he is reckoned to be that much nearer ordination, though no firm indication is given of the sort of teaching he should have received so as to meet the bishop's demands. The monastic route was clear enough, and we have a good idea of the sort of training he would have had in one of the new monastic schools in Latin, theology and pastoral care. It is certain also that there was a positive charge on the old minsters and, as they grew in number, on parish priests to provide a degree of elementary schooling that could serve as a basis for better things. We must recognise, however, that there is a vast difference between instructing children so that they could recite the Creed and the Ten Commandments in their own tongue, and teaching ordinands to the point where they could at least have access to the Bible and some of the work of the Early Fathers in Latin. The persistent lament of the homilists tells us that even this modest ideal was never fully reached, nor should we expect it to be. Surprising probability remains that there were enough literate parsons as well as monks in the reigns of King Ethelred and Cnut to pass on the torch of sound learning.

---

25 *Wulfstan's Institutes of Polity*, xxiv, '*De ecclesiasticis gradibus*', especially pp. 225–36; C.A. Jones, 'The Book of the Liturgy in Anglo-Saxon England', *Speculum* 73, 1998, pp. 691–5.

By an odd chance of survival, some of the best insights into the state of the clergy come from a document relating to the north of England, though admittedly probably from Wulfstan's pen and certainly under his inspiration in the early 1020s. The so-called 'Law of the Northumbrian Priests' consists of sixty-seven clauses, some of which are subdivided, and is by no means a simple document.[26] The first forty-five clauses deal directly with the priests, with some possible interpolations from a slightly later date, and the remainder mostly with the laity. The threat from the heathen was greater in the North than the South, a fact powerfully emphasised in the code, though not to the point where its evidence for the general state of the English Church should be belittled. Wulfstan's influence was widespread throughout the kingdom, central to the legal activities of King Cnut's court. In consequence the code's value is great as evidence for the state of the clergy in Kent or Wessex or Mercia as well as for the Northumbrians to whom it is primarily addressed.

The code as it stands has a concise beginning and end, which gives an impression of a unitary creation, though the contents suggest some elements of stitching together, in other words of a composite origin, even if written by the same hand and directed by the same mind. It is memorable in the annals of church history for two special reasons. By implication it suggests that many, perhaps most, of the local clergy were non-celibate. It also gives one of our very rare authentic references to an archdeacon and his court operating in Anglo-Saxon days.[27] A priest was to be cursed, presumably excommunicated, if he left a woman and took another, a penalty invoked for desertion and loose-living, not for the basic sin of clerical marriage or concubinage. Archdeacons receive frequent mention as key people in the administration of a large diocese.

The detailed decrees of the code and the order in which they are presented demand some attention. The opening clauses deal with the compensation received if any wrong is offered to a priest. All his colleagues were asked to help, with the support of the bishop. They were to be in every matter of law just as if 'one heart and soul'. This initial concentration on the corporate sense of the clergy makes one reflect on guild statutes such as those for pre-Conquest Cambridge, Exeter, Bedwyn or Abbotsbury, all for laymen but with a strong religious involvement and sanction. No priest was to buy or receive another's church except in the presumably exceptional circumstances where the incumbent had committed a capital crime and

---

26   Law of the Northumbrian Priests. *EHD* i, no. 52, pp. 471–6.
27   Cl. 6. A penalty of 12 ores was to be imposed for failing to answer the archdeacon's summons.

so rendered unworthy to serve at an altar. Severe penalties attended such usurpation, including money payments. The term 'ora' (ore) is used to express such payment, a Scandinavian term initially signifying an ounce of silver but coming to mean 16 silver pence, or, in some cases, 20. The priest guilty of illegal dispossession was subject to a payment of 20 ores to the bishop, 12 to the priest he had ousted from his church, 12 to his colleagues, and whatever he had paid to obtain wrongly the church that belonged to a priest. On top of all that he was to provide himself with 12 sureties who would guarantee his future observances of what is called bluntly the priests' law. Such emphasis so early in the code (clause 2) suggests some significant abuse but, even more important, illustrates the attempt made under force-ful reforming bishops to impose solidarity on the clergy.

The rest of the code divides relatively simply. Up to clause 45, the concern is with matters of offence against clerical order and the compensa-tion to be paid. For roughly half the clauses (up to clause 24), compensation is calculated in ores. From clause 25 to 45, a compact subsection, com-pensation is insisted on, though at no fixed level. A close look at the substance of offence reveals the reason for this difference. The first group deals with failure on the part of the priest to perform routine duties and would by implication be a matter for the archdeacon and his court operating within an agreed level of monetary penalties for offences (clauses 3–18, with an intermediate sub-group 19–24 involving the church's status). The second group (25–45) contains more elements of a complex nature involving public courts. One powerful element throughout was an aim to strengthen epis-copal discipline. An offending priest was to pay 20 ores to the bishop if he celebrated mass after the bishop's prohibition as well as making amends for his other offences. A similar sum was to be paid if he neglected the bishop's own summons or if he referred a cause to a layman when it should have gone to an ecclesiastic. A lesser sum, though still substantial, of 12 ores was to be exacted as a standard rate for a whole series of more or less standard offences: neglecting the archdeacon's summons; celebrating mass in spite of the archdeacon's prohibition; refusing baptism or confession; not providing chrism at the right time; failing to see that a child was baptised at the proper time; misdirecting a fast or a festival; obtaining ordination out-side the diocese; celebrating mass in an unconsecrated building or without a consecrated altar, in a wooden chalice, or without wine. The same sum of 12 ores was exacted if he neglected the host or if he celebrated mass more than three times a day. Special attention was naturally placed on his duty to see to the baptism of infants (clause 10). A penalty of 6 ores was imposed if a child was not baptised within nine days. If the child died heathen within nine days through carelessness, no secular fine was exacted but the priest was instructed to make his amends to God; if after nine days, amends again were to be made to God, but with an additional fine of 12 ores because the child had remained heathen so long.

The opening section of the code ends with a small group of clauses (19–24) that deal with offences made against the priest or his church but still well within the firm control of ecclesiastical courts. Violation of sanctuary was to be compensated in proportion to the church's status. A standard penalty, the *lahslit* (12 ores for a man of *ceorl*'s, i.e. ordinary freeman's, status) was invoked for anyone trafficking with a church, or for anyone driving a priest from a church. A priest's person was placed under special and expensive protection: anyone wounding a priest was to pay compensation for the wounds and a further 12 ores to the bishop for the insult to the altar (4 ores only in the case of a deacon). If a priest were killed, a full wergeld was to be paid, with an additional 24 ores to the bishop (12 ores if a deacon). The clergy were still subject to their kin-law, unlike the monks, but had the weight of their clerical order also in support. The seeds of their corporate strength as a body set apart, which were to bear fruit in the full theocratic claims of the Hildebrandine Church in the late eleventh century, were already burgeoning in this relatively remote corner of the Western world.

A significant change comes over the law code in the following section (clauses 25–45). The compiler reverts to offences on the part of the priest, although now mostly of a wider social nature as opposed to neglect or mishandling of church duties. For these offences no specific money penalty was mentioned. We are merely told that a priest was to make composition. The reason for this is quite clear. The degree of damage done would be variable and compensation would also be variable and presumably decided at a variety of courts, some ecclesiastical, some secular, some perhaps the equivalent of a meeting of the wiser and senior men of a priests' guild. The bishop is referred to in only one case: if a priest fought with another, he was to pay compensation both to his fellow priest and to the bishop. Some of the role of protector of his kin was undoubtedly firmly embedded in episcopal minds when they considered their position in relation to the priests of the diocese.

The medley of offences contained in this section of the code reveals the social complexity of the world the priests inhabited. There was concern for decorum within a church and for proper order. A priest was not to put unsuitable things in a church (the mind boggles at the possibilities), to remove church goods, or to desert the church to which he was ordained. He was to ring the hours or sing the hours at the appointed time, not to enter the church with weapons, nor to perform the annual services of the church in the wrong sequence, nor to conduct the ordeal wrongly. There was great concern over a priest's personal appearance and his conduct.

Scorn or insult by word or deed had to be met by compensation. He was not to act as an accessory to ill-doing, nor to refuse lawful help to another, nor to leave him unwarned. Compensation was demanded if he neglected the shaving of his beard or the cutting of his hair: no long-haired prophets were to be encouraged within this decorous church. Perhaps there is significance in the fact that concern over a priest's hirsute appearance (clause 34) is followed immediately by the famous decree that anathema was the penalty if he left a woman and took another (clause 35). If he covered up fraud, practised drunkenness or became a glee-man or tavern-minstrel, he was to pay compensation. This section concludes with a reversion to ecclesiastical matters and to more general affairs. A priest was not to conceal what wrong was rife among men in his parish (his *scriftscir*), nor to leave his yearly dues undemanded, nor to stay away from a synod. Some indication is given of the disciplinary procedures that could make a reality out of all the somewhat pious invocations when we are told that if a priest will not submit and resists the commands of his bishop, he is to be cut off from the community of those in Holy Orders and to forfeit both fellowship and every privilege unless he resumes obedience and atones deeply for his misdeeds. However roughly, a true attempt was being made to build up an integrated clerical community imposing its own rules on its members.

The compiler of this lengthy code concludes with decrees (clauses 45–67) that were of wider and more general importance, still with a heavy ecclesiastical input but no longer exclusively priest-centred. Penalties were to be imposed for heathen practices, witchcraft and idol-worship, with arrangements made for compurgation according to the rank of the offender. Establishment of sanctuaries built around a stone or a tree or a well (or any such nonsense, as the manuscript has it[28]) had to be atoned for by the payment of the standard *lahslit*, half of which was to go to the church and half to the lord of the estate. Sabbath observance was strict. Markets, public assemblies and all carrying of goods was forbidden on Sundays, with merely a tenuous allowance for travellers in perilous times who were empowered to take enough for their needs within six miles of York. Failure to observe these rules involved a fine of 12 ores for a freeman or a flogging for a slave. The same amount, a fine of 12 ores, was exacted as penalty for violation of a festival or a legal fast. Rome pennies, that is to say, Peter's Pence, were to be paid to the bishop's see by St Peter's Day, 29 June; two trusty thegns and a mass-priest from each wapentake were to collect it and hand it over to the bishop. Penalties were imposed for withholding tithes and a complicated set of regulations attempted to make sense of marriage law and sexual

---

28   Cl. 54: *swilces ænigge fleard* (any such nonsense – or trifles [*nugae*]). *EHD* i, p. 475.

behaviour. No man was to have more than one wife (presumably at one time), legally betrothed and wedded. Atonement was to be made and paid for to the bishop for infringement of the laws of consanguinity. No one was to marry within the fourth degree of kindred nor within the spiritual bonds involved in the relationship of godparent and godchild. Intercourse with a nun meant that both parties were liable to the full payment of their wergelds. Separation was possible for a married pair, but the separated partners were then expected to live chastely. The whole code is rounded off in a typical combination of homily and the practical with an insistence on the validity of the purchase of land and of legal rights. In typical Wulfstan phraseology, the writer declared that there should ever be one Christianity and one royal authority in the nation. The high theory of medieval theocratic kingship could scarcely be better expressed. Chance survival of this one tract relating primarily to the northern province enables us to probe the thoughts of the reformers in the age of Aelfric and Wulfstan as they confront the reality of the state of the clerical order in England.

CHAPTER THREE

The Church *c.* 1016–66:
King Cnut to Edward the Confessor

It is all very well to talk of an age of Aelfric and Wulfstan, and yet a political historian may then take reasonable exception to the apparent neglect of what was surely one of the critical events in the flow of English history, the Danish Conquest effected by Sweyn and his young son, Cnut, between 1014 and 1016. Justification can come through an insistence on the continuity of ecclesiastical life, somewhat in contrast to happenings during the first Danish onslaught in the days of King Alfred and Edward the Elder, when large sections of the English Church in the Danelaw suffered severe dislocation. This continuity is marked in the career of Archbishop Wulfstan. We have already discussed the importance of the laws given to the Northumbrian priests, but the influence and forceful guidance of Wulfstan is evident elsewhere throughout the land. He lived on until 1023, seven years after Cnut's success in battle had settled the immediate political future of England.

A community that desired peace more than anything at first acquiesced in and then substantially welcomed the Danish conqueror. There was no recorded resistance after 1017 or early 1018. The young Danish ruler in turn revelled in the wealth his conquest brought him and sensibly took the most effective course to ensure its continuity. Already Christian, he intensified his support for the Church, using Wulfstan as his willing principal instrument. The result was an assured strengthening of existing church government. In Denmark the Christian Church was new-fledged, a tender plant of recent growth, drawing its bishops and leading priests from Germany and England. King Cnut himself was a convert, and many of his followers, Norwegians and Swedes as well as Danes, were still heathen. The contrast here with the Norman Conquest half a century later could not be more marked. William of Normandy had the resources of a Norman

Church to draw on, a Church that was moving steadily along a reforming path. Cnut had virtually no one, unless the Anglo-Danes of the Danelaw can be taken into account. He, therefore, conformed to existing English practice, making sure that it was indeed to his advantage to do so. His appointments to high office in the Church conformed to custom and were respectable. Some were made from monasteries within the diocese concerned. Others were royal priests drawn from the immediate entourage of the king. Later in his reign, when his confidence in his personal knowledge of the men concerned was that much greater, the courtly element is more pronounced. Aelfwine, who became bishop of Winchester in 1032, and Duduc, promoted to the see of Wells in the following year, were prominent among the king's personal followers. Aelfweard, abbot of Evesham, who was made bishop of London in 1035, the last year of Cnut's life, was said to be a kinsman of the king. Respect was shown to the monasteries from the beginning, even when there were political consequences of the monks' actions. In 1020 the Christ Church monks elected Aethelnoth as their Dean, an action which led to his succession to the archbishopric in the November of that year.[1]

King Cnut showed himself a consistent and generous patron of his favoured churches, though, if the record does not lie, he was distinctly selective in his gifting both in land and treasure. Christ Church, Canterbury, and the Old Minster, Winchester, were high in his favour, and many other churches prospered during his reign, many from grants by local aristocrats approved and supported by the king. Waltham in Essex and Bosham in Sussex fall into this category, the origin of their prosperity dependent on the Godwin family with full acquiescence from King Cnut and his followers. Abingdon, Durham, Ely, Evesham and Sherborne are among the great churches benefiting from personal relationships with the king, though there were moments of strain recorded at Ely and at Sherborne, and also possibly at Ramsey and at Wilton. If Cnut rewarded, he expected a return in general loyalty and in specific help, notably in supplying literate servants. Some great churches where one might expect to find evidence of royal patronage, notably Worcester, London and Glastonbury, are curiously and possibly significantly silent. Their wealth and influence later in the century suggests that they did not suffer greatly, if at all, under Danish rule, but there is nothing positive to go on. Worcester is a strange example. Uncertainty over the liaison with York persisted in some measure through to the 1060s. Wulfstan had held both sees (1003–16), but his successor Leofsige (d. 1033)

---

1 *Encomium Emmae Reginae*, ed. Alistair Campbell, 1949, p. 40: '*vir omni virtute et sapientia praeditus*'.

suffered a disputatious tenure of office, with both Lyfing (d. 1046) and Aelfric Puttoc (who united York and Worcester briefly in 1041) enjoying consecration and temporary success in the bishopric in the 1020s. Such episcopal turbulence inhibited patronage. King Cnut seems to have been well content to leave the see, prosperous and well endowed thanks to the ministrations of St Oswald and of Wulfstan, in peace to enjoy its wealth and prestige.[2]

Far and away the best example of Cnut's fostering of the church in England comes from Winchester. We have already discussed the key role played by Winchester in the early stages of the tenth-century reformation, but it is appropriate now to stress the importance of Winchester in early eleventh-century history.

Recent archaeological work at Winchester, coupled with a close investigation of literary remains, notably the great *Liber Vitae* of New Minster (1031), has brought the reign of Cnut into sharp perspective as a key moment in the life of the city.[3] At Easter 1019, King Cnut issued a charter in favour of New Minster, 'situated in the famous and populous city of Winchester in which the wonderful bodies of the illustrious confessors Judoc and Grimbald to this day are efficacious in miracles'. In the following year, or possibly in 1021, at a great council convened at Winchester, under the direct supervision and active construction of Wulfstan, archbishop of York and former bishop of Worcester, a code of laws was issued, bringing up to date the legislation of the previous century, and indeed enduring as an authoritative statement of law deep in to the Norman period. An extensive tract of the code (Cnut I) dealt with ecclesiastical law, echoing the promulgations of late Ethelred and also of Edgar. The abbot of New Minster, Byrhtmaer (1012–30), has emerged as one of the key figures, with Wulfstan, among those who ensured continuity over the Danish Conquest. It was during his abbacy that Cnut presented New Minster with a great gold cross, depicted at the frontispiece of the *Liber Vitae*. The cross was destroyed in a conflagration during the civil war of Stephen's reign (August 1141) and we are told that from the ashes of the cross, Bishop Henry of Winchester (Stephen's brother) recovered 500 pounds of silver and 30 marks of gold, as well as three diadems and as many foot-rests of the purest Arabian gold, decorated all over with precious stones, and made with most exquisite and wonderful workmanship. It seems more than likely, as Dr Keynes has

---

2 Aelfric Puttoc's general reputation remained high. He was referred to as very venerable and wise in the notice of his death: *Anglo-Saxon Chronicle* (D), *s.a.* 1051.

3 *Winchester in the Early Middle Ages*, ed. Martin Biddle, *Winchester Studies i*, 1976 and 'The Study of Winchester: Archaeology and History in a British Town', *Proc. Brit. Acad.* 69, 1983, pp. 93–135. *The Liber Vitae of the New Minster and Hyde Abbey, Winchester*, ed. Simon Keynes, EETF, Copenhagen, 1996.

suggested, that the portrayal of King Cnut and Queen Emma in the *Liber*, presenting the golden cross to New Minster, was comparable, deliberately comparable,[4] to the picture of King Edgar, placed at the beginning of the New Minster Charter of 966. In this, as in so many other ways, notably legal, Cnut and his advisers seem to be emphasising the direct link between the Christian Danish ruler and King Edgar, the most highly regarded of his predecessors. It was as advantageous to Cnut and his ecclesiastical advisers to foster the myth of a Golden Age in the reign of Edgar as it was to King William a generation or so later to foster the ideal of a Rule of Law under Edward the Confessor. The big difference was that while Cnut's ecclesiastical advisers were exclusively drawn from the existing English establishment, William's were mostly new men, predominately Norman, sensitive to advanced European thought.

Winchester itself indeed enjoyed something of a golden period in the reign of Cnut, whose favoured residence it was. The formidable monastic precinct, the Old Minster, New Minster and Nunnaminster flourished and played a critical part in educating the next generation of influential clergy. Deliberate concentration on Wessex, with Winchester its chief town bearing the attributes we associate with a capital, ensured Cnut's immediate success, even though it did not bring permanence to his dynasty. The influence of the womenfolk, notably that of Emma, Cnut's queen and a Norman princess, became inseparably attached to Winchester. Not that other traditional centres lacked importance. Bath, Canterbury and Westminster enjoyed a time of prosperity. Glastonbury prospered. Cnut's peace over a period of twenty years allowed for a time of economic and especially urban recovery. But Winchester and its allied port of Southampton grew into special prominence; and it is not too unreasonable to speculate on the possibility that they might have continued at least for a generation or two to have outranked London and Westminster, had Cnut lived longer or had an even stronger king succeeded Cnut.

Some indication of the dominance of Winchester in politics and finance comes from the situation immediately after the king's death. Cnut died at Shaftesbury on 12 November 1035, and was buried in the Old Minster at Winchester. The key people in deciding the succession were his widow, Queen Emma, and Earl Godwin of Wessex. It is notable that the dominant figures in the politics of the succeeding generation, immediately leading to the Norman Conquest, were all new men or their sons, men in other words who owed fame and fortune to the Danish Conqueror. Queen Emma was well placed in control of the principal royal treasury at Winchester, and

---

4 *Liber Vitae*, p. 38.

initially with the help of Earl Godwin she negotiated a settlement which left Wessex in the hands of her son by Cnut, Harthacnut, who was absent in Scandinavia at the time of his father's death. The more forceful Harold Harefoot, the son of Cnut and Aelfgifu of Northampton, was left in charge of England north of the Thames. Harthacnut's failure to return to England, coupled with rumours that Emma was negotiating with her other two sons, Alfred and Edward, sons of King Ethelred and exiles at the Norman court, prompted a change of heart on Godwin's part. Harold moved south, took charge of the treasury, and in 1037 forced Queen Emma into exile in Flanders. Harold Harefoot was recognised as sole king (1037–40). His early death on 17 March 1040 was followed by a recognition of Harthacnut as king (1040–42) and a return from exile of Queen Emma. Poor Harthacnut seems to have been a singularly inept young man, possibly mortally sick, who died as he stood at his drink at a wedding feast on 8 June 1042.[5] One recension of the Chronicle (s.a. 1040) says that he did nothing worthy of a king as long as he ruled. In 1041, his half-brother, Edward, Queen Emma's son, was brought back from exile and recognised as heir. On Easter Day, 3 April 1043, he was crowned king, significantly at Winchester.

A sinister figure at the back of all these political intrigues was the priest Stigand, who had served Cnut in the 1020s, had received preferment from him, and had become a close counsellor to Queen Emma. There is a clear thread of a powerful group exerting sometimes decisive influence on events during the seven years following Cnut's death. His sons cannot have been more than late teenagers at his death, subject to heavy pressures from older folk, men and women. King Edward, very early in his reign, was forced, probably by discontent over his mother's authority, to assert himself. In November 1043, he descended on Winchester and deprived Emma of control of her vast treasure. Stigand, who had been rewarded with the bishopric of East Anglia at Elmham, was also deprived of his bishopric. At the top political level, sheer force often outweighed legal niceties. Emma was allowed to remain in Winchester, where she continued to be an influential figure as queen mother through to her death in 1052. Stigand also recovered, was reappointed to Elmham in 1044, and translated to the see of Winchester in 1047. From this tortuous story, resulting in the establishment of a king of the ancient dynasty in the person of Edward (later known as the Confessor), Winchester played a vital part in the decade following the death of Cnut, a focal point one suspects also for the involvement of the Church in the high politics of the period.

---

5 *Anglo-Saxon Chronicle, s.a.* 1042. Versions C and D of the Chronicle refer to Edward's succession, as his natural right.

As background to the reign of Edward the Confessor (1042–66) and the prelude to the Norman Conquest, there are some matters and developments in Cnut's reign that proved long-lasting and demand discussion. Emphasis is now properly put on the creation of what was virtually a new establishment, if that term may fairly be used, even if it operated in traditional ways.

At the secular level the nature of the earldoms was modified as new men were introduced into office; and the use of the term 'earl' to replace 'ealdorman' at that level was no mere empty linguistic quirk. Concentration of power over many shires had been as firm a characteristic of tenth-century England as the eleventh, but Cnut's right-hand men turned out to be truly new men, less dependent on the network of kindreds which supported leading provincial figures of an earlier age such as Athelstan Half-King, the chronicler Aethelweard or Byrhtnoth, the hero of the lost battle of Maldon in 991. From a veritable tangle of secular offices, three men emerged whose families were to dominate political life in the middle years of the eleventh century: Earl Godwin (d. 15 April 1053) in Wessex; Earl Leofric (d. autumn 1057) in Mercia; Earl Siward, who was Danish, in Northumbria (d. 1055). These three men had been Cnut's appointments: Godwin by 1018, when he attested charters as *dux*; Leofric probably in the mid-1020s and certainly before 1032; Siward before 1033. The policy in secular affairs was clearly moving towards allotment of regional authority over many shires to trusted men.[6]

Royal attitudes towards the Church were less dramatic and yet more complex, with a surprisingly strong Roman theme present in them. At a council held at Cirencester at Easter 1020, a formal letter was read out from King Cnut (who was in Denmark), setting out the royal intention to act as a positive Christian ruler.[7] At such a comparatively early stage in his reign the king is still thinking in terms of the traditional administrative structures and asks for full co-operation from his ealdormen and reeves, with the basic shire and royal manorial arrangements very much in mind. He refers specifically to the letters and messages which Archbishop Lyfing had brought to him from Rome, and charged his ealdormen that they should help the bishops and archbishops in furthering God's right and his own royal dignity with proper regard for the benefit of all the people. Archbishops and bishops are fully integrated into the process of creating a just society, indeed are central to the whole process. It was Cnut's will that

---

6   Simon Keynes, 'Cnut's Earls', *The Reign of Cnut*, ed. A.R. Rumble, Leicester, 1994, pp. 43–88.

7   *EHD* i, no. 48, pp. 452–4.

all the nation, ecclesiastical and lay, should steadfastly observe Edgar's law, which men had chosen and sworn to at Oxford. The two elements which emerge from this letter are clear: a firm link with the idealised practice of the age of the Christian King Edgar, and contact with Rome. This latter point was greatly strengthened later in Cnut's reign when he felt himself secure enough to make the perilous journey to Rome on the occasion of the Emperor Conrad II's Coronation by Pope John XIX on Easter Day, 26 March 1027. At the height of his power, King Cnut addressed a solemn letter to his two archbishops, Aethelnoth of Canterbury and Aelfric of York, and the whole race of the English, styling himself King of all England, Denmark, of the Norwegians and some of the Swedes.[8] He informed them that he personally had interceded for his people in connection with unjust tolls exacted on merchants and pilgrims in imperial territories (Burgundy) and also in connection with excessive sums demanded of his archbishops when they visited Rome to receive their pallia. The letter was written when Cnut was *en route* from Rome to Denmark. Part of the purpose of the letter is revealed – and the reason why it was directed to the archbishops – in its concluding paragraphs, which itemise the payment of ecclesiastical dues: Peter's Pence, from towns and villages; tithes of the fruits of the year (curiously in mid-August); church-scot or the first-fruits of the grant on St Martin's Day (11 November) to the church of the parish where each man resides. The *quid pro quo* of interchange between church dues and royal protection could scarcely be better illustrated.

Reinforced contact with Rome and a firmer integration with the European Church is therefore to some measure a rather unexpected feature of the Danish Conquest. This is not such a paradox as at first appears. Cnut needed the Church for moral support and also for financial and social reasons. He also needed it for active help in his attempt to convert and to deepen the conversion to Christianity of his Scandinavian empire. England had been conquered politically but there was also a reverse movement that one neglects at peril. The English Church had passed the zenith of its cultural achievements but it was far from torpid in the reign of King Cnut. It still had much to offer in the missionary field.

Cnut died in 1035, still a young man. We have already seen how the succeeding six or seven years were a period when neither of his sons, Harthacnut and Harold, proved capable of taking control. Ineptitude or illness stood in their way. One can sense during this troubled time a new group of English clerics and powerful earls striving to keep the kingdom intact while recognising that the Danish empire was falling apart. Eventually

---

8   Ibid., no. 53, pp. 474–8.

Edward the Confessor succeeded to the throne in 1042 with remarkably little opposition. His mother, Queen Emma, and Earl Godwin were key figures in bringing about this succession, but majority support also came from those of Danish as well as of English stock who had done well out of the peace imposed by Cnut and had no wish to see their gains wasted in civil wars. This is even more true of the Church. The insistence, so palpable from the records of Cnut's reign, on continuity of law and the Church, with King Edgar held as the model of Christian king, now bore fruit. King Edgar's grandson, the half-Norman Edward, was accepted peacefully as the lawful king of England.

Views on the character of Edward have undergone a dramatic change in recent generations. For long it was fashionable to treat him as a pious nonentity, memorable for his work on Westminster Abbey but for little else. Thanks largely to the work of Frank Barlow, we can now see that this picture was far from the truth.[9] His piety was deep-rooted enough, and advantageous; but he was no nonentity. Reliant initially on the support of Godwin and his family, he showed himself capable of independent action at critical moments throughout his reign. He was even able to create something of a balance in the political structures of the kingdom, intruding some, though not an inordinate number, of his own Norman friends into key positions, and keeping an uneasy rapport with all the three great families of earl's rank that had emerged in the preceding generation, with the kindreds of Leofric of Mercia and Siward of Northumbria as well as with Godwin and his sons. Above all he succeeded in maintaining substantial peace in very troubled times over a period of twenty-four years. Some of his success should properly be attributed to his use of the spiritual powers implicit in his Christian kingship exercised in the diplomatic field. He was childless and, for the last fifteen years of his reign at least, doubts over the succession served as a powerful counter in his efforts to preserve his own royal authority. His nephew, Edward the Atheling (d. 1057), Harold Godwinson, William, duke of Normandy (Edward's mother's great-nephew), and his own young great-nephew, Edgar the Atheling, all at different times to different bodies of opinion, appeared as possible legitimate successors. Our principal concern must be with his relationship to the Church. In itself the Church in England did not appear to voice any coherent thoughts over succession to the throne.

Edward was crowned king at Winchester on Easter Day, 3 April 1043, with great ceremony by the two archbishops, Eadsige of Canterbury and Aelfric Puttoc of York. Winchester was associated, as we have seen, with

---

9   Frank Barlow, *Edward the Confessor*, 1970; also *Vita Aedwardi Regis*, ed. Barlow, 1962.

the central traditions of church reform and royal government from the days of King Edward to Cnut, and it must have appeared at that moment as if its proud position would be maintained and fostered. Instead Edward's affections were diverted elsewhere. If there is one single symbol of Edward's kingship that came to dominate the minds of contemporaries and of future historians it is his support for the rebuilding of Westminster Abbey. Edward had experienced the life of an exile in Normandy for most of his younger years and was careful in his expenditure. Yet on Westminster he lavished resources on a massive scale. Proximity to London was perhaps the most powerful reason for the choice. London had been ravaged by the Danish wars but survived as the most wealthy mercantile centre of the kingdom with an immense potential in the reviving economy of mid-eleventh-century Western Europe. It was also of relatively easy access to Canterbury, and gave Edward a chance of asserting his own independence from what he may well have regarded as the stifling influence of the Winchester establishment. The site of Westminster Abbey itself had not been conspicuous in the first wave of tenth-century monastic reform. There is likely to have been some sort of ecclesiastical organisation there before the reign of King Edgar, but it was not until St Dunstan and the young king started their reforms that Westminster and the Isle of Thorney came into any prominence. The site itself was not inviting. Tidal waters on the treacherous banks of the Thames where the Tyburn brook entered the main stream did not make the situation attractive. It is not certain at what stage in King Edgar's reign a formal monastery was set up. Some good sources suggest this was done at an early stage, perhaps even 959 or 960 when St Dunstan was bishop of London. Others favour a later date in the early 970s as part of a systematic programme attributed to the reformers by which they planned to establish twenty new monasteries in the kingdom. The monastery was not initially well endowed. When Edward decided on the rebuilding, virtually a new foundation, it was referred to by the rather contemptuous term of *monasteriolum*, a petty little monastery.[10] There is again some uncertainty over the exact date when the decision was made, probably in the 1050s, though possibly even earlier. All agree that Edward planned it as his own special church, his *eigenkloster*, symbolically as an assertion of his independence, ultimately as his burial place. Henry III's rebuilding in the thirteenth century has left very little trace of the masonry but a surprising amount is known or can be inferred from literary accounts, from its representation in the Bayeux Tapestry, and from Norman cognates, notably, although not exclusively, Jumièges. Edward's Westminster was a superb example of Romanesque,

---

10   David Sullivan, *The Westminster Corridor*, 1994, p. 56.

immediately inspired by contemporary Normandy, though with Burgundy in the background. The abbey was built of Reigate stone with a long nave of six double bays, alternating massive and simple piers, and with a central lantern tower overlooking the crossing – the feature that most impressed contemporaries. As one would expect from a Norman-inspired work of the period, it had clean lines without a clutter of over-ornamentation. With a royal palace also established near at hand, Westminster had come to rival Winchester as principal centre of royal and ecclesiastical influence. When Edward was mortally ill, it was to Westminster that the great Council was summoned for the Christmas festivities in 1065. Edward was too ill to attend the solemn consecration of the abbey on 28 December, and within the first week of the New Year the king died, was buried, and his successor, Harold Godwinson, was elected, all within range of the gleaming new abbey.[11]

Westminster Abbey must be given pride of place, but it does not stand alone in the chronicle of great churches that were founded or developed in the reign of the Confessor. Queen Edith, Godwin's daughter, was responsible for founding the nunnery at Wilton, which was dedicated in 1065. Harold Godwinson spent time and energy building up Waltham, endowing it and seeing to its consecration at a splendid ceremony in the early 1060s. Waltham was, according to later historians, planned as his burial place, and indeed it was believed at Waltham that his body was brought there and buried after the battle of Hastings, a story that some good Waltham people found hard to square with strong local traditions of his survival after Hastings and life as a hermit.[12] Concentration on the great churches gives only a part of the picture. There is also a strong inference from many parts of the country that this was a time when there was a significant increase in the number of manorial churches. The expertise involved in the urge to permanence and building in stone characteristic of the Benedictine Reformation seeped through to the lesser churches of England in this generation before the Conquest.

The problem of general Norman influence on church life and organisation is one that vexes all historians who examine the evidence relating to the nature of the Church and the attitudes of the Confessor. Edward had spent well over twenty years in exile in Normandy and was heavily influenced by the political turbulence and ecclesiastical vitality of the duchy. When he returned he was accompanied by some of his friends and companions,

---

11 *The Bayeux Tapestry*, ed. David Wilson, 1985. Plate 29 brings out clearly the Anglo-Norman affinities, archetypal Romanesque.
12 *The Waltham Chronicle*, ed. and trans. Leslie Watkiss and Marjorie Chibnall, 1994, pp. xliii–lviii.

though initially he sustained a solid continuity with the advisers close to his Danish predecessors. Indeed there was something of a reaction against some direct Norman influence associated with his mother, Queen Emma, at Winchester. Edward's reliance in those early years of his reign on Earl Godwin was strengthened when, some forty years of age, he married Edith, Godwin's daughter, on 23 January 1045. She was herself anointed and crowned at the marriage ceremony, after which the king and the queen dined separately, the queen with the abbots and abbesses of the realm.[13]

The twin pillars of Edward's supports, the Godwins and the Church, were brought into close conjunction. And yet it is about this time that the first significant Norman intrusions into the ecclesiastical hierarchy became apparent. Stigand, it is true, had been restored to favour, possibly at Earl Godwin's insistence, in 1044, but another figure to assume great prominence enters the scene in the person of Robert Champart, abbot of Jumièges. There are mysteries surrounding his career. To leave his high office in Normandy and accompany Edward, possibly as head of his household, or even his domestic chaplain, is a step still unexplained. His reward came at some time between 1044 and 1046. In 1044 the see of London fell vacant and by 1046 Robert was subscribing charters as bishop. Two others of Edward's companions in exile also received substantial rewards in the mid-1040s. Leofric, an Englishman brought up in Lorraine, was consecrated bishop of Crediton in 1046, later moving his diocesan centre to Exeter (1050–72). Hermann, also from Lorraine, was made bishop of Ramsbury (1045–58), later of Sherborne (1058–78). The intrusion of these three men, none of whom would have been unaccompanied by congenial followers, into three influential southern sees marks a significant, though not yet overwhelming, change in the composition of the episcopacy.[14] Stigand still remained a powerful figure, very experienced in the ecclesiastical politics of the day. With strong backing from the Godwin family he was made bishop of Winchester in 1047.

Ecclesiastical and secular politics now merged to precipitate the major political crisis of the reign in 1050–51, a crisis which had repercussions on events leading directly to the Norman Conquest. On 29 October 1050, Eadsige, archbishop of Canterbury, who had for long been a sick man, died, to be followed in a short space of time by his fellow archbishop of

---

13 Barlow, *Edward the Confessor*, p. 65. Her coronation was according to the tradition accepted by Osbert of Clare.

14 Frank Barlow, *The English Church, 1000–1066*, 1963, p. 86. To some contemporaries Robert Champart was something of an evil genius: *Vita Aedwardi Regis*, ed. Barlow, pp. 17ff.

York, Aelfric Puttoc (d. 22 January 1051). Two parties were now formed, reflecting tensions generated in the preceding five years, a group close to the king and another group more directly directed to the Godwin interest. Earl Godwin's sons were growing both in political stature and notoriety at this stage and election to Canterbury provoked conflict. Stigand seems seriously to have been considered a candidate for the archiepiscopal throne, backed by a Godwin faction, but at the Easter Council, held in March 1051, Edward and what was now his court party won the day. Robert of Jumièges was appointed archbishop of Canterbury. Spearhafoc, abbot of Abingdon and also the king's goldsmith, replaced Robert as bishop of London, and a Scandinavian bishop, Rothulf, became abbot of Abingdon. We shall never know the detail of the balance of forces that determined these appointments, but consequential actions are enough to suggest serious underlying conflict. Secular disputes, including a notorious riot at Dover and a dramatic confrontation in arms in Gloucestershire where civil war was narrowly averted, resulted in the exile of Earl Godwin and his family in the autumn of 1051. A twelvemonth later they returned with armed force and achieved a settlement on terms.

It was during their absence that a serious attempt was made to increase Norman influence in depth on the Church. Robert visited Rome to receive his pallium, and it is highly likely that in the course of his journey he opened negotiations over possible succession to the throne with Edward's young kinsman, William, duke of Normandy. Reputable sources talk of a personal visit by William to England at this time.[15] On his return, Robert, acting on papal orders, refused to consecrate Spearhafoc to London and the bishopric passed instead to a Norman, William. Rumours of simony, even that he had paid Stigand for his promotion, later circulated to explain Spearhafoc's demotion. For some months in 1052 Norman influence seemed paramount in the hierarchy, with Robert at Canterbury, William at London and Ulf, also a Norman, recently appointed to Dorchester. Godwin's return in the autumn altered the political balance; and yet the immediate repercussions were by no means simple. The personal nature of the dispute came out strongly. Robert of Jumièges went into exile, pleaded his case energetically but died abroad probably in 1053, casting a long shadow over the English Church as a legitimate archbishop falsely removed from his office. Ulf also disappeared into obscurity. William, after an initial hasty escape, returned to prove a key element in preserving elements of continuity

---

15 *Anglo-Saxon Chronicle* (D), *s.a.* 1051. David Bates, *Normandy before 1066*, 1982, p. 84, reminds us that controversy over Harold's and William's claims to the English throne is littered with as many corpses as was the field at Hastings.

over the Conquest. He retained his London bishopric until his death in 1075. Stigand was the immediate beneficiary of Godwin's return. Canterbury was declared vacant on Robert's flight. Stigand was moved into the archiepiscopal office, still preserving his bishopric of Winchester. An uneasy political balance was achieved with the respectable Cynesige appointed to York (1051–60) and the much more interesting Ealdred (1044–69) consolidating his hold first on Worcester (1044–62), and then, after a doubtful intermediary period when he held both sees, on York alone (1062–69).

It is not easy to draw clear lines out of the developments in the English Church during the last fourteen years of Edward's reign. This was a period of considerable turmoil within the Western Church. The Papacy itself was undergoing reform on a scale that was to lead to the crisis of the Investiture Contest in the 1070s. At the papal curia the theoretical basis was laid which would loosen ecclesiastical dependence on secular authority and open the way to effecting moral reform, freeing elections, removing the stain of simony and establishing the norm of celibacy among the clergy. There are clear signs in England of closer contact with Rome and the Continent, but also much conservative retention of the old order. One feature worthy of close examination is the consolidation of authority within the Church in the hands of relatively few men. Two extraordinary figures stand out, Stigand and Ealdred.

The example of Stigand is well known, not least because he appears at critical moments, the death-bed of Edward and the coronation of Harold, in the Bayeux Tapestry. For eighteen years, 1052–70, he held the see of Winchester as well as Canterbury. At first sight this was inexcusable and one can see how earnest reformers at Rome could have regarded it as a flagrant example of pluralism, one of the abuses they were most anxious to oppose. William of Malmesbury, a fair-minded historian, though writing some two generations after the events, declared that Stigand alone also possessed many abbacies, referring to the long vacancies, perhaps unduly prolonged, during which he controlled the revenues of some of the most prestigious monasteries in the kingdom, St Augustine's at Canterbury, New Minster at Winchester, Ely and St Albans. He may well have regarded East Kent as a paltry endowment for his archbishop's rank and prestige. His careful promotion of two of his men, Siward to the subordinate see of Rochester (1058–75) and Ethelric to Selsey (1058–70), left him in effective episcopal control of the South-East, south of the Thames. He retained wealth and interest in his home territory of East Anglia, where his brother Aethelmaer succeeded him in the diocese of Elmham (1047–70). Stigand's reputation for wealth – and also it must be admitted for generosity and artistic taste – was well merited. In short he represented a fine example of the old unreformed order of the Church, primarily a capable administrator, appreciated as such by Edward and to some extent William in his early years. As a secular he was distrusted by the monks over whom he exercised authority. At Rome he never quite escaped the odium attached to one who had forcibly replaced a legitimate archbishop, Robert of Jumièges. Only in 1058 (and then again briefly in the early years of William's reign) did Stigand consecrate bishops; and his action, taken after he had at long last received the pallium from Benedict X, himself regarded by the reformers as an intrusive pope, was regarded as unlawful. Both Ethelric and Aethelmaer were deposed by the papal legates in 1070.[16]

Stigand's reputation therefore has undoubtedly clouded discussion of the state of the English Church. Yet he was not alone in creating what amounted to an ecclesiastical empire and in throwing emphasis on the administrative as opposed to the pastoral. The reputation of Stigand's fellow archbishop, Ealdred, came to be as high as Stigand's was low, but the similarities in their career patterns are striking.[17] Ealdred, it is true, was a monk, which made some difference. Trained at Winchester and already abbot of Tavistock in Cnut's reign, he was promoted to the important and wealthy bishopric of Worcester in 1046. Politically the border with Wales remained an active interest, and Ealdred appeared to retain the trust of both the royal court and the Godwin family during the crisis of 1050–52. He had fought against the Welsh in 1049, had been sent to Rome as a royal envoy in 1050, and played a somewhat dubious role in the confrontation between the king and the Godwin family in 1051. After Bishop Leofgar of Hereford's death in battle against the Welsh in 1056, Ealdred took on the administration of that extensive and turbulent diocese for a period of four years. He also controlled the bishopric of Wiltshire for some three years (c.1055–58) during the withdrawal of Hermann (Ealdred's companion on a mission to Rome in 1050). Hermann appears to have been something of an alter ego to him. Soon after Hermann's return, Ealdred set out on a long journey which took him to Hungary and then to Jerusalem. Cynesige, archbishop of York, died shortly after his return. Ealdred then, accompanied by Harold's two brothers, Tostig and Gyrth, set out again, this time for Rome to receive the pallium and also to do business on behalf of the king. He pleaded, with plentiful precedent, for the retention of his diocese of Worcester, but the papal attitude was now clear-cut, and to his great disappointment he had to yield Worcester to the English monk, Wulfstan, later to be honoured as

---

16 F.M. Stenton, *Anglo-Saxon England*, 3rd edn, 1971, p. 661: Ethelmaer of Chichester on dubious grounds, questioned by the Pope.

17 R.R. Darlington, 'Ecclesiastical Reform in the Late Old English Period', *EHR* li, 1936, pp. 385–428, gives a good insight into Ealdred's importance.

St Wulfstan, bishop of Worcester (1062–95).[18] Ealdred concentrated in this last phase of his career on the diocese of York itself, crowning William in 1066 and easing, initially at least, the strains and tensions of the Conquest. But from the middle years of Edward's reign he stands out, just as prominently as Stigand, as an old-fashioned prince-bishop with elements anticipating those of a later Lord Marcher. Yet again a sense of proportion has to be maintained. Ealdred was absent from England for a whole year in Cologne. He made two visits to Rome and one to Hungary and Jerusalem. He left a good name for generosity and also for administrative and diplomatic success. The implications are clear. There must have been a whole bevy of efficient and now anonymous subordinates capable of carrying through effective business in their lord's interest.

Stigand and Ealdred stand out for accumulation of control over ecclesiastical offices, but they were not alone in striving for concentration of authority and increased central efficiency in episcopal office. Hermann, the bishop of Ramsbury, on his return from his long journey in Ealdred's company, moved the diocesan centre of his see to Sherborne (1058–78) and planned a further move to Salisbury in the 1070s, so uniting the shires of Wiltshire and Dorset into one wealthy influential bishopric. The foreign clerk, Leofric, probably Cornish in origin but trained in Lorraine, had been appointed to the see of Crediton in 1046, but moved its headquarters to Exeter (1050–72), exercising effective office over the shires of Devon and Cornwall. Priests from Lorraine were prominent in English affairs in the last generation of Anglo-Saxon England. Duduc, probably from Lorraine, though possibly from Old Saxony, had been appointed to the see at Wells as early as 1033, and on his death in 1061 was succeeded by Giso, who had been born in Saint-Trond in the diocese of Liège in Lower Lotharingia.[19] Giso exhibited typical administrative talents in his diocese, playing no great part in the high politics of the age, consolidating his lands and finances and those of the canons of his church, and surviving the three kings under whom he served, Edward, Harold and the Conqueror. He had been a royal priest at Edward's court since the 1040s but appears to have had little difficulty in maintaining continuity. On his visit to Rome in April 1061, he received from Pope Nicholas II a papal privilege safeguarding his possessions. It is the shadow of the Ottonian Church rather than the reformed Papacy that seems to be heavier on these men of Lorraine who achieved high office in the English world.

---

18 Emma Mason, *St Wulfstan of Worcester, c.1008–1095*, 1990.

19 Simon Keynes, 'Giso, Bishop of Wells (1061–88)', *Anglo-Norman Studies* xix, 1997, pp. 203–71.

The same could well be said also of the direct Norman influence. Under direct ducal control, the Church in Normandy in the first half of the eleventh century bore all the marks of Ottonian attitudes towards reform. The archbishops of Rouen were kinsmen of the duke in unbroken succession from 989 to 1084. William (later the Conqueror) could intrude his half-brother Odo into the rich diocese of Bayeux before the young man had reached the age of twenty. Yet reforming elements were vigorously at work, reflecting in some curious ways the situation in England. A generation after the monastic revival in England, under the direction and inspiration of William of Volpiano, the Norman monastic situation was transformed. There were only six monastic houses in Normandy in 1026; by 1070 there were thirty-three, including seven nunneries. The establishment of Bec by Herluin in the 1040s brought international fame to the Normans, but it is well to remember that there was already a fruitful seedbed of monastic thought and practice in the duchy. Lay control had brought the secular church into some disrepute, but from the 1020s and much more so during the 1050s there was a clear growth of authority on the part of the bishops of all seven dioceses, a reorganisation of landed wealth followed by a rapid growth and evolution of chapters in the 1060s and 1070s coinciding with the conquest of England. Even more impressive is the building activity: new cathedrals were started, mostly in the 1020s and 1030s, though completion was delayed. As Professor Bates has shown, most appear to have been essentially of the second half of the eleventh century, with the exception of Rouen. Avranches indeed was not even consecrated until the 1120s.[20] Norman energy was more productive of quick results in England, when they had the pride and authority of conquerors to spur them on.

Bishops were undoubtedly great men in the eleventh century and showed marked signs of becoming greater in Edward's reign. Elements of the reforming impulse of the Benedictine Reformation were still strong and the saintly Wulfstan II of Worcester (1062–95), who succeeded Ealdred in the West Midlands see, carried on the tradition through the Norman Conquest deep into the Norman period. But the general tendency was more in the direction of administrative bishops, men trained in the royal curia, carrying on the familiar pattern of close co-operation between the king and his bishops so characteristic of the late Carolingian and Ottonian periods on the Continent. There was certainly (and to some extent surprisingly) no favouring of monks during Edward's reign. By 1064 more than half of the fourteen bishops in office had been royal clerks. It is important not to underestimate the importance of bishoprics as vital elements in national

---

20   Bates, *Normandy before 1066*, p. 214.

finance and therefore national defence. Ecclesiastical lands were as much part and parcel of the geldable resources of the kingdom as secular lands. Some bishops, Ealdred himself and bishop Leofgar of Hereford, for example, and many abbots too were willing and able to play an active role on the battlefield. The Anglo-Saxon Chronicle is not altogether approving of Leofgar. We are told that he was one of Earl Harold's priests, and that he 'wore his moustaches during his priesthood until he became a bishop'.[21] Even then his military instincts were not suppressed. In the same year that he became a bishop (1056) he abandoned his spiritual weapons, took up his spear and his sword and went on campaign against the Welsh, who killed him in battle (16 June 1056). It has been pointed out that Stigand's agglomeration of ecclesiastical offices, taken with his patronage of other bishops and his own personal wealth, made him a key figure in providing resources for the defence of the long coast-line of the South-East and South, substantially from Southampton to the Wash. Comparison with Odo of Bayeux in the following generation would not be out of place. Ealdred's position up to the time of his severance from his Worcester see held a comparable status in relation to the Welsh Marches. York and, even more so, Durham were equally potent in feeding into northern defences. The sadness for the historian is the shortage of good evidence for the composition of the episcopal households. If only we knew more in detail about their precise organisation we would be much happier over our assessments of the strength and weakness of the Old English Church.

We are not completely without knowledge, of course, of church administration at the lower levels, even if much of it has to be teased out of Domesday Book and allied documents, and then reflected back from that later generation on to the reality of the Edwardian Church. Difficulties of terminology abound, and while we can be sure that functions later associated with *choriepiscopi*, deans, priors, and archdeacons, were freely exercised, the use of such terms is rare. Homilists in their exhortations placed an immense burden of pastoral duties on the bishops, so much so that it is hard to see how even a sizeable fraction could be done without massive delegation, especially in the larger dioceses and amalgamation of dioceses. The household clerks of the bishops, their *clerici* or *ministri*, were the men most likely to be trusted with such delegated duties. There remained some things that had to be done by the bishop alone. The most time-consuming of these activities was the act of confirmation. This could not be delegated. Wulfstan II's biographer stressed the bishop's special concern for his pastoral duties and told how, both at Worcester and at York, he conducted

---

21 *Anglo-Saxon Chronicle, s.a.* 1056.

mass confirmations, claiming that he dealt with literally thousands of children in a single day.[22] Orthodox doctrine expected children to have reached an age of discretion, seven or nine, before confirmation, but there was a strong undercurrent of opinion, probably based on sheer physical necessity, that confirmation could quickly follow baptism, and indeed even accompany it at the same ceremony.

Visitation of all parts of the diocese was also a serious obligation hard to meet even by the most conscientious of the bishops. Many dioceses were split into smaller units, later in Norman days to be fossilised into territorial archdeaconries. Recent concentration on the importance of the minster churches has also enabled us to understand better a widespread phenomenon whereby minsters were often associated with hundreds or wapentakes. The senior priests at such minsters were the natural guardians of episcopal interests at hundred and at shire courts. When matters of moment were brought forward, a bishop would indeed attend a shire court and set claim to a share in the presidency over it, though it is far from certain that such an attendance was a matter of routine. Changes in the structure of the Church were throwing more weight on the smaller units and on more compact agrarian localities. As we have said, minsters were still important, but village churches were becoming increasingly common in the eleventh century. As always, the truest test of health in the Church rested with the humble priests and deacons, of whom we have only spasmodic record. Many of them in King Edward's day must have been trained in the monastic schools set up as a direct result of the Benedictine Reformation. Monks and clerics who had been taught in the early decades of the century by Aelfric, Wulfstan and their contemporaries would still be active in the 1040s and 1050s. Their pupils in turn would constitute the majority in pastoral office.

It was commonplace among Norman writers to disparage the state of the Old English Church as lifeless and lacking in reforming zeal. A more balanced view would suggest that there was still much strength in the structure, in the administrative expertise developed in episcopal and monastic households, and in the traditions of homiletic teaching and instruction inherited from an earlier generation. No other country in Western Europe showed such a firm allegiance to literary and educative activity in the vernacular. There were imperfections. Charges of pluralism could be maintained at the highest level; and the Pope's firm rejection of Ealdred's plea to retain Worcester when translated to York is a whiff of what to the Roman curia appeared a scandal. Accusations of simony seem on the whole to have been vague and unsubstantiated, and on celibacy England seemed no

---

22   Mason, *St Wulfstan of Worcester*, p. 169.

more at fault than other Western European Churches. Royal involvement in appointment to high ecclesiastical office and landlord control of many lesser offices remained intense. It has been well said that the Old English Church in the eleventh century up to 1066 existed in a period of slack water between two tides of reform.[23] That main stream was receiving a sharp definition precisely during the reign of the Confessor from the time of the Synod of Sutri (1046) to the 1060s, when Cardinal Hildebrand, later to be Pope Gregory VII (1073–85), was assuming an ascendancy at the papal curia. For this period, with its emphasis on instruction in the vernacular, its support for church building, and its accumulation of wealth in land and treasures, one recognises that there was great potential locked up in the institutions of the Old English Church.

---

23   Barlow, *The English Church, 1000–1066*, p. 27.

CHAPTER FOUR

The Norman Conquest

The Norman Conquest was a political and military triumph of the first order, and dramatic political and military consequences of a permanent nature flowed from it. Effects on the ecclesiastical life of England were also intense, even if, initially at least, they were not so dramatic. Most of the great churches lost some of their temporal possessions, it is true, to the advantage of Norman newcomers, but only exceptionally, as at New Minster, Winchester, were there large confiscations by way of punishment for active resistance. Most alienations were suffered at sub-tenant level because the tenants had fought against William and stood in array against him at Hastings or later; and there was quite a degree of recovery as new Norman bishops and abbots took over administration of their estates.

King William was anxious to stress the legitimacy of his succession, and it is quite surprising to find how strong was the element of continuity in the first three or four years after the battle of Hastings. Stigand remained archbishop of Canterbury. Papal strictures against his position and status were unheeded. In late 1067 or early 1068, Remigius, elected to the vacant see of Dorchester-on-Thames, went to him for consecration, a step studiously avoided by Anglo-Saxon bishops in Edward's reign. Ealdred at York, the most experienced of all the other bishops, proved, until his death in 1069, a key figure in ensuring relative peaceful ecclesiastical continuity. The same may be said of Wulfstan, bishop of Worcester (1062–95); and because of his long life and personality his example proved even more telling. Throughout the reign of William I, and well into that of William II, Wulfstan stood out as one toiling to keep the peace, and so supporting the legitimacy of the new Norman ruler. English survivors of moderate estate from many parts of England turned to him for leadership in complex ways. The Life of Wulfstan, written in Anglo-Saxon by Colman, the monk, soon after Wulfstan's death, was translated into Latin by William of Malmesbury. It tells stories of miracles and of church consecrations in places outside his diocese. Wulfstan was declared a saint in the 1120s. It is clear that his elevation to sainthood was a reflection of the way in which he had acted as peacemaker and reconciler over the trauma of the Conquest.[1] Giso at Wells (1061–88) exercised a similar role, though, as a foreigner, in a lower key.[2] At London, the Norman bishop William, in office since 1051, continued to exercise a powerful influence until his death in 1075. Clearly his bishopric did very well out of the Conquest. He did not share in the castle building in London itself but at some stage, with royal support, set up a castle at Bishops Stortford (Hertfordshire) and succeeded in picking up many useful estates in Hertfordshire and Essex, laying the foundation for the substantial bishop's fee of Domesday Book, something in the nature of a purchased lordship. Already by 1066 he had advanced the internal organisation of his bishopric, separating off episcopal from chapter estates to the point where the canons were reckoned to hold most of their estates from the king. The strength of St Paul's in the ecclesiastical polity, often overlooked because of the towering figures of Lanfranc and then Anselm, at Canterbury, is a point often neglected in discussion of the relative ease of transition from Anglo-Saxon to Anglo-Norman.[3]

London was a special case. A dramatic general turning point in ecclesiastical affairs in England came in 1070. William, Duke of Normandy, had undertaken his conquest with the full backing of the reforming element in the Western Church. Hildebrand, a most powerful member of the Cardinalate, later to be the formidable Pope Gregory VII (1073–85), gave him active support. Indeed at a time of tension between King William and the Papacy in the late 1070s, Gregory deplored in retrospect the bloodshed that had been caused by the Conquest. For all this papal support, there was no immediate attempt to bring England in line between 1066 and 1069, probably because there was just too much to do to establish the secular pattern of settlement, but in the later 1060s, above all after the death of archbishop Ealdred on 11 September 1069, action was needed. A papal legation was invited to the kingdom, headed by Ermenfrid, cardinal bishop of Sitten, and two cardinal priests. The initiative for the mission presumably came from the Roman curia, but William must have given it his approval. The anomalous position of the archbishop of Canterbury had to be rectified

---

1 Emma Mason, *St Wulfstan of Worcester c.1008–1095*, 1990.
2 Simon Keynes, 'Giso, Bishop of Wells (1061–88)', *Anglo-Norman Studies* xix, 1997, pp. 203–71.
3 Christopher Brooke with Gillian Keir, *London, 800–1216: The Shaping of a City*, 1975, p. 29.

if first steps towards curial ambitions to create something of the nature of a papal monarchy were to be taken.

At a Council held at Winchester in 1070 decisions were taken vital to the reshaping of the upper echelons of church government.[4] Of the fifteen English sees, York was vacant and Durham in disarray, with its bishop, Aethelwine, hostile to King William and soon to be exiled and outlawed. Four bishops represented foreign appointments, made in the reign of the Confessor: William of London, Hermann of Sherborne, Giso of Wells and Walter of Hereford. Leofric of Exeter, though English or Cornish by birth, had been brought up in Lorraine. Wulfstan of Worcester and the rather negative Siward of Rochester were native-born but of impeccable appointment. Remigius of Dorchester was the most recently appointed, consecrated by Stigand, it is true, but in all other respects acceptable, foreign-born and foreign-trained. That left five Englishmen, all Edwardian appointments, open to harsh scrutiny by the legates. Stigand was the critical figure. After more than three years under Norman rule, trusted to some extent by the Norman incomers, he seems to have been taken by surprise when the papal legates moved to his deposition. The old question of exercising archiepiscopal office when his predecessor was still alive, together with what must have looked to the reformers as flagrant pluralism (he held the major sees of Canterbury and Winchester, and many other lucrative offices), was at last decisive. He died two years later, still complaining about his treatment. Leofwine, bishop of Lichfield, was married. Aethelmaer of Elmham, Stigand's brother, was tarred with the same brush of venality as his brother. Aethelric of Selsey presented a more complicated case. He had been very close to Stigand and had been appointed to his see in 1058 during the brief period when Stigand had received papal recognition. The Council at Winchester hesitated over his case, but Ermenfrid, acting alone after the departure of the cardinal priests, declared him deposed at a second council held at Windsor. Pope Alexander II expressed some unhappiness over Aethelric, who left some good reputation for legal sagacity.

The actions of 1070 left the board clear after the Whitsun Council at Windsor for a set of new Norman-directed appointments to the episcopate. Both the archiepiscopal sees were vacant, together with a number of other key offices, including Winchester. This gave perfect opportunity to the reforming elements in the Church, supported by the king, to intrude their men into high office legally. As similar opportunities occurred in the abbacies, as abbots died, corresponding intrusions were made, firmly though with

---

4   *Councils and Synods, 871–1204*, part II, pp. 563–75 (Legatine Council at Winchester),
7 or 11 April; pp. 577–80 (Legatine Council at Windsor), 24 May.

regard to proper legal procedures. No Englishman henceforth was appointed to the highest ecclesiastical offices during the reign of King William I; and substantially this was true with only minor exceptions throughout the reigns of his sons. In personnel the effect of the Norman Conquest on the English Church was revolutionary. Bishops and abbots for the two generations after 1070 became almost exclusively French-speaking and trained in the liturgy and mores of the Continental Church, mostly Normans, with a sprinkling from France, Italy and Lorraine; and mostly men who had made their way through royal service.

The biggest immediate problem was the Canterbury appointment. The deprivation of Stigand left King William with a problem to delight the heart of any political leader with a taste for legality. At the great Whitsun Council, action was taken over York and Winchester. Thomas of Bayeux, royal chaplain and distinguished scholar, was appointed to York (1070–1100). A near-contemporary described him as famous for his knowledge of literature, secular prudence and good morals; and pre-eminent for his love of music.[5] Walkelin, also a Norman, reputedly a kinsman of the king, was moved into the Winchester see. There remained Canterbury, the most important prize of all. It is likely that the Norman establishment had already made up its mind. Lanfranc, abbot of St Stephen's, Caen, since 1063, was one of the most eminent scholars in the Western Church. Of Italian origin, he had become one of the principal teachers and ornaments of the vigorous new reformed Benedictine abbey of Bec. He was no mere acquiescent yes-man to William, and their relationship had at times been stormy. Yet William marked him out for the headship of his own new prestigious monastic foundation at Caen, and in 1067 had offered him the archbishopric of Rouen. Lanfranc refused, but now in 1070 the even more remarkable offer of Canterbury was made to him. After many protestations of unworthiness, some conventional, some not, he accepted the offer. Among the genuine elements in his protestations were his plea of ignorance of the English language, and his awareness of what he saw as the backwardness and remoteness of the English people. Pressure from the king and from his former abbot, the saintly Herluin of Bec, probably determined acceptance. Lanfranc crossed to England and was consecrated in the damaged metropolitan church at Canterbury on 29 August 1070. This highly experienced

---

5 *Ordericus Vitalis*, vol. ii (Books 3 and 4), ed. Marjorie Chibnall, 1969, p. 238. Thomas and Walkelin, who was promoted to Winchester, are described as men of foresight, full of kindness and humanity, venerable and loving to men, venerating and loving God in their inmost souls.

scholar-monk and administrator in his fifties now began one of the most effective and successful tenures of archiepiscopal office known to English history.[6]

He started his period of office (1070–89) with many positive assets. His accord with the king was strong and indeed proved absolute in England. Their interests were too coincident for either to risk open breach, in spite of the strains and tensions of this exceptionally turbulent decade in European Church–State relationships. Not that there was always full agreement between the two powerful men. At the outset the position of Archbishop Thomas of York had to be considered. His consecration had been delayed until Lanfranc himself was in office. To King William's displeasure, Lanfranc insisted on a written declaration of obedience from Thomas. It took both expressions of royal wrath and exercise of royal diplomacy to effect a compromise by which Thomas provided a personal declaration to his fellow archbishop, leaving the question of permanent subjection of York to Canterbury as an open matter for adjudication later. From Lanfranc's point of view it was essential to confirm supremacy over York if he were to implement general reforms within the English Church; and indeed within a twelvemonth he received written professions of obedience from other bishops as well. Both Lanfranc and Thomas visited Rome in 1071 to obtain their symbols of office, their pallia, from the Pope. Their reception differed dramatically. Lanfranc was honoured by Pope Alexander but Thomas was threatened with deposition and made no headway whatsoever with his claims to jurisdictions over some of the southern sees such as Worcester, long entangled in late Anglo-Saxon days with the archiepiscopal see of York. From that point onwards, Lanfranc was confident in his control and well set on his course to reorganise the English Church.

Lanfranc's main instruments for reform were thoroughly traditional, much in line with what was aimed at by the better reforming elements in Normandy itself in the 1060s and 1070s. The secret was to ensure the appointment of good bishops and clergy, to hold regular councils and to issue (and as far as possible implement) decrees that would bring England in line with advanced Continental thinking on the status and function of the clerical order. Synods and circuits were the key to success. In England Lanfranc and his supporters were able to harness such means to reformation

---

6 Z.N. Brooke, *The English Church and the Papacy*, 1931 (reprint 1968), ch. viii, pp. 117–31. Frank Barlow, 'A View of Archbishop Lanfranc', *Journal of Ecclesiastical History* xvii, 1965, pp. 163–77; Margaret Gibson, *Lanfranc of Bec*, 1978. The *Acta Lanfranci* may now be studied in a good edition, *Anglo-Saxon Chronicle, MS A*, ed. Janet Bately, 1978.

more efficiently than in Normandy. As conquerors, they had a free hand in dismissing what they regarded as evil customs, much freer than when faced with the entrenched rights of triumphant barons and clerics in the Norman homeland. The result is a certain time lag in favour of England. In many respects it is not until after the Council of Lillebonne in 1080 that the Norman Church shows signs of catching up, displaying then, as Professor Bates has shown, a professional quality outstanding in contemporary Northern France.[7]

Lanfranc himself was well placed in 1070, with much more scope than he would have had if he had accepted Rouen three years earlier. His prestige, his seniority, his ability to work on fundamentals with King William, ensured success. William had selected him to preside as abbot over his new foundation, St Stephen's, the *abbaye aux hommes*, at Caen, and it was universally recognised that it was his reputation as scholar and teacher at Bec that had done so much to set the Norman Church on the right path to revival. Yet we must not praise Lanfranc to the neglect of others. The sheer weight of evidence relating to him and his doings can be misleading. Full credit should also be given to the astonishingly vigorous and able bench of bishops who came to work and flourish both centrally and in their dioceses during his archiepiscopate. After 1070 there is a sense of group solidarity among them, brought about by their origins, by their consciousness of common purpose, and by their awareness that they were operating in conquered territory. All new bishops in Lanfranc's time came from the Norman side of the Channel. Wulfstan of Worcester and Giso of Wells had been appointed before 1066 and outlived the Conqueror and Lanfranc in full possession of their sees, but everywhere else there was change: Normans, French, Lorrainers, Italians, but no English. They tended to be appointed young, to live long and to endure, wearing well in office. At the time of Domesday Book, in 1086, there were fifteen bishops in England, eleven Normans, two from Lorraine, one Italian (Lanfranc), and only one Englishman (Wulfstan). Their length of tenure was remarkable. Five of the fifteen occupied their sees for thirty years or more, another five for more than twenty. Of the remainder, four enjoyed tenure between sixteen and nineteen years. At peril we ignore this simple fact which did so much to ensure institutional continuity and stability to the English Church. Edward the Confessor's policy of drawing some good men from Normandy and Lorraine into high office now bore full fruit. Of our fifteen Domesday Book bishops, five were monks and ten drawn from the secular clergy, though it might well

---

7   David Bates, *Normandy before 1066*, 1982, p. 212.

be argued that the presence of Lanfranc himself (and also of Wulfstan, representing an earlier manifestation of the monastic) threw a notable emphasis on the side of the puritan, monkish element.[8]

Lanfranc was sufficiently in the mainstream of the ecclesiastical thought of his age, even if he was himself something of a pre-Investiture Contest man on the papal issue, to know the force of and need for continuous legal insistence on moral reform. The agency for implementation of this legal activity was close at hand in the shape of provincial councils, a device which further enhanced the group solidarity of the bishops. Councils were held regularly, probably annually, and we have record of two (styled general councils) in 1072 and 1075, and also of further councils at Winchester (1076), London (1078), and Gloucester (1081, and late 1085). Some were held in conjunction with royal councils or witans. Vocabulary was still uncertain and the distinction between an ecclesiastical council and a synod non-existent. At the great royal Council over Christmas 1085 at Gloucester where Domesday Book was planned, we are told that after the king held his court for five days the archbishop and clerics had a synod for a further three days. Three bishoprics were filled at that meeting, all by clerks from the royal household, for Norfolk, Cheshire and for London.[9]

As for the substance of reform, it is clear from surviving evidence that the general thrust was in accord with advanced clerical thought, though with special arrangements attributable to English peculiarities. Matters concerning simony, parish arrangements, pluralists, vagrant monks and the recognition of Anglo-Saxon saints were all dealt with. Two special concerns merit attention. At some stage in the early 1070s, possibly as early as 1072, King William issued a famous writ, two copies of which have survived. It dealt with matters of ecclesiastical jurisdiction and reflected the deliberations of all parties, the magnates as well as the spiritual leaders. It was not a clear-cut separation of ecclesiastical and secular jurisdiction, but it undoubtedly represented a serious stage in that direction. Bishops and archdeacons were forbidden henceforth to hear pleas relating to the episcopal laws in the hundred court. With full support from the king and his officers, the bishop was to hear such cases at his seat or in some appointed place. This was contrary to the custom of the country and was not immediately allowed. Nevertheless it is a positive pointer to the increased prestige of ecclesiastical

---

8   Frank Barlow, *The English Church, 1066–1154*, 1979, pp. 57–8, and a useful diagram on p. 318; H.R. Loyn, 'William's Bishops: Some Further Thoughts', *Anglo-Norman Studies* x, 1988, pp. 223–35.

9   *Anglo-Saxon Chronicle, s.a.* 1085.

law and ecclesiastical jurisdiction and a delicate step towards the movement of clerical influence from the hundred court.[10]

The other special case concerns the problem of clerical marriage. Norman councils in 1064 and again even more firmly in 1072 followed the central reformist line, insisting on clerical celibacy, even though the custom was opposed and indeed met with fierce resistance when bishops attempted to enforce it. At a council at Winchester in 1076, Lanfranc issued a decree which suggested an element of compromise. It forbade, not altogether effectively, the future marriage of priests but also ordained that there should be no compulsion for priests, whether in towns (*castellis*) or in villages, to put aside their wives. Those who were unmarried were forbidden to marry. Bishops were enjoined to take care not to ordain priests or deacons unless they first made sure they had not wives. In practice, decisions rested with the diocesan bishop. The Englishman Wulfstan of Worcester, monk and reformer, was zealous in implementation. He gave his clergy the clear choice of their wives or their churches.[11]

Fortunately, a reasonably full account has been preserved of this Winchester Council which gives a fine illustration of the co-operation between royal government and the reforming element in the Church.[12] The separation of courts was tacitly affirmed and royal fines invoked to ensure that episcopal jurisdiction was effective. Priests were to be made safe against intrusions by vagrant monks and also against abuse by landlords. A priest was to give only accustomed service in return for his benefice. Lanfranc attempted, though not with complete success, to make the blessing of a priest necessary for a lawful marriage. A man was enjoined not to give his daughter or kinswoman in marriage without priestly benediction. In 1076, the very year in which the ecclesiastical tradition of co-operation between king and Church was being torn apart in Europe by the struggle between Pope and Emperor, King William and Archbishop Lanfranc in England, were operating in a unison reminiscent of the days of Charles the Great or Otto the Great and their immediate successors.

Bishops were the key figures in bringing about Lanfranc's reorganisation of the English Church, but it would be wrong to regard them as revolutionary. They worked in the full tradition of the Church in England, as well as that of the Continental Church in Western Europe. In one respect they were able to reinforce a move that had already started in England. The

10   *EHD* ii, 2nd edn, 1979, *s.a.* 1085.
11   Emma Mason, *St Wulfstan of Worcester*, 1990, p. 163; *Vita Wulfstani*, ed. R.R. Darlington, Camden Society, 1928, 53–4.
12   *Councils and Synods, 871–1204*, part II, no. 93, pp. 616–20.

nature of the conversion of the English to Christianity and the endowment of churches in the early centuries had left many bishops in a rural setting. A foretaste of what was to come was offered in 1050 when the headquarters of the see for Devon and the South-West was moved from Crediton to Exeter. Now Lanfranc, with full royal support, was able virtually to complete the urbanisation of episcopal sees. Need for defence and security played its part. Norman garrisons could protect Norman bishops. Even more important was the administrative and legal need. Towns and boroughs were becoming more central to the fabric of eleventh-century society. Shire courts, trade, mints and coinage were all associated with them. Diocesan order demanded a safe centre. As early as 1072, Lanfranc ordered bishops to appoint archdeacons and other ministers of the Holy Order, presumably with the prime object of facilitating routine government over what were sometimes very large dioceses. Three years later, further ordinances were made concerning episcopal order and decisions taken which resulted in the transfer of the central church of the sees of Lichfield, Sherborne and Selsey to Chester (to 1102), Salisbury and Chichester. After 1102, bishop Robert de Limesey moved his see from Chester to Coventry, and by the early thirteenth century both Coventry and Lichfield were recognised as the episcopal centres for the north-western diocese. In East Anglia, Thetford had taken the place of Elmham before 1072 and ultimately Norwich was selected as the cathedral site. The biggest change of all came in the great see based on Dorchester-on-Thames, which, by historical accident had come to stretch from the Thames to the Humber. Before the end of the reign of the Conqueror, probably about 1080, Remigius (1067–92) had transferred fully his episcopal seat to Lincoln, and it is very likely that initial steps had been taken in that direction as early as 1072, the year in which the royal writ of King William appears to have been issued, notifying the transfer of the see to Lincoln. Authorisation to do so had been received from Pope Alexander II (d. 1073). Remigius was still 'bishop of Dorchester or Lincoln' in the record of the London Council (1075), but after 1080 and throughout Domesday Book he is bishop of Lincoln alone.[13] All this centralisation of power and wealth had a direct effect, as we shall see in the following chapter, on the physical structure of the Church in England. The late eleventh and early twelfth century constituted one of the greatest building booms in English history, cathedrals, abbeys and castles on a spectacular scale.

Norman reorganisation of the secular church was, at the top level, highly successful. With some necessary qualification, the same can be said of the

---

13   David Bates, *Bishop Remigius of Lincoln, 1067–1092*, Lincoln, 1992.

regular, the monastic element, though in some quarters, as we shall see, local Saxon loyalties created problems. Initially William looked directly to Cluny for support, but, when this was not forthcoming (manpower was limited), rather surprisingly, chose the French house of Marmoutier-on-Loire to sponsor his new prestigious and symbolic house of Battle Abbey in Sussex. It was unusual in its French patronage. For the most part, and especially after the appointment of Lanfranc, William and his advisers turned to much more natural sources in Normandy, and it is from the Norman houses of Bec, Mont-St-Michel, Jumièges, Fécamp and Caen that the bulk of abbatial appointments were made. Methods of royal control resembled those applied to the secular church. The legal niceties were observed, and the formalities of election followed faithfully. Selection of fit candidates for election was another matter. Royal interest was inevitable and in practice royal influence was overbearing. Something approaching a seventh of the landed wealth of England was in the hands of the abbots by 1086 at a time when the duties that went with such wealth had been increased by the introduction of feudal military service and the sharpening of legal responsibility both in the hundreds and in the spiritual courts.

The facts of appointment speak for themselves. In October 1066, of the thirty or so known abbots or priors of cathedral chapters, only one was an obvious foreign intrusion: Baldwin, royal physician, former monk of St Denis, abbot of Bury St Edmunds from 1065 until his death late in 1097. By 1087 the picture was vastly different.[14] All the heads of important houses were foreign-trained and of foreign birth, with only fringe exceptions: Pershore, where Thurstan, a former monk at Gloucester, died in 1087; and Ramsey, where Aelfsige was replaced by Herbert Losinga in the same year. The pattern was continued substantially through the succeeding generation, and it has been estimated that over sixty foreign appointments were made to the office of abbot between 1066 and 1135, mostly from Normandy, seven direct from Caen, seven from Fécamp, with Winchester, Old Minster and Christ Church, Canterbury, acting as intermediate staging-posts and training grounds for thirteen more (eight from Caen, five from Fécamp). Promising monks from Normandy were installed safely there, ready to take high office as opportunity served.

In the nature of things such a dramatic change in personnel created tensions, more so in the monasteries than in the secular church. The traditional picture of monks loyal to the old Anglo-Saxon order at Peterborough,

---

14 H.R. Loyn, 'Abbots of English Monasteries in the Period Following the Norman Conquest', *England and Normandy in the Middle Ages*, ed. David Bates and Anne Curry, 1994, pp. 95–103.

Ely, Exeter, Worcester or Glastonbury has some truth to it. There were also Anglo-Saxon abbots who conformed comfortably. Abbot Aethelwig of Evesham (1058–77) is a conspicuous example, and it was he who was prominent in suppressing the first serious Norman rebellion against William in 1076. At Bath, Burton, Coventry, Pershore, St Benet Holm and Sherborne, long-lived Anglo-Saxon abbots survived (at Sherborne until 1099) and were left in peace. Tensions sometimes erupted into violence, at St Augustine's Canterbury, and notoriously at Glastonbury, where in 1085 Abbot Thurstan turned his men-at-arms loose in the abbey, slaying some of the monks so that blood ran from the altar to the floor. Occasionally the contempt of the new rulers for the conquered Anglo-Saxons seeps through. The abbot of Abingdon refused to honour the feasts of saints Aethelwold and Edmund, dismissing them as English rustics. Abbot Paul of St Albans went even further, destroying Anglo-Saxon tombs and describing his own antecessors as rude and unlettered. Many simple monks were in fact drawn from good Anglo-Saxon families, and it is no wonder that troubles sometimes occurred.[15]

In this new post-Conquest world, however, monasticism may truly be said to have flourished. The impetus at this stage was solidly Benedictine and Cluniac. It was left to a later generation to enjoy the variety that came to be expressed in new Orders, notably the Cistercian. Lanfranc's part in the enterprise was not as clear-cut as might be expected, and some historians express surprise that this product of reformed monasticism at Le Bec, the 'father of the monks', as he has been termed, was so busy with affairs of the secular church and with high politics. Such surprise underestimates his contribution to monasticism in two special fields. In England he found one established custom much to his taste. At Christ Church, Canterbury, at Winchester Old Minster, at Sherborne and at Worcester the cathedrals were run on monastic lines, with the bishop operating as abbot or prior in charge of a monastic chapter. Lanfranc encouraged this system and strove to extend it. Rochester followed the example of Christ Church. After many vicissitudes, Ely became the central see for a new diocese, though not until 1109. Successful attempts were made to link the rich abbey of Bath with the poor see at Wells, though similar efforts to involve the abbey of Bury St Edmunds with an East Anglian see failed. The wily and powerful abbot Baldwin resisted pressure, and Norwich ultimately emerged as the proper diocesan centre. In the North-West, as we have seen, there was a further linking of the rich abbey at Coventry with a poorer see at Chester. Lanfranc

---

15   Ibid., p. 96; *Gesta abbatum Sancti Albani*, ed. H.T. Riley, Rolls Series, 3 vols, 1867–69, vol. i, p. 62.

was clearly happy both with the principles of urbanisation and with the intimate involvement of the regular clergy with the secular church. He was also concerned over the inner life of monastic communities. His 'Monastic Constitutions', which he provided as a customary for his monks at Christ Church, Canterbury, shows him in full vigour, not as an innovator but as a reformer. Drawing material from other customaries, principally but not exclusively Le Bec, but also with Cluniac and Flemish additions, he set out a pattern for regulating the liturgical year. It owed little to Anglo-Saxon precedent. Lanfranc's customs came to apply to at least a dozen abbeys and cathedrals in England, including Rochester and the abbey at St Albans, where Lanfranc's personal influence was strong.[16] Traditional autonomy within the Benedictine houses precluded absolute uniformity, but there can be no doubt that Lanfranc's towering personal prestige had immense impact. The abbots themselves belonged to a small, intimate group, mostly trained in the same few Norman houses. They bore within the limits of their monastic discipline characteristics of conscious superiority, gifted rulers of men and of materials, able builders and administrators. They produced no saints but were, as far as we can judge, mostly celibate and tolerably virtuous, not unlike the better elements of the higher echelons of the Indian Civil Service in the days of the British Raj.

The chance of survival of historical record has enabled us to learn more about the activities and motives of many of these men than we might have any reason to expect. It was not usual for any biographers to attempt a full-scale life of any bishop as such, and yet one able author wrote a biography of Gundulf, bishop of Rochester, 1077–1108, probably within a decade or so of the bishop's death.[17] As an insight into the nature of a monk-bishop of the age, the *Vita* is invaluable, bringing together the two strands most powerful in the making of the Norman Church, the ascetic, saintly, monkish and the active governor, experienced and effective in external affairs. Gundulf grew up in the shadow of Lanfranc, very much the archbishop's man, first at Caen and then at Canterbury and finally at Rochester. He was the archetypal useful man of his age, his saintly qualities matched by practical sense and business acumen. William the Conqueror knew of his work at Caen and Canterbury and used him to supervise the building of the White Tower in London. Rufus, although not as close to him as his father had been and his younger brother, Henry I, was to be, arranged for him to replace the timber castle at Rochester with one of stone. Gundulf's first task in episcopal office was to see to the rebuilding of the cathedral. He built a

---

16 David Knowles, *The Monastic Customs of Lanfranc*, 1951.
17 *The Life of Gundulf, Bishop of Rochester*, ed. Rodney Thomson, 1977.

convent at Malling together with a church dedicated to the Virgin Mary. His concern for organisation shone through his activities within his church. When he arrived at Rochester there were only five monks in the chapter, but he built numbers up to a reputed sixty. What is more, he saw to it that the resources were available to support such a chapter and his concern to add estates to the patrimony of Rochester is a steady element in his active life. As a diplomat and adviser he was cherished by William I and Henry I. He was also a natural choice as a participant in great ecclesiastical ceremonies. Indeed the *Vita* tells us that Gundulf was called upon whenever there were any dedications of importance to be performed or translation of holy relics. Incidental references show him present at the opening of the Confessor's grave in 1073, the ceremony of the translation of the body of St Augustine during the Canterbury vacancy in 1092, and the dedication of Battle Abbey in 1094. He also seems to have been chiefly responsible for the establishment of an effective confraternity at Rochester, possibly based on an existing Anglo-Saxon guild but more likely a new creation inspired by Cluniac ideals and models. Under its terms gifts were made, some very substantial, by laymen and -women, a number of whom adopted a monastic habit on their deathbed. Service was then performed for them at death as for a monk. A precious text embedded in the *Textus Roffensis* of the 1120s preserves a list of more than fifty charters associated with the fraternity. A high proportion of the donors were English, sub-tenants of great Norman lands such as Odo of Bayeux, Lanfranc, William d'Aubigny or Ernulf of Hesdin. It has been well argued that such a fraternity may have helped to consolidate a feeling of community in Kent after the trauma of the Conquest. Gundulf himself may have been influenced by Bec in setting up this eleventh-century 'Friends of Rochester Cathedral', perhaps at a time when, following example elsewhere at Canterbury and at London, he was separating the monks' property from his own. In his combination of wise stewardship and holiness he represents the ideal monk-bishop of his period, exhibiting both pastoral and administrative virtues of the highest order.[18]

In the purely monastic sphere, new foundations were not plentiful as a result of the Conquest. Chester was founded, direct from Bec. Selby, Shrewsbury (very much under the influence of the Montgomery family), Cranborne and Tewkesbury all became influential in their local areas. Battle Abbey was naturally a special case. It was treated as the personal territorial church of the Conqueror, its high altar erected on the spot where Harold fell. No expense was spared in its construction. By 1071 a substantial church was in

---

18   R.A.L. Smith, 'The Place of Gundulf in the Anglo-Norman Church,' *EHR* 58, 1943, pp. 257–72 and also his 'The Early Community at Rochester, *EHR* 60, 1945, pp. 289–99.

existence of a new design, incorporating a combination, rare in Normandy, of an eastern apse and an ambulatory with radiating chapels. Its pattern was followed in England at St Augustine's, Canterbury, Bury St Edmunds and Gloucester. Some 225 feet in length, it did not reach the sheer size of later creations at Winchester (533 feet), St Augustine's (349 feet) or Norwich (440 feet). The Old Minster at Winchester, planned and started in 1079, seems to have inaugurated this period of extra grandiloquence in Norman architecture; but, even so, Battle was impressive enough. As a royal foundation, a thank offering for victory and also a symbol of penitence after the slaughter of Hastings, it retained a special force, useful indeed in maintaining its independence, often in vigorous conflict with the bishops of Chichester, anxious in their own right to assert what they saw as legitimate authority in Sussex.[19]

Indeed one cannot help having a certain feeling of sympathy for the bishops of Chichester, who also faced difficulty in their relationships with another of the most interesting of post-1066 monastic foundations. William had looked first to Cluny for support in founding Battle Abbey, but Abbot Hugh had refused, with the rather curious consequence, noted above, that William had turned to the French house of Marmoutier. A decade or so later, at some time between 1078 and 1081, William's loyal tenant-in-chief, William of Warenne, and his wife, Gundrada, were more fortunate. Although still reluctant, Abbot Hugh permitted four of his Cluniac brethren to set up the first Cluniac priory in England under the patronage of William and Gundrada at Lewes in Sussex. By 1100, Lanzo, the first prior, had built a cloister, dorter and reredorter, and refectory and chapterhouse, establishing Lewes as a distinguished Cluniac house.[20] Warenne's example was not followed widely. Alwine, a wealthy London merchant, established a priory in Bermondsey, and by the middle of the twelfth century there were some thirty-six Cluniac foundations, most of them small. The influence of Cluny was great but appears to have been disseminated through the Benedictine Order in general as much as through Cluny itself and its dependent priories.

The most significant innovations in the monastic world came in the North of England, originating in the activities of the two most powerful English survivors from the Church of the reign of Edward the Confessor, Wulfstan, bishop of Worcester, and Aethelwig, abbot of Evesham. Within his diocese Wulfstan consistently supported monasticism both in his own tradition and in the tradition of the new men. In 1072, King William had

---

19 Eleanor Searle, *Lordship and Community: Battle Abbey and its Banlieu, 1066–1538*, 1974 and *The Chronicle of Battle Abbey*, ed. Searle, 1980.

20 Brian Golding, 'The Coming of the Cluniacs', *Anglo-Norman Studies* iii, 1981, pp. 68–77.

appointed Serlo, a monk from Mont-St-Michel, as abbot of a struggling little Benedictine house at Gloucester, reduced to only two monks and eight novices at the time of his arrival. Serlo was one of the many success stories of this generation, leaving an inheritance at his death in 1104 of a thriving house with some 100 monks, enjoying one of the great Norman building achievements in the abbey, begun in 1089 and dedicated on 13 July 1100.[21] Old English scholarship continued to flourish in the diocese, preparing the way for the basic interest in history and record that made possible the work of the Worcester historians of the early twelfth century. Bede's Ecclesiastical History and the tradition of St Oswald and above all St Cuthbert proved the inspiration for the move north. In 1073–74, Aldwin, a prior of Winchcombe, Reinfrid, a *conversus* of Evesham, and Aelfwig, a monk, re-established a monastic house at Jarrow; other small houses were set up at Tynemouth, Wearmouth, Whitby and Durham. The revival was extended to Scotland, to Melrose in the borderlands and to St Andrews. A small house was established at York itself. By 1100, the time of the death of Thomas of Bayeux, archbishop of York, these small and unpretentious new Benedictine foundations were firmly established. They provided a Benedictine presence familiarising the North to monks and so providing the immediate background in which the dramatic Cistercian movement could succeed in the following generations. They also provide a superb though neglected example of the way in which both Anglo-Saxon and Norman traditions could converge to enrich the religious pattern of the kingdom.[22]

One result of all the reorganisation that attended the Conquest was the elaboration of administrative structures within the dioceses and to some extent also with the greater abbeys, where, for example, the burden of dealing with military service at Bury St Edmunds led to a delegation to a non-monastic officer (in this instance the abbot's brother) who took on responsibility for seeing to this substantial part of the abbey's public obligations of service. Indeed Bury St Edmunds provides a splendid, if somewhat anomalous, example of how a great abbey could flourish under the conditions of Conquest. Unlike its neighbour, Ely, or Peterborough, or New Minster, Winchester, its abbot was in a powerful political and social position. Baldwin, a monk of St Denis and prior of the great abbey's dependency in Alsace, had been attracted to England by Edward the Confessor because of his known skill as a doctor. He was rewarded with the church

21 Emma Cownie, 'Gloucester Abbey, 1066–1135', *England and Normandy in the Middle Ages*, ed. Bates and Curry, pp. 143–57.

22 David Knowles, *The Monastic Order in England*, 1940, pp. 143–71. Anne Dawtry, 'The Benedictine Revival in the North: The Last Bulwark of Anglo-Saxon Monasticism', *Studies in Church History* 18, 1982, pp. 87–98.

at Deerhurst and the manor of Taynton (Oxon), held under the lordship of St Denis. In 1065 he was promoted to the key office of abbot of Bury St Edmunds. His reputation as a physician continued to be great and he served both the Conqueror and William Rufus in that capacity. He died at the end of 1097, probably on 29 December.

Baldwin's role in providing a strong element of continuity with the Anglo-Saxon past has probably been underestimated. A later biographer, Jocelyn of Brakeland, writing a century or so after Baldwin's death, has preserved precious details about the abbot, telling us that he spoke his English with a Norfolk accent, that he was a commanding figure in every way, and that he was capable of using his bushy eyebrows to great effect.[23] The abbey was already well endowed before his arrival, enjoying the special liberty of $8^1/_2$ hundreds in West Suffolk and his right to have a moneyer, virtually exercising regalian rights over nearly a third of the shire. The liberty had been held by Emma, the Confessor's mother, up to 1043 or 1044. In land alone by 1086 Baldwin had added some £73 worth to the abbey estate, a sum only paralleled in its increase by the amount Gloucester received under Abbot Serlo (1072–1104). The total increase in value was close on 50 per cent with benefactors drawn from high and low, ranging from the king, the queen and leading barons to local landowners and humble English sub-tenants. Baldwin was also a considerable diplomat, operating on an international scale even to the Papacy, resisting successfully attempts to transform his abbey into an episcopal see. Loyalty to the abbey itself seemed to ignore the political upheavals following the Conquest, and such loyalties from the population at large in Bury and St Albans and Ely and elsewhere may have done much to ease the transition to new French-speaking overlordship.

A feature of Baldwin's tenure of office that demands special emphasis was his fostering of the cult of St Edmund, a deliberate encouragement of maintaining strong links with the Anglo-Saxon past. It is a reminder to us that the new lords after the Conquest were not uniformly hostile to what went before them. It was all very well for Abbot Paul at St Albans to fulminate against his predecessors as primitive and stupid, and yet we hear of a chapel dedicated to St Cuthbert, of a tapestry depicting the passion of St Alban, and of a conscious encouragement of a cult of St Alban in the magnificent new abbey to the point where resources were spilled over on the embellishment of a splendid new shrine. St Etheldreda was honoured at Ely. Elsewhere and widely, Norman churchmen indulged in hagiography that linked their churches with the origins of Christianity in England.

---

23   *The Chronicle of Jocelyn of Brakeland*, ed. H.E. Butler, 1949, pp. 39–40. Antonia Gransden, 'Baldwin, Abbot of Bury St Edmunds, 1065–97', *Anglo-Norman Studies* iv, 1982, pp. 65–76.

Lanfranc, it is true, was initially hostile, complaining before accepting appointment that the language was unknown to him and the native races barbarous, but Eadmer, writing about him a generation later, probably got the balance right when he explained that the great man, while still new to England, changed some things, often with good sense, that he found unacceptable, and others principally to assert his own authority.[24] Lanfranc was probably hostile to many of the local obscure saints, seeing them as masks for early pagan-based revelation of holy wells, groves or other holy places. At Evesham, Abington, Malmesbury and St Albans itself contempt for things Anglo-Saxon was at times expressed. And yet, as a modern commentator shrewdly wrote, with Baldwin at Bury in mind, 'in terms both of publicity and of veneration the Norman Conquest was perhaps one of the better things ever to happen to Anglo-Saxon saints'.[25]

If Baldwin, with his regulation of military service, and systematic analysis of the abbey's resources, represents one side of ecclesiastical ability over the period of Conquest, he was by and large a representative of a general phenomenon. Terminology was still fluid in the secular, more so than in the regular, field, and priors, deans, archdeacons and deacons did not always conform to a stable pattern. Archdeacons, as is shown by a famous writ of *c*.1072, present some perplexing problems. In the larger dioceses, such as that of Remigius of Lincoln, a division into manageable administrative units was essential. Remigius himself, bishop of Dorchester/Lincoln (1067–92), was an important figure in the settlement of conquered England. He had been present at the field of Hastings and was much in favour with the ducal house, to which he may have been related. Henry of Huntingdon, writing when memory of Remigius was still green, tells us that he was very short in stature, though great in heart, and had a dark complexion and a charming manner.[26] His administrative gifts were formidable. He was placed in the great rambling diocese of Dorchester, as it then was, as early as 1067, and consecrated by Archbishop Stigand. His diocese was probably in areal extent the largest in settled Europe. Very sensibly and with full royal support (the writ has still survived) he moved the centre of the diocese from Dorchester to Lincoln, probably initiating the move soon after 1072. Faced with this mammoth task of supervising the church in a swathe of county from the Humber to the Middle Thames, he divided the diocese into seven units, within which clerks of his household, among whom there were some

24 Eadmer, *The Life of St Anselm, Archbishop of Canterbury*, ed. R.W. Southern, 1962, p. 51.
25 S.J. Ridyard, '*Condigna Veneratio*: Post-Conquest Attitudes to the Saints of the Anglo-Saxons', *Anglo-Norman Studies*, ix, 1986, p. 206.
26 Bates, *Bishop Remigius*, p. 4.

described as archdeacons, carried out such episcopal offices as were permissible within their chosen area. We begin to hear also of clerks who were in charge of minsters, often coinciding with the boundaries of hundreds. These developed, possibly more quickly than the written evidence permits us to say, into rural deaneries.[27] For all the attempts made to establish separate ecclesiastical courts to deal with ecclesiastical business, clerks remained deeply embedded in secular affairs, natural parts of rural communities at the time of the Domesday survey, essential witnesses at causes concerning lands and rights at the secular courts. At the level of cathedral clergy, Archbishop Thomas of York seems to emerge as a key figure in ordering chapters not of a monastic nature. Under his guidance the pattern was established which became more or less standard throughout the Middle Ages, offering a four-square division of responsibility between dean, treasurer, precentor and chancellor. But the ramifications of responsibilities of the episcopal household went far beyond the ordering of the cathedral itself.[28]

Men of the calibre of Wulfstan of Worcester, Giso of Wells, Abbot Baldwin of Bury St Edmunds and Abbot Paul of St Albans ensured the stability of the Norman settlement. Towards the end of King William's reign, they, with their colleagues, took part in the massive and unique survey of the kingdom that produced Domesday Book. With the contents of Domesday Book we shall have to deal when we attempt in our next chapter to assess the nature of the English Church in the last decades of the eleventh century. For the moment it is enough to note the production of the survey, to recognise the part played by the Church in its construction, and to acknowledge that in itself the survey represents an act of supreme confidence on the part of the Normans. All manner of anxieties may have prompted the effort: fear of renewed Scandinavian pressures, desire to perpetuate tax systems that would uphold the military structures of the new Norman world, a basic wish to ensure continuity and legitimacy. The very haste with which the project was carried through illustrates the strength of the administrative machine which the Normans had inherited and refined. Plans to undertake the survey were set in motion at the Christmas feast of 1085–86. By the time William left England, as it turned out for the last time, in the autumn, a substantial bulk of the material that was to be compressed into the final record, the first volume of Domesday Book, had been brought to him.[29] On campaign against the French king, his own liege lord, William was hurt as

---

27   C.N.L. Brooke, 'The Archdeacons and the Norman Conquest', *Tradition and Change*, ed. Diana Greenway, Christopher Holdsworth and Jane Sayers, 1985, pp. 7–12.

28   D.E. Greenway, *Le Neve: Fasti Ecclesiae Anglicanae, 1066–1300*, vol. iii, Lincoln, 1977, pp. ix–xi.

29   *Anglo-Saxon Chronicle, s.a.* 1085: and all these records were brought to him afterwards.

he devastated the town of Mantes, and on 9 September 1087 he died and was buried at Caen in the monastery dedicated to St Stephen which he had built and richly endowed. The Anglo-Saxon Chronicler attempted a lengthy assessment of his reign, his character and achievements. He praised his good peace and his dignity. He did not conceal his bad points, his cupidity and sternness and violence. On religious themes he took a positive view and in a famous passage summed up his qualities:

> He was gentle to the good men who loved God, and stern beyond all measure to those people who resisted his will. In the same place where God permitted him to conquer England he set up a famous monastery and appointed monks for it, and endowed it well. In his days the famous church at Canterbury was built, and also many another over all England. Also, this country was very full of monks and they lived their life under the rule of St Benedict, and Christianity was such in his day that each man who wished followed out whatever concerned his order.[30]

William left three sons, but the immediate succession problem was eased by the support of Archbishop Lanfranc, who saw to it that William's wishes were carried out and his second son, William Rufus, succeeded to the English throne. An anonymous monk of Caen left a moving account of the dispositions made by the dying king, what should be given to churches, to the poor and finally to his sons. He gave his crown, his sword and his sceptre studded with gems to Rufus. After special pleading by the Norman archbishop of Rouen he was persuaded to leave Normandy to Robert, his eldest son, in spite of his unfilial behaviour. The monk does not mention the youngest of the brothers, the later Henry I, but other sources tell us of the large fortune that passed to him, though no land.[31] In a concise summary of the Conqueror's characteristics, his strength, wisdom and temperateness, special concentration is laid on his piety. Less than two years later, on 24 May 1089, Lanfranc, the other giant figure of the ecclesiastical scene, died. Between them, King William and Archbishop Lanfranc had steered the Church along a reforming path without ever submitting to the extreme claims of the Hildebrandine Papacy. We must pick up with the complex questions of contact with Rome again in the following chapter. Respect for Rome, but not submission to Rome, seems indeed to have been the policy agreed and followed by both men, the consequences of which were to be further played out in the following generation. It is perhaps an accurate

---

30 Ibid., *s.a.* 1087.
31 *EHD* ii, no. 6. Included in some manuscripts of the *Chronicle of William of Jumièges*, ed. J. Marx, 1914, pp. 145–9.

measure of the achievements of both king and archbishop that their deaths did not disrupt the general pattern of development of the English Church. Rufus proved to be a very different man, morally and spiritually, from his father. Anselm, in temperament and character, differed from Lanfranc at many points. Yet there is no great break to be noted at the end of the 1080s. The consequences of the Conquest continued to be apparent in an unbroken line of development.

CHAPTER FIVE

Domesday Book: Ecclesiastical Organisation at the End of the Eleventh Century

To understand the development of church organisation in the late eleventh century is a worthy objective and yet in a sense only touches the surface of things. We have, always important, sometimes dominant, the evidence of Domesday Book to take into consideration. Whoever tries to approach the problems connected with the nature and status of the English Church at this period sooner or later has to grapple with the mass of information contained in this record. Historian after historian has attempted the task, often starting with reservations and hesitations, and sometimes with querulous complaints. Some of the complaints are justified. Domesday Book will not tell us what we want to know; and moments of sheer frustration occur when we realise how much was known and not recorded. Yet by and large the historian has much more to be grateful for than to see as matter for complaint. No other community in medieval Europe has so much information packed in relatively uniform style that covers so much of its life, including its ecclesiastical life.

If we approach the problems at three levels, the advantages to us of the Domesday evidence, even more than the difficulties, become apparent. To take first the most prominent level, that of the great dignitaries, new Norman prelates for the most part, exercising power and influence at the centre and in their various localities. Exactness cannot be wished for, but we know that roughly a fraction of something between a little over a quarter and a fifth of the landed wealth of England was in the hands of the Church.[1] We can tell also, sometimes directly, often by inference, that the systems of exploitation

---

1 W.J. Corbett, *Cambridge Medieval History*, vol. v, 1926, pp. 507–11, gives a good general statistical basis, though there have been many attempted refinements since his day.

and accounting on the church lands tended to be more efficient than that on secular estates. Only the royal administration, conducted itself by clerics, could equal the skill of the officers of Lanfranc, the bishop of Salisbury or the bishop of Durham, or, to take an example from a surviving English prelate, that of the Worcester episcopate. Let us look in detail, for example, at Wiltshire, where the bishops of Winchester and Salisbury ranked among the greatest of the landowners. Both bishops won reputations as administrators of the first order. Walkelin of Winchester (1070–98) matured under William Rufus to become, with Ranulf Flambard, the chief financial officer of the Crown. Osmund of Salisbury (1078–99) was a more complex character. He had been king's chancellor from 1070 to 1078, presiding over the royal writing office at a time when Latin finally replaced English as the sole official language of government. He made substantial contribution to the ordering of liturgy according to the 'Use of Sarum'. He appears to have acted as a commissioner for the Domesday survey in the south-western circuit; and there is some evidence that suggests that the circuit return known as the Exeter Domesday may have been written at Salisbury. The arrangements made by Bishop Osmund for his lands in Wiltshire were a model of their kind. His estates were grouped into four great manorial complexes with a smaller holding at Charnage, assessed at 5 hides for tax and worth £4 in 1086. The four centres were all convenient for tax collection. Potterne paid gold for 52 hides and was valued at £60. Bishops Canning was also worth £60 to the bishop, with complex attached holdings worth another £35. Before 1066 it had paid tax for 70 hides. Ramsbury, a former episcopal see, was the third centre, with a tax obligation for no less than £90 in 1066. The total value was given at £70, of which £52.15s was the bishop's. Salisbury itself constituted the fourth great holding, with a geldable capacity of 50 hides and a value of £47 in the bishop's demesne and £17.10s in the other men's holdings. A mass of detailed information is also given, including the names of many sub-tenants, a high proportion suggesting survival of Saxon landholders at that level. The concentration of financial rights and duties illustrates admirably Norman use of existing late Anglo-Saxon structures to good purposes. Great churches could and did spring up at places like Bishops Canning, providing for ecclesiastical fiefs safehouses as effective as castles were to prove for the secular lords.[2]

Indeed the presence of substantial churches at sub-cathedral level brings us to reconsider the second level at which the evidence of Domesday Book gives effective meaning. We have already discussed the minster churches of late Anglo-Saxon England, and modern scholars, notably John Blair, have

---

2 *DB* i, Wiltshire, ed. Caroline and Frank Thorne, 1979, p. 3 (66a).

rightly emphasised their continuing importance into the twelfth century. In a vastly influential paper which opened up the topic to serious consideration, Blair surveyed the secular minster churches of Domesday Book.[3] He brought together evidence for what he called the 'superior' churches of the survey, some of which enjoyed the services of two or more priests or canons, others where the priest or the church held more than the normal share of arable, more than a hide in some cases, indeed as much as two hides in some rare instances. He also brought correctly into the picture descriptions of churches which went outside the normal pattern in the estimate of separate tenancies or separate values. All this helped to alter the balance of thought concerning the nature of ecclesiastical structures in the later eleventh century. There had been a general understandable consensus that such minsters of the older types, some serving areas equivalent to ten or more later parishes, had had their day by 1066. Undoubtedly the future did not lie with them. The effects of the monastic revival, coupled with the multiplication of manorial churches in late Anglo-Saxon England, diminished their role. But we must now recognise that that role was still far from negligible in 1086. A wide range of what may properly be called collegiate churches continued to exist, many based on old minsters, others new, many served by groups of *clerici* or *presbyteri* or *canonici*. Exercise of traditional rights such as churchscot or rights over subordinate chapels was a mark of their special position; and a great number of them enjoyed royal or episcopal patronage. We suspect that the austerity of the Exchequer Domesday Book has concealed their true number. The fortunate survival of the *Domesday Monachorum* of Christ Church, Canterbury, describes twelve East Kent minsters, only six of which are recognisable in Domesday Book itself.[4] There are significant regional variations. South of the Thames in Hampshire, Wiltshire, Berkshire and parts of Sussex and Somerset superior churches are common, though for the most part of relatively small size. In Devon and Cornwall they are fewer but more substantial, which has led many of us to see them as more directly analogous to the *clas* churches of early medieval Wales. The Welsh border, too, sees a heavy concentration, whereas they decrease in number progressively as we move east and north into the Danelaw. Even so, no area exists without some superior churches, and overall they can be numbered in their hundreds. Some were clearly akin to the houses of canons drawn into coherent order and discipline by the second

---

3 John Blair, 'Secular Minster Churches in Domesday Book', *Domesday Book: A Reassessment*, ed. Peter Sawyer, 1985, pp. 104–42.

4 *The Domesday Monachorum of Christ Church, Canterbury*, ed. D.C. Douglas, Royal Historical Society, 1944; also S.P.J. Harvey, 'Domesday Book and its Predecessors', *EHR* 86, 1971, pp. 753–73.

move of monastic reform in the late eleventh and early twelfth centuries when the example of St Augustine of Hippo rather than that of St Benedict proved the guiding light.

The origin of these secular minsters was complex. Surviving literary sources justify us in concentrating on the Benedictine revival in late Anglo-Saxon England, but they serve also to observe another ecclesiastical phenomenon, and that is the introduction of knowledge of Carolingian rules for the exercise of uncloistered canonical life. As early as the reign of Athelstan, the Rule of Chrodegang was being copied in England to apply to *clerici* who wished to live canonically with all honesty and reverence.[5] St Werburh's at Chester, St Oswald's at Gloucester and, possibly, St Alhmund's at Shrewsbury were early examples of royal interest in strengthening Mercian religious life before the full revival of Benedictine observance under King Edgar. Yet, as we have seen, such foundations, as at New Minster, Winchester, were regarded as too slack by the zealous monastic reformers of the late tenth century; and much was made of the need to replace canons who had lost their austerity (and presumably their celibacy) by monks committed to the disciplined and celibate life of their corporate communities. Even so, patronage continued by royalty, by great earls, and by lesser men; and in the background of the Domesday evidence must be placed our knowledge of patronage given to such foundations. Mercia again is rich in examples – at Leominster, Wenlock, Chester (St John's, and continued support for St Werburh) and Stour – and similar evidence can be found elsewhere. The most striking and well-documented example, which we have already discussed, was Harold Godwinson's full-scale support for Waltham.[6] Set up under strong influence from Lorraine, it was strictly governed, though the canons lived in their own houses, enjoying their own prebends. The spiritual impact of such establishments was as variable as it was incalculable.

The evidence of Domesday Book highlights one element that proved a source of weakness and, in some instances, of scandal. They were valuable assets and only too easily treated as property. Some of the leading administrative officers had already by 1086 benefited from this characteristic. Regenbald, who might well have been the first known formal chancellor, owned no fewer than five minsters, including Cirencester (where he was buried), Milborne Port and Frome.[7] Ranulf Flambard held the great minster

---

5   *The Old English Version of the Enlarged Rule of Chrodegang Together with the Latin Original*, ed. A.S. Napier, EETS 150, 1916.

6   *The Waltham Chronicle*, ed. and trans. Leslie Watkiss and Marjorie Chibnall, 1994, pp. xix–xxx.

7   Simon Keynes, 'Regenbald the Chancellor (*sic*)', *Anglo-Norman Studies* x, 1987, pp. 185–222.

at St Mary's, Dover, and Christchurch and Godalming. Most important of all is Harold's Waltham, where the canons appear to have set up a school and to have been thoroughly active in all the secular charges within their ambit. For a long period the discipline held, but by the 1170s there was need for extra support and sanction, and Waltham, with all the mystique of Harold's purported shrine, passed under the control of the Augustinian Order. Financial advantage certainly swirled around these substantial churches of middle rank. In a famous example, recorded in detail in Domesday Book, we learn that St Mary's at Huntingdon had belonged to Thorney Abbey, but the abbot had pledged it to the burgesses. Even so, as the claim has it, King Edward had given it to two of his priests, Vitalis and Bernard. They in turn had sold it to Hugh, King Edward's Chamberlain. That was far from the end of the matter. Hugh had then sold it to two priests of Huntingdon, a transaction for which they had the royal seal. In spite of all this – and the mind boggles at the possible legal complications, charges and countercharges – Eustace the sheriff now held it without proof of delivery, without writ and without seisen. The case was still *sub judice* and so one must not jump to conclusions about ultimate rights and wrongs, but the crabbed record makes the point clearly enough. A church of some standing can still be treated as a piece of property, subject to normal property law over transmission and proof of ownership.[8]

The fate of many of these superior churches is hinted at in Domesday Book and rapidly becomes clear in the twelfth century. Reorganisation of secular cathedrals had impact on their survival, though often in distorted form. The general move in a non-monastic context, as at York or Lincoln or Salisbury, was towards a system of named prebends with the stalls firmly allotted to specific churches. London is the outstanding example, where Bishop Maurice was the creative force. Appointed in 1086 after eight years' service as royal chancellor, his private life was a matter of great scandal. A libertine of the first order, he had the endearing temerity to claim that his sexual exploits were necessary for the preservation of his health. His public life more than compensated for his rather untypical misdemeanours. He set up an enduring system of thirty prebends serving his cathedral at St Paul's, a model for fair distribution of revenue as well as a secure means of maintaining continuous exercise of clerical duties at the cathedral. Some of the stalls were held by important national figures: by Robert, bishop of Hereford; by the almost inevitable Ranulf Flambard; and by Ingelric, the refounder of the church of St Martin-le-Grand. A network of power, influence

---

8   *DB* i, Huntingdon, ed. John Morris, 1975, p. D1 (208a).

and financial expertise protected St Paul's. Ingelric was a key active figure in the background. St Martin-le-Grand developed under his guidance into a collegiate church that trained a succession of leading administrators, feeding into the royal chapel, something of a Balliol of its day. Such collegiate churches fitted in easily to the mores of the age. Many enjoyed exercising patronage over them, and with it opportunities for building ventures. New monastic impulses, notably the evolution of the Augustinian, and then later of the Premonstratensian, canons, helped to muddy the lines of succession and complicated matters of status.[9]

Secular lords were also not slow in using the flexibility offered by these churches of middle rank to their own advantage and purposes. Again the evidence from Domesday Book is precise. Roger Montgomery, earl of Shrewsbury, held no fewer than twelve superior churches in Shropshire, with a further six on his Sussex lands. In Shropshire he used his rights freely to support the clerks and others of his elaborate household. The bishop of Hereford is also shown to have been a great exploiter of the resources of ancient minsters. Traditional local revenues were sufficient to satisfy the needs of an administrative system at the headquarters of a diocese or of a great fief and still leave enough over to support, rather after the fashion of Chaucer's poor parson or Trollope's poor curates, priests who would serve the everyday needs of what became virtually their parishioners. Much still needs to be done to make the picture intelligible in many parts of England, but the general trend is clear and in some instances capable of close analysis. Even where bishops or great magnates were involved, a tendency existed for ancient minsters to split into their component parts. John Blair has pointed to a telling and possibly archetypal example at Bromfield in Shropshire, a minster served by twelve canons which had been patronised by Edward the Confessor. The canons preserved much of their land with six prebends, still active until 1155, when the church was annexed to Gloucester Abbey. It seems likely, however, as Blair suggests, that the other six of the basic prebends, strewn along the valleys of the Teme and of the Onny, had already developed into heavily localised village churches by that date.[10]

It is appropriate, therefore, that we recognise the importance of the superior churches, many of which bear the character of collegiate churches, over the crisis of the Norman Conquest. Many were located naturally in

9 C.N.L. Brooke, 'The Composition of the Chapter of St Paul's, 1086–1163', *Cambridge Historical J.*, 1951, pp. 111–32. C.N.L. Brooke with Gillian Keir, *London, 800–1216: The Shaping of a City*, 1975, pp. 310–12 (Ingelric), pp. 340–2 (Bishop Maurice).

10 Blair, 'Secular Minster Churches in Domesday Book', pp. 128–36.

central places and some offered opportunity for stimulating urban growth. They provide a practical lesson in continuity from the Anglo-Saxon past. Even if a large part of their revenues was hived off to the advantage of new lords, the active priest or deacon in charge of their everyday needs would continue to exercise his regular round of preaching and teaching in the English tongue. Pressure on them from above from cathedrals, the monasteries and new feudal lords was accompanied by pressure from below to institute a regular pattern of parish churches. Their influence and very existence diminished in the course of the twelfth century. Some survived in tolerable good shape, notably those able to resist episcopal pressure, as at Dover or Wolverhampton. The new Orders, especially the Augustinians, inflicted further pressure to move away from a canonical structure to a monastic one. Heavily patronised by Henry I and his advisers, the Augustinians flourished, but some more amorphous groups of *clerici* persisted throughout the Middle Ages. At Bampton in Oxfordshire a community recorded in the 950s was served by three vicars in the thirteenth century, still jealously guarding rights over tithes and burial fees, and surviving in recognisable direct line of descent as late as 1845.[11] Sometimes a local cult helped to preserve them as a respected central place for worship, a relic of astonishing continuity from Anglo-Saxon days.

This movement towards the third level of ecclesiastical activity, the concentration on the individual local church, represents a further field where Domesday Book evidence, carefully handled, can cast fresh light. The future lay at the local level, as all can admit, with the parish church, heading towards the familiar pattern of one priest, helped by assistants, a deacon or a curate, possibly with oversight of an ancillary small church or chapel. Domesday Book itself was not primarily concerned with the location of village churches nor with their value, except as they represented tangible financial assets to their landlords, spiritual or lay; and information about that value was often subsumed in other aspects of the Domesday record. The result is that the record is spasmodic and scattered. In Suffolk and Huntingdonshire, however, the enumerators exceeded their brief and the record appears to be reasonably full. There are 85 places mentioned in the Huntingdonshire survey, and in 53 there is reference to the existence of churches. Suffolk is a much larger shire with some 639 places (including towns and hamlets). Churches are referred to in no fewer than 352 villages. Even in Suffolk there are some areas where the record is poor. Nevertheless the ample coverage helps to confirm a conclusion drawn from other

---

11 Ibid., p. 139.

evidence, legal and common sense, namely that opportunities for easy access to public worship were open to almost all the inhabitants of England.[12]

In detail, complications abound relating to uncertainties on the part of those who collected information for the survey and also from the final compression of information into Domesday Book, skilful though the master scribe might be. There are many examples of churches being mentioned at only one of the villages on the property of thegns who held a variety of estates; and one is justified in inferring that the named church was a point used for the collection of geld or other church dues. This inference is stronger where thegns bearing a territorial name occupy estates at which a priest is mentioned. In Hertfordshire, Aethelmaer of Benington Lordship and Anschil of Ware fall into this category. Some thegns had interests in many churches, a reminder to us of the complications arising out of any oversimple explanation of the evaluation of a parish system. Edwin, a wealthy thegn in the reign of the Confessor, bequeathed land on his death to twelve churches, eleven of them in Norfolk. From such diversity of patronage it is easy to see how a set of parishes could evolve rather differently from the manorial norm dependent on a local resident lord and also from a splitting up of the holdings of ancient minster churches. Cornwall, with its exclusive references to the collegiate, stands on a touchstone of contrast, though there, as we have already suggested, the establishment of parish churches for each village with dependent hamlets was certainly delayed in the Celtic West. Domesday Book provides our central body of information but there is much ancillary material also, some prepared in readiness for its construction, others quite independent. The Kentish evidence is particularly strong. Documents survive relating to matters such as the reorganisation of chrismmoney and other dues, dating to the early years of Lanfranc's period of office. From them we know that there were many churches, probably 400 or more, in Kent. Even after taking into account the advanced nature of the shire, with its easy access to the Continent, this is a significant number, pointing again to the conclusion that there were few inhabitants of eleventh-century England outside convenient range of a church.[13]

The general move towards a more uniform parish system was well under way by 1066 and was vigorously extended in the early Anglo-Norman period. St Wulfstan of Worcester encouraged church building throughout

12 H.C. Darby, *Domesday England*, appendix 4, 1977, p. 346. His figures for Huntingdon and Suffolk are slightly amended from those given in the earlier volumes on Eastern England, published in 1952.

13 Reginald Lennard, *Rural England 1086–1135*, 1959, pp. 293–4, with reference to *Domesday Monachorum*, pp. 5–15 and 77–9; to *Chronica Angliae*, 20 vols, ed. Thomas Hearne, 1720, pp. 228–31; and to Gordon Ward's work in *Archaeologica Cantiana* xliv and xv, 1932–33.

his diocese, building them on his own manors and consecrating those founded by thegns and sub-tenants at, for example, places as diverse as Wycombe in Buckinghamshire, Longney in Gloucestershire and Ratcliffe in Nottinghamshire.[14] In the Berkshire folios of Domesday Book we find a famous and classic case for new building. At Whistley, some three miles from the big church at Sonning, the inhabitants found it difficult to attend church because of flooding at the fords. The abbot of Abingdon owned the manor, and it was agreed that he should establish a priest there, having all oblations reserving the rights of the bishop of Salisbury (the lord of Sonning) and giving him half a mark annually.[15]

It is fair to assume that where we find an entry in Domesday Book referring to a church, there was also a priest. At Market Bosworth in Leicestershire there was a priest with a deacon, and the familiar picture comes to mind, probably accurately, of a vicar with his curate. Some churches were wealthy. Long Melford in Suffolk, a village later famous for the size and beauty of its church, had land of the order of 240 acres under its control, a substantial estate indeed.[16] Most holdings, when specified, were of a more modest order, much in line with what one would expect from a moderately prosperous villager. Priests were freemen, and it is reasonable to assume that they were normally expected to enjoy at least the normal peasant holding in the arable. Variation is the keynote in the erratic Domesday evidence, and where the arable holdings have been described, examples have been found varying from 4 or 5 hides to half a virgate (15 acres). The rather strange entries in the Middlesex folios are the most revealing. Only eighteen priests are mentioned in the whole shire, but the holdings of all of them are recorded. Three priests held a whole hide (120 acres), one held 90 acres, five held 60, six a modest 30 and three only 15.[17]

A priest would, then, be regarded as among the more prosperous of the villagers in most parts of the country. He would have an interest in the tithe, though he would receive only a portion of it. The lords of village churches found the granting of tithes to favoured monastic houses in Normandy or England a convenient and painless way of endowing their favourite houses. Royal servants such as Regenbald, described as 'the first great pluralist', could benefit from the grant of churches, leaving the active local

---

14   Emma Mason, *St Wulfstan of Worcester, c.1008–1095*, 1990, pp. 145–6.

15   Lennard, *Rural England*, pp. 314ff.

16   *DB* i, Leicester, ed. Philip Morgan, 1979, land of Grandmesnil; *DB* ii, Suffolk, ed. Alex Rumble, 1986, land of Bury St Edmunds. The whole estate at Long Melford consisted of 12 carucates (1440 acres), and was well stocked. The manor had appreciated in value from £20 to £30.

17   Lennard, *Rural England*, p. 314.

clerics substantially impoverished. Three of the most influential bishops of the first generation after the Conquest, Maurice of London, Osmund of Salisbury and Osbern of Exeter, were conspicuously adept at exploiting their control over local churches. Ownership of churches in their secular attributes was regarded very much as ownership of any property. But occasionally from the Domesday record we have a glimpse of something nearer our picture of an eighteenth-century squarson. At Martell in Dorset there were four priests who were substantial sub-tenants, one of whom held $2\frac{1}{2}$ hides, one $1\frac{1}{2}$ hides, another $1\frac{1}{3}$ hides and yet a fourth with 1 hide. Details relating to the land owned by the priest with $1\frac{1}{2}$ hides specify that his estate comprised two ploughs, four villeins, two bordars, a mill which rendered 5 shillings, 11 acres of meadow, some woodland and no fewer than eleven houses in Wimborne.[18]

The age-old division into fat livings and poor livings undoubtedly existed; and not surprisingly many of the fat livings were held by men of high rank, or by men who would serve the king, the bishop or the great magnate as household officers. The resident priest could be ill paid. He could also, although this may have been unusual, be subject to direct personal service. In Archenfield, a border district of Herefordshire where Welsh custom was powerful, the priests of three churches that belonged to the king had the duty of conveying messages from the king into Wales and also of saying two masses a week on his behalf.[19]

For long, and probably for all the Anglo-Norman period, the resident village clergy remained English, with few exceptions. Celibacy remained the ideal, but the practice depended much upon the vigour and beliefs of the individual bishops. Charges of illiteracy and of drunkenness and general moral turpitude were to become frequent, particularly as moral fervour in the hierarchy became more intense as the teaching of the Hildebrandine reformers seeped through. Given the energy of the late eleventh-century bench of bishops, it is highly likely that a reasonable proportion of priests continued to exercise their office without major scandal. The survival of many Anglo-Saxon manuscripts, especially from the scriptoria of Canterbury, Exeter and Worcester, suggests that the teaching and preaching experience of late Anglo-Saxon England continued to be influential. Rare but significant references to the work as village priests early in their career of such major figures as Wulfric of Haselbury in Somerset or, even more so, of

---

18 *DB* i, Dorset, 1.31, ed. Frank and Caroline Thorn, 1979, Hinton Martell.
19 Ibid. The Archenfield entry precedes the Hereford folios proper and constitutes a document of maximum importance for any examination of Welsh customs. Archenfield, ch. 1.

Gilbert of Sempringham in Lincolnshire hint at solid continuity in pastoral work on the part of priests throughout the trauma of Conquest.[20] In the monastic world the religious impulses proved at times quite sensational. It is unlikely in the extreme that this period of church building left the standard of ministration impaired in the villages of England.

Much of this evidence from Domesday Book, if properly addressed, has a bearing on the vexed questions of what was involved in lay ownership. There are enough indications from a variety of sources, principally legal sources relating to the evolution of canon law, to show that the dominant trend was away from ownership on the part of the laity towards patronage. By the end of our period the process is accelerated. The strength of church courts during Stephen's reign, increased sensitivity towards Roman law coinciding with the work of Gratian on the Continent, point to the fertility of the 1140s. But already in England the dislocation of lordship over many local churches caused by the Norman Conquest imposed some radical thinking over the relationship of lay lords to resident priests. An Anglo-Saxon thegn was expected to own his church and his bell-house. New owners, even if they moved to found new churches, would be more open to pressure to conform to a reformed position in return for the spiritual benefits they expected to receive, and to be content with the authority visited in them as patron rather than to apply the full rigour of landlord control.

Any attempted assessment of the state of ecclesiastical organisation towards the end of the eleventh century has to take into account these underlying attitudes towards lay ownership. Yet it would be wrong if, even with the massive support of evidence from Domesday Book and its satellites, we concentrated too exclusively on the internal English situation. The Norman Conquest admittedly distorted the picture. It could always be argued that England was a special case. But England was still an integral part of Western Christendom, and there remains one field of activity which demands attention if we are to begin to understand the Church in England in the reign of the Conqueror and his immediate successors. In European terms the period is often referred to as the age of the Investiture Contest. At the centre of events was the public quarrel between Pope Gregory VII (Hildebrand), 1073–85, and the Emperor Henry IV, 1056–1106. Relationships between Church and State suffered such a crisis that the old tradition of co-operation involved in the so-called 'Carolingian compromise' was shaken to its very core. And yet in England this compromise survived with the king and the archbishop working in close accord to bring elements of advanced moral

---

20   Lennard, *Rural England*, pp. 234–8. *The Book of St Gilbert*, ed. Raymonde Foreville and Gillian Keir, 1986.

and organisational reform into an old-fashioned Christian kingdom where the king still effectively controlled appointment to key offices in the Church. How did this state of affairs come about, and to what extent were contacts with the Papacy amicable and not subject to strain?

One thing is certain: Pope Alexander II (1061–73), ably assisted at the papal curia by Archdeacon Hildebrand, had given full legal support to William's invasion of England in 1066. The Norman case was apparently accepted, and Harold portrayed as an usurper and an oath-breaker who consorted with clerics, especially Archbishop Stigand, of doubtful title. With ideas of papal leadership in Europe taking feudal shape, it was natural that many at the Roman curia should consider conquered England as a papal fief. King William himself did little to dispel this notion in the early years of his reign. He paid great deference to papal legates. He approved the payment of Peter's Pence, a tax which was regarded by the Papacy as a recognition of lordship. He supported fully the reforms initiated by Lanfranc. He wanted a moral Church. But as king of England, he was also heir to traditions and special customs that left him with much authority over the Church. He showed every inclination, for example, to exercise full powers over the matter of appointment to episcopal office. When the energetic and dynamic Hildebrand succeeded Alexander II as Pope Gregory VII in 1073, difficulties were inevitable. As part of a conscious centralising policy, the Pope attempted to enforce attendance at Rome from the prelates of England and Normandy. He aimed above all and specifically at establishing a claim for fealty from William for the kingdom of England. A critical point in English affairs came in 1079–80. Gregory, at the height of his second big quarrel with the Emperor Henry IV, wished to rally support. He had shown anger over Lanfranc's failure to visit him. He now summoned two bishops from each of the English and Norman provinces to attend his Lenten Synod at Rome in 1080. Their failure to do so re-opened tensions over the question of fealty. Either orally or in writing he made a formal request to King William that fealty should be sworn. William's reply has survived and is rightly hailed as a diplomatic masterpiece. He rejected fealty sharply on the grounds that he had never promised it, nor had his predecessors ever paid it. However, he apologised for negligence in paying Peter's Pence during the past three years, when he himself had been out of England. He promised to make good the deficiency, sending some by the papal legate and stating a firm intention to send the rest by the envoys of his trusted archbishop, Lanfranc. A possibly ominous note is sounded at the end of his letter when he thanks the Pope for his prayers, and expresses the earnest hope that he will continue to love the Pope and to hear him most obediently. Hildebrand, busy elsewhere, sensibly let matters rest. King William continued to respect him, but also continued to be political master of his own Church in his own duchy and kingdom.[21]

Perhaps, indeed, one should not marvel too much at the persistence of this old-fashioned relationship between the king and the English Church. Wise men at the Papacy were willing to put up with it, recognising the special circumstances existing in an England ravaged by the uncertainties inevitably following the processes of Conquest and settlement. Discipline was needed to bring a measure of peace and order into the land-holding position; and only the king had the immediate authority to impose such discipline. From the beginning of William I's reign to the end of Stephen's, surviving legal evidence tells the same story, with the survey that resulted in Domesday Book as the supreme example of royal initiative in this field. Disputes involving claims by churches of dispossession by new Norman lords, disputes between churches over legal ownership of lands or rights were almost without exception settled in royal courts, sometimes involving the king or special commissioners (notably Geoffrey of Coutances in the first generation), often directed to shire courts with witness taken in traditional fashion from the men of good standing in the hundreds.

A famous and revealing cause was pleaded quite early in the Conqueror's reign, probably in 1072, at Penenden Heath near Maidstone in Kent.[22] Conflict arose between two of the greatest men in the realm, Odo of Bayeux as Earl of Kent, and Archbishop Lanfranc. Odo had taken full advantage of his position as a key person in the settlement from the very earliest days to encroach on the lands and liberties of the archbishopric in Kent. Lanfranc, tough and experienced, though arriving late, in 1070, fought for his new interests. Matters were aired and partly settled in a long hearing, presided over by Geoffrey of Coutances, and extending over three days. Evidence was taken from Englishmen well versed in the law, and incidentally anxious to be freed from the bad customs which Odo, acting as vicegerent as well as earl, had imposed on them. In a spectacular move, Aethelric, bishop of Chichester, a very old man, was brought specially to Penenden Heath in a chariot at the king's command to discuss and expound the old legal customs. The result was a success for the archbishop. With only minor exceptions calculated to preserve royal rights over the highway, Lanfranc was to be free from interference by royal officials. Geoffrey of Coutances

---

21 *EHD* ii, no. 101. *Lanfranci Opera*, ed. J.A. Giles, 1844, p. 32.
22 *EHD* ii, no. 50. John le Patourel, 'The Reports of the Trial on Penenden Heath', *Studies in Medieval History Presented to F.M. Powicke*, 1948, pp. 15–26. David Bates, 'The Land Pleas of William I's Reign: Penenden Heath Revisited', *BIHR* 51, 1978, pp. 1–19.

presided over similar tribunals elsewhere, notably over a major dispute between the bishop of Worcester and Evesham Abbey concerning the nature
of episcopal rights in the tract of country in the West Midlands known
as the Oswaldslaw.[23] The long-drawn pleas concerning spoliation of the
lands of the abbey of Ely were matters of great concern to the king, who
attempted restoration on the basis of sworn testimony of Englishmen who
remembered the state of affairs at the time of King Edward. King William
even ordered a written report from Archbishop Lanfranc as a result of the
sworn inquests concerning the lands of Ely.[24] Elsewhere it is a similar story.
The two great abbeys of St Albans and Westminster were often at daggers
drawn; notably over lands on the borders of their interests at Barnet, Radlett
or Aldenham. Abbot Frederick of St Albans claimed that he had leased
Aldenham to Westminster for a limited period only, but royal support to
Westminster ensured that the manor was retained by them.[25] The testimony
of the English was important to the king and his advisers because of his
basic claim that he was the true successor of the English dynasty. William
was perfectly willing to rely on able survivors such as Bishop Wulfstan of
Worcester and Abbot Aethelwig of Evesham, a man described as holding
great secular power because he surpassed everyone by his intelligence, his
shrewdness and his knowledge of worldly laws (the *only* ones he was held to
have studied!).[26]

The same pattern of activity in vital ecclesiastical business continues
under the sceptical William Rufus, the ruthless Henry I and again to some
extent under Stephen and Matilda. Time and time again litigation occurs
in the royal courts, leading to establishment of proof of tenure (deraignment,
dirationare), and the continuity in use of the hundred jurors, or the wisest of
the English, is a thread running through our admittedly scrappy surviving
evidence. Burial rights, even details such as the holding of wakes or the
tolling of bells, were brought forward as well as matters concerning tenure.
Rufus showed his scepticism when fifty men accused of forest offences went
to the ordeal of the hot iron and were adjudged innocent. He introduced a
discordant note by asserting that his royal justice was to be preferred to the
apparent wayward judgement of God.[27] Eadmer told a revealing story of
Henry I in action, showing the dangers as well as the advantages of royal

23 W.L. Warren, *The Governance of Norman and Angevin England, 1066–1272*, 1987, p. 29.
24 Edward Miller, *The Abbey and Bishopric of Ely*, 1951 and 'The Land Pleas in the Reign of
    William I', *EHR*, lxii, 1947, pp. 441ff.
25 Barbara Harvey, *Westminster Abbey and its Estates in the Middle Ages*, 1977.
26 R.R. Darlington, 'Aethelwig, Abbot of Evesham', *EHR* xlviii, 1933, pp. 1–22; Mason,
    St Wulfstan of Worcester, pp. 126–7.
27 Frank Barlow, *William Rufus*, 1983, p. 111.

support. After the strong prohibition against priests associating with women made at the Council of London in 1102, Henry I ordered his ministers to act against them. But many were innocent and therefore not enough money was collected in fines. Henry I therefore levied a general tax on the parishes, so involving a pathetic appeal by priests. Some 200 of them turned up in alb and stoles, though barefoot, only to be driven away. They appealed to the queen, who dissolved into tears but was too frightened to intervene. Yet to what other quarter than the royal could churchmen turn in routine matters? After Easter 1132, Henry I heard disputes over boundaries between Llandaff and St Davids. In 1148 Stephen judged in favour of Battle Abbey, which claimed exemption from the episcopal authority of Bishop Hilary of Chichester.[28] We shall see how the authority of Rome grew in legal matters in the first half of the twelfth century; and yet the royal court remained a magnet for those wanting decisions in routine ecclesiastical affairs.

The judicial attributes of Domesday Book, the noting of complaints and dispossessions concerning ecclesiastical land, fit easily and naturally into this ongoing picture of royal concern for good order in the Church. Such attributes speak equally of the Church's need for royal support in order to achieve good order. One final comment is perhaps imperative. We can see how by its very nature Domesday Book can tell us little of the inner life of the Church in England. We have also seen that it can tell us much of the wealth of the Church. If we take our conservative estimate of something like a quarter of the landed wealth of England resting in ecclesiastical hands, with a roughly even division between the secular church and the monastic, we sense a further complication and yet also a further hint at this inner life. The situation is admittedly complicated by the existence of monastic chapters in some of the leading sees and by Norman efforts to link prosperous abbeys with impoverished bishoprics, successful in Bath and Wells, ultimately successful in the Chester, Lichfield and Coventry arrangements, and unsuccessful in East Anglia, where Bury St Edmunds maintained its monastic integrity, though Ely became the centre for a new see. Cathedral or abbey, prosperity did not always yield spiritual success, but by and large William and his advisers and his energetic bishops and abbots could pride themselves on the existence of a Church under royal control

---

28 Martin Brett, *The English Church under Henry I*, 1975, makes the point (p. 95) that the king's court was frequently engaged in determining matters that one might suppose more properly the preserve of the archbishop. His analysis of archiepiscopal and episcopal jurisdiction is essential to modern study of the problems, especially, pp. 91–100 and 148–61.

exhibiting most of the characteristics that might be expected in the reforming climate of the late eleventh century.

Conspicuously this reforming zeal made itself manifest in building projects. The generation after 1066 witnessed one of the biggest building booms in medieval English history. In the 1070s six great ecclesiastical buildings were begun: Canterbury (Christ Church), Lincoln, St Albans, Rochester, Hereford and Winchester (Old Minster). Presumably work at Battle Abbey was already under way. In the 1080s four more were started: Ely, Worcester, Chichester and Gloucester. In the 1090s another four were added: London, Chester, Durham and Norwich. The impetus for such enterprise must have received central direction, and Lanfranc may personally have been involved in advising such activity. Nor was the impetus halted by the death of William I. Initiation and continuation of the construction of our typically massive Norman great churches continued through the reigns of his sons.

The construction did not lack ornament. Wall paintings were in use in great churches and in small. Lanfranc provided Canterbury with paintings, as did the priors of the next generation, Ernulf (1093–1107) and Conrad (1107–26). Gilbert the sheriff founded Merton Priory in 1114 and handsomely decorated it with paintings and other images, as was the custom. At St Albans a painting was placed above the high altar of the new church (1077–93). Attention has been drawn to indications of a positive talented school of wall painting in Sussex.[29] We neglect at peril the continuity of effort in church building and ornamentation from 1066 to 1120, especially in great churches, but also and perhaps with extra thrust in monasteries and lesser churches at the end of our period. Builders and craftsmen had golden opportunities and many thrived. The movement at the top of society from the Conqueror to William Rufus and Henry I, even to Stephen and Matilda, had little impact in detail on these important manifestations of the vitality of Anglo-Norman religious life.

---

29   David Park, 'The "Lewes Group" of Wall Paintings in Sussex', *Anglo-Norman Studies*, vi, 1984, pp. 200–37.

CHAPTER SIX

The Anglo-Norman Church:
The Sons of the Conqueror, 1087–1135

Continuity is the main theme to be isolated in any examination of the Anglo-Norman Church from the reign of William I to the reigns of his sons, William II (1087–1100) and Henry I (1100–35). A willingness to accept the best of Continental moral reform, especially when to the newcomers' advantage, was coupled with an awareness of English peculiarities and a very positive attitude to the building and ornamentation of churches, sometimes on a massive scale. There were, however, differences, some of which can be attributed directly to the personalities of the kings themselves. William I was harsh and unyielding in insisting on what he considered his regal rights, but his support of moral reform in the Church was unquestioned. This could be said of neither of his sons who succeeded him, Robert in Normandy nor William Rufus in England. William II in England quickly gained an evil reputation as a despoiler of the Church. He supported, it is true, some good causes, the abbey at Battle, or the new Cluniac priory at Bermondsey, and he acquiesced in the appointment of Anselm, a truly great theologian and spiritual leader, to the archbishop's see at Canterbury (see below). However, these acts were heavily outweighed in the minds and pens of the succeeding generation by scandals over his personal life and sexuality and over what amounted to a systematic policy of financial exactions from the Church at large. His father had seen to it that the Church was integrated into the new Norman world of military service and William II had close advisers, notably Ranulf Flambard (later bishop of Durham, 1099–1128), who knew how to exploit to the full financial duties owed by the great churches for their ecclesiastical fiefs. A bishop-elect paid what amounted to a relief on entering his see. Vacant sees or abbeys were treated after the fashion of lay fiefs, and the king as their lord took the revenues of the church during the vacancies. To zealous reformers all this looked very like the sin of simony. In 1100, at the time of the king's death, there were no fewer than eleven of the wealthiest abbeys and three of the bishoprics in the hands of king's officers, true *exactores regis*.[1]

The most dramatic events of Rufus's reign in ecclesiastical matters took place in connection with the archiepiscopal see at Canterbury. For four years after the death of Lanfranc in 1089, the see at Canterbury had been left vacant. The obvious successor was Anselm, abbot of Bec, already regarded as one of the leading theologians and scholars of the age. Rufus and his advisers found it exceedingly profitable to keep the see vacant and so to control the wealth connected with the Canterbury revenues. The problem was resolved dramatically in the spring of 1093. In early March the king fell seriously ill, and was taken to Gloucester, where it was thought he was likely to die. Among his acts of repentance and atonement, the most conspicuous was the acquiescence in the nomination of Anselm to Canterbury. At this stage Anselm himself, who was on a long, protracted visit to England, resisted, complaining graphically that to elect him would be to yoke an old and feeble sheep to an untamed bull, but, at a royal court held in Winchester in September, he was ultimately prevailed upon to accept the archbishopric and became the king's vassal for his Canterbury lands, almost certainly following the accepted practice, as had Lanfranc, of performing homage and swearing fealty to the king.[2] He was enthroned at Canterbury on 25 September, consecrated by Archbishop Thomas of York on 4 December, and spent the Christmas feast with the king at Gloucester, apparently in full amity.

Such amity soon broke down. Temperamentally the men were poles apart and there were deep matters of dispute between them. Rufus was willing to concede restoration of lands to the see, though there were rough edges to the detailed definition of archiepiscopal lands. As the vassal, Anselm had ultimate responsibility for the military service exacted from his see and the soldier-king was dissatisfied, possibly with reason, with the troops sent from Canterbury. The main issue of contention lay, however, with the recognition of Pope Urban II. Heavy intrigues, from which no party emerged unspotted, resulted in May 1095, in superficial success for Anselm when he received the pallium, his badge of office, from the altar of his cathedral, but Rufus had also won success over the admittance of papal legates and letters (always and only with royal assent). Further friction, again over practical matters, the inefficiency of the Canterbury troops sent on Welsh campaign,

---

1 R.W. Southern, *Medieval Humanism*, 1970, contains a revised version of 'Ranulf Flambard and the Anglo-Norman Administration', *TRHS*, 1933, pp. 95–128.
2 Z.N. Brooke, *The English Church and the Papacy*, 1931, pp. 154–5. N.F. Cantor, *Church, Kingship, and Lay Investiture in England, 1089–1135*, 1958, p. 62.

brought matters to a head. In November 1097 Anselm went to Rome to discuss difficulties with the Pope. He left England without royal consent, and for the last years of Rufus's life the Canterbury revenues were again in the hands of royal agents.

During his absence on the Continent, first at Rome and then at Lyons, Anselm found himself in the mainstream of theological thought, and built up his own reputation, notably with the writing of his great treatise on the incarnation, *Cur Deus Homo*. As far as the Church in England was concerned, the result of the exile was not good. Papal diplomats had no wish to alienate the powerful English king, no matter what honour and respect they might be prepared to offer Anselm. Within England, royal agents were given a free rein to exploit what Rufus saw as legitimate feudal dues and rights.

After the king's death in the New Forest in August 1100, Anselm played a great part in ensuring the legitimacy of the new king, William's younger brother Henry, even though he could not be present at the coronation itself. Henry was crowned by Maurice, bishop of London, but hastened to write to Anselm, assuring him that if delay had been possible there was no one from whom he would have preferred to receive his crown. He begged Anselm to return and told him that money for his expenses would be available as soon as he reached Dover. Prospects for reconciliation and peace appeared good. The elderly archbishop (he was now in his late sixties) and the young, more amenable and dutiful youngest son of the Conqueror (b. 1068) seemed ready for full accord. Henry I's coronation charter promised positive and active support for a reformed Church. Nothing could be further from the truth.

William Rufus was killed, probably accidentally, at a moment when in political and military terms his reputation appeared in the ascendant. Nevertheless the nature of his death, unshriven, with no time for repentance, gave monastic chroniclers their chance to draw out all evils and injustices and to see his sudden death as an act of God. The Anglo-Saxon Chronicle followed the general pattern. It specifically charged him with avarice, harassing the nation with military service and excessive taxation. His oppressions on the Church were described in detail: on the day he died he had in his own hands the archbishopric of Canterbury, the bishopric of Winchester, and that of Salisbury, and eleven abbacies, all leased and for rent.[3] Henry, the new king, in common with all incoming governments throughout time, blamed his predecessor for injustices, promised to make redress for the unjust exactions imposed on the Church and for the evil

---

3   *Anglo-Saxon Chronicle*, s.a. 1100.

customs, and to move back to the good old days of his father, William I, and the laws of King Edward.

The opening years of Henry I's reign passed peacefully enough, but there was now an added complication. England up to this point had escaped the ravages of conflict over the technicalities involved in the investiture to office of bishops and abbots. Even Anselm himself had conformed to custom, and had paid homage to Rufus, receiving the gift of the pastoral staff from him, when he was appointed to Canterbury. Anselm's years of exile had sharpened his awareness of the details of the conflict. He now pleaded the case for papal sanction before submitting to what he recognised as the custom of the country. The conflict was conducted in a dignified and reasonable manner but initially proved incapable of resolution, in spite of a succession of embassies, including a journey by Anselm himself to Rome at Easter 1103. Failure at this meeting prompted Anselm to remain abroad in exile, a step which brought criticism even from supportive friends and clergy. Pope Paschal II, at first intransigent, came to recognise that compromise was essential and both in France and then in England an accord was reached by the terms of which the kings gave up their rights to spiritual investiture by ring and pastoral staff, though continuing in practice to retain their right to approve appointments and (the heart of the matter from the point of view of feudal kings) to receive homage from the bishops-elect. The careful historian William of Malmesbury, reflecting on the situation within a generation of this compromise of 1107, agreed that Henry gave up in perpetuity investiture by ring and staff, though is a little vague in his account of what was retained, describing it as the privilege of election and regalian rights (*retento tantum electionis et regalium privilegio*).[4] Eadmer, whom one might have expected to be explicit on these matters on which he had first-hand knowledge, is even vaguer, saying merely that within the bounds prescribed by the Apostolic See, King Henry settled all the outstanding points in the controversy and satisfied Anselm's wishes in the various issues for which he had striven.[5] The settlement made finally in 1107, in which Henry's sister, Adela of Blois, and the great theologian Ivo of Chartres played a part, was altogether reasonable. Bishops and abbots were powerful rulers of men, great feudal vassals and often prime agents in the machinery of government at both national and local level: it was sensible that the king should have a say in their appointment, and in their continued loyalty. Arrangements made in England and

---

4   A.L. Poole, *From Domesday Book to Magna Carta*, 1951, pp. 125–81; William of Malmesbury, *Gesta Regum Anglorum*, vol. 1, ed. and trans. R.A.B. Mynors, R.M. Thomson and Michael Winterbottom, 1998, p. 754.
5   Eadmer, *The Life of St Anselm*, ed. R.W. Southern, 1962, p. 137.

France in 1107 proved the basis for the wider settlement made by the Concordat of Worms in 1122, which brought to an end the tempestuous struggle between popes and emperors that we call the Investiture Contest. Anselm himself had returned to England in September 1106, and remained at peace with the king until his death on 21 April 1109.

The publicity that was naturally given by contemporary writers to the disputes between the popes and the kings and the archbishop and the kings has led to an obscuring of the main developments within the English Church at the time. In this second generation after the Norman Conquest, much was achieved that was to set a permanent imprint on the medieval English Church. The elaborate building programmes at urban cathedral centres and also at Benedictine abbeys such as St Albans around which urban communities were growing were the outward symbols of profound inner social change. The key to such change in the reign of Henry I has been well isolated by Martin Brett when he described the Church as 'an essentially Anglo-Saxon institution moving slowly towards a later Latin norm'.[6] Up to 1100 a preponderance of bishops was Norman before succeeding to English sees. After 1100 most had held office in England as archdeacons, canons or priors. Their family and cultural origins were still heavily Continental, Norman or Lotharingian, but their experience was more often than not in the English Church. By the middle of Henry I's reign there was indeed a significant reverse movement from English benefices to Normandy. Hugh, a native of Amiens, but a monk at Lewes before becoming the first abbot of Reading, was appointed to the archbishopric of Rouen in 1129. Nevertheless, group sentiment became much more attuned to the English situation, even though abbots continued to be appointed from Normandy, usually after an intermediate English office.

In itself the remarkable flowering of historical scholarship in the 1120s bears witness to the changes that were coming about. Historians of the first rank such as William of Malmesbury and Florence and John of Worcester busied themselves with recovering English history, translating the essence of the Anglo-Saxon Chronicle into Latin and consolidating it with scholarly additions into a form acceptable to the Latinate world. The Chronicle itself was kept up to date at some of the traditional centres in an English language that was visibly changing from Anglo-Saxon to early Middle English. At Peterborough this was continued to 1155, the entries up to 1121 having been copied from a version associated with St Augustine's Canterbury.[7] Pride in the Anglo-Saxon past was beginning slowly to replace

---

6   Martin Brett, *The English Church under Henry I*, 1975, p. 7.
7   *The Peterborough Chronicle, 1070–1154*, 2nd edn, ed. Cecily Clark, 1970.

the contempt which informed some comment and much action among the first generation of Norman prelates. At Canterbury, Eadmer wrote an important account of recent times and a Life of Anselm fundamental to historians' knowledge of the detail of the career of that great man. He also wrote lives of Anglo-Saxon saints and bishops, of Wilfrid, Oda, Dunstan and Oswald. The work of Bede was venerated, and William of Malmesbury consciously in his history tried with considerable success to fill the long gap between the end of Bede's own history of the English Church (c.731) and his own day. Eadmer, more than most, was aware that to be English was still in his day to be excluded from easy movement into high office. In a famous passage he wrote of Englishmen who had not obtained preferment during the reign of Henry I that their nationality was their downfall. If they were English, no virtue was enough for them to be considered worthy of promotion; 'if they were *foreigners* (*alieni*) the mere appearance of virtue, vouched for by their friends, was sufficient for them to be judged worthy of the highest honour.'[8]

The compromise over investiture reached with Anselm left the Church in control of the formalities of transmission of the spiritual offices, though the king retained the substance of appointment. The archbishoprics were a special case, and rumbling uncertainty over the question of precedence between Canterbury and York remained a feature of the reign. In one respect Henry proved no more careful of ecclesiastical rights than had his brother William II. The four-year vacancy after Lanfranc's death was regarded as something of a scandal. After Anselm Canterbury was left *sede vacante* for no less than five. It was not until 1114 that Henry I filled the see. At that point, however, according to Eadmer, Henry permitted a true element of choice to enter the election. He himself favoured his doctor, the monk Faricius, abbot of Abingdon. The secular bishops objected and a compromise candidate was eventually chosen, Ralph, bishop of Rochester, a man popular among the monks and people of Canterbury. Again in 1123 something approaching a genuine choice was made in the person of William of Corbeil. The Anglo-Saxon Chronicle is a prime source for this election, stating bluntly that the king ordered that they should choose whomsoever they wished as archbishop of Canterbury and he would grant it to them.[9] In fact the other bishops and the king himself saw to it that the prior and

---

8   Eadmer, *Historia Novorum in Anglia*, ed. Martin Rule, Rolls Series, 1884, 224.

9   *Anglo-Saxon Chronicle, s.a.* 1123. Opposition came from the simple fact that William of Corbeil was a clerk not a monk. The church at Canterbury, the papal legate and, initially at least, the Pope himself were opposed. Indeed on William's visit to Rome the Pope refused to meet him for a full week, though, as the Chronicler wryly comments, he was eventually persuaded to give him the pallium by judicious use of gold and silver. That which overcomes all the world overcame Rome.

community of Christ Church, Canterbury, were not left with an unfettered choice. A short-list of four seems to have been selected. Even so, the incident is significant. An element of consensus was certainly present. York was a different matter, and Henry's three appointments were all conducted on a more arbitrary basis: Gerard, bishop of Hereford and former chancellor (1100–08), Thomas II (1108–14) and Thurstan (1114–40) both royal chaplains. Elsewhere, too, appointment of ordinary diocesan bishops seems to have been conducted very much after the pattern set by William I. Simony, in the strict sense of payment for office, seems to have been rare, though Roger de Clinton was reported to have given the large sum of 3000 silver marks for the relatively poor bishopric of Chester (1129–48). Prolonged vacancies, on the other hand, constituted an abuse: Durham (1128–33), Hereford (1127–31) and Chester (1117–21 and 1126–29) all suffered heavily in this respect. Bishoprics were regarded as a fitting reward for royal administrators, especially for the chancellors of both the king and the queen. Until 1125 all bishops were chosen from among the king's immediate servants and it is only after that date the king moved more widely, introducing a reformist element that was to make great impact on the inner legal life of the Church, making it much more open, for example, to the parallels provided by papal jurisdiction. One of the most important appointments of the century was made when Henry of Blois, brother of Stephen, was elevated to the see of Winchester (1129–71); he had been trained as a monk at Cluny and was already abbot of Glastonbury. Gilbert the Universal, a scholar learned in revised Roman law, was bishop of London (1128–34). Robert de Béthune, influential again in law, a former prior of Llanthony, held the see of Hereford (1131–48). Some element of genuine religious sentiment may have inspired these appointments. Of Robert it is said that the king declared that he wished to leave at least one godly bishop behind him.[10] All these men proved influential both at local and national levels, some well into the middle of the century. More traditional appointments also continued to be made. Nigel, the treasurer, was made bishop of Ely (1133–64) and Durham passed into the hands of the chancellor, Geoffrey Rufus (1133–41). The episcopal bench provided more than its fair share of strong characters, well versed in the arts of government, patient of the needs of the king and his council.

The strength of the liaison between king and bishops provoked some natural reaction at the Papacy. The contrast between the promises made by Henry in his coronation charter and his practice as his hold on the throne

---

10   Brett, *The English Church under Henry I*, p. 112, where the phrase from the *Vita Roberti* is quoted in which Henry refers to Robert as '*una radix bona post dies nostros in ecclesia*'.

grew more secure became ever more pronounced. He practised simony. He kept bishoprics and abbacies vacant for long periods and exploited their revenues. He even claimed a right to the personal effects of a deceased bishop, an abuse which provoked a sharp letter of rebuke from Pope Honorius II. Henry of Huntingdon recorded with some humour that after the death of Gilbert the Universal in 1134 royal officials took away the bishop's boots, filled with gold and silver, to the royal treasury.[11] On celibacy, Henry was quite willing to see the ecclesiastical councils repeat the reformers' decrees imposing celibacy on priests. He was equally willing to exact substantial fines from them so that they could continue to live as before. Even at the higher level, celibacy was sometimes not observed. Roger of Salisbury, great administrator, described as *secundus a rege*, lived openly with his mistress, Matilda of Ramsbury. Papal legates were received with respect but exercised no power. Invoking the ancient customs of the realm, the king and his advisers claimed that it was the special function of the archbishop of Canterbury to act as the papal vicar in England, a position ultimately agreed to in 1125.

On one crucial political question papal support was much needed, and that is on the question of precedence between Canterbury and York. Under the litigious Thurstan, former secretary to the king, archbishop of York (1114–40), the matter became something of a *cause célèbre* at the curia. Canterbury evidence, based on the historic testimony of Bede and a succession of documents not acceptable and coolly received at the curia, was not held to be sufficient, though the reality of precedence remained with the southern wealthy see. But Rome was active and the nature of Rome as the supreme legal authority in the Western Church was strengthened by the dispute.[12]

Partly because of the positive efforts made by the Papacy to assert effective headship of the Western Church and partly because of the close Anglo-Norman involvement in moral reform, the Church in England was drawn more closely into the inner workings of the reform movement. Monasticism provided a renewed and vital element in the process. Under the Conqueror, important advance had been made along traditional Benedictine lines, with help from Cluny and with a notable extension to the North of England. With the turn of the century, a fresh inspiration came about. Religious enthusiasm of the sort expressed in military terms in the First Crusade (1095–99) was also directed into forms of monasticism more

---

11 Henry, archdeacon of Huntingdon, *Historia Anglorum. The History of the English People*, ed. Diana E. Greenway, 1996, p. 601.
12 R.W. Southern, 'The Canterbury Forgeries', *EHR* lxxiii, 1958, pp. 193–226.

austere than the old Benedictine Order, and new institutions, notably the Carthusian and the Cistercian, began to take root. These were cosmopolitan movements and as such brought a deeper consciousness of the stature of Rome to men's minds. It is only late in Henry I's reign that the new orders begin to have serious impact, but reform generally had a significant feedback on the still dominant Benedictine houses. Efforts on their part to win exemption from diocesan control bore mixed success. Ultimately seven of the great houses, Bury St Edmunds, St Albans, Battle, Malmesbury, Evesham, Westminster and St Augustine's, Canterbury, were to achieve success, which involved freeing the abbot from attending the diocesan synods and paying its tax. Exemption also entitled successful abbots to wear what were termed the pontifical insignia in various forms. Claims were complicated, suits were complicated, deep questions of limits of jurisdiction often unresolved. For the moment and in connection with the reign of Henry I it is enough to note that such claims and friction between bishops and abbots more often than not brought recourse to the Papacy into play. Difficulty over travel and uncertainty over procedures and the efficiency of judgement did not hinder the development. In common with the rest of the Western world, dispute on matters relating to the spirituality opened the legal route to Rome.

Contact with Rome was not confined to legal affairs nor yet to the purely spiritual. There remained the question of hard cash, of Peter's Pence. We have already seen how this proved an important factor in the negotiations between William I and Hildebrand over the payment of fealty. Many legatine visits to England were made throughout Henry I's reign, and in most, probably in all if we had complete record, the issue of Peter's Pence was raised. A crisis occurred in 1128–29. Henry I's most conspicuous act of patronage was his foundation of the great abbey of Reading with suitable endowments in 1125. The first abbot was a distinguished figure, Hugh, who, as noted above, had been a Cluniac monk at Lewes before his elevation, and who was to go on to be archbishop of Rouen in 1129. Hugh's ability was well known, and in 1128 Pope Honorius summoned him to Rome, apparently with the intention of keeping him there as a member of the curia. At Rome Hugh negotiated a new rate at which Peter's Pence had to be paid. The figure reached in these negotiations was accepted, and indeed appears to have remained the standard which was to endure in theory until the Reformation.[13] Papal authority had also to be involved on matters of vital political significance such as the creation of new sees. The

---

13 *Papsturkunden in England*, ed. Walther Holtzmann, vol. iii, Berlin and Göttingen, 1952, nos 15–23: H.R. Loyn, 'Peter's Pence', *Lambeth Palace Library Annual Report*, 1984, pp. 10–20.

complex moves by which the see for north-west Mercia had its diocesan centre moved from Lichfield to Chester in 1075, again to Coventry in 1102, were determined by feudal as well as ecclesiastical politics, but the Papacy had to be informed. Completely new sees were even more open to papal notification. After long negotiations the abbey of Ely became the centre of a new see in 1109, when Harvey, who had been expelled from the see of Bangor by the Welsh, took over. At Carlisle towards the end of Henry's reign in 1133, a see was created for the North-West by Thurstan of York and a papal bull has survived authorising him in general terms to divide or to unite dioceses. The new bishop, an Augustinian canon, who bore the very English name of Aethelwulf (Aldulf), had been the king's confessor and prior of Nostell.

There is one general characteristic of Henry I's reign which should positively be taken into account in connection with papal affairs. The world of the early twelfth century was becoming increasingly more mobile. Travel was easier. Pilgrimages and especially the extraordinary phenomenon of the Crusades had opened the Western world to relatively safe movement along accredited safe routes; and the most important routes led to Rome. Up to 1100, Rome was respected, visited occasionally by archbishops and leading clerics almost always no more than once in a lifetime, and remote. After 1100, visits became comparatively commonplace, and the practices of the papal curia much better understood. The reality of appeals to Rome rather than the symbolic invocation of papal appeal became manifest. In human terms the working out of the implications of papal monarchy in law, in finance, and also in respect shown to moral judgement became better known and formed a groundswell of important public opinion in mid-century England.

Increased reliance on the written record in the twelfth century has left us with a much more precise picture of the everyday activities of the Church in England. Large collections of letters were put together as records and as examples for the future: more than 300 of Anselm's letters have survived from his period as archbishop alone. Bishops and abbots were men of great potential wealth and power. If they themselves were sometimes so involved in national affairs that they appear remote from their dioceses, their officers were not; and episcopal and abbatial influence were everywhere powerful. The increase in number of surviving episcopal charters points to the busyness of the bishop and his household in enforcing his canonical rights to supervise presentation to lesser churches. In jurisdictional affairs the Church claimed authority over the laity in all sexual matters. Vigorous attempts were made to enforce Christian marriage. Anselm notably launched a campaign against what he saw as the widespread practice of unnatural vice. Over the clergy claims were virtually absolute on personal behaviour or clothing, on drinking, on the practice of usury, on proper decorum in the conduct of the priestly office. Above all there was heavy and consistent concern over clerical marriage.[14] Conciliar decrees represent high theory rather than practice, but even so they show a hardening of opinion since Lanfranc's day. In 1102 there was express condemnation of marriage, with some evidence for subsequent excommunication of offenders at Canterbury. More specific penalties were imposed in 1108 not only on offenders but on those, archdeacons and deans in particular, who had failed to deal with offenders. In 1127 attitudes reached a high point in severity. Any former clerical concubine who repeated her offence was to be tracked down by the bishop's servants, brought to judgement, and reduced either to ecclesiastical discipline or to episcopal servitude. By that time late in Henry I's reign it is clear that ecclesiastical courts existed in some profusion. A bishop had always exercised dominical jurisdiction over his household. Quite commonly synods attended by the clergy of the diocese were held twice a year and these were convenient occasions on which the bishop would deliver judgement. Procedures were likely to be traditional at this stage. The full force of the legal revival was not felt in England until the reign of Stephen and Henry II and causes both on property and person would be decided by witness, tradition and precedent very much on the pattern of the secular courts.

For everyday administration the bishop depended on his household and by 1135 we have fuller evidence concerning its normal composition. A steward was a key figure when it came to dealing with secular business. At Canterbury, York, London and Salisbury the office of steward was well on the way to becoming hereditary. Their office was held as of knightly service and it is likely that arrangements for their sustenance were made along the lines of those associated with lay fiefs such as Rayleigh in Essex, where a cluster of knights' fees surrounded the lord's principal holding at Rayleigh Castle, or at the great abbey of St Albans, where Childwickbury, a couple of miles distant from the abbey itself, bears witness in its name to holdings belonging to the abbey's knights.[15] Their service was direct and concentrated on the episcopal honour where the steward would be the first in rank among a group that would consist of chamberlains, responsible for finance, butlers, constables and dispensers. According to the splendid sequence of Norwich charters, which gives the best insight into these affairs, other officers,

---

14 C.N.L. Brooke, *The Medieval Idea of Marriage*, 1989.
15 H.R. Loyn, 'Rayleigh in Essex: Its Implications for the Norman Settlement', *Studies in Medieval History Presented to R. Allen Brown*, ed. C. Harper-Bill, C.J. Holdsworth and J.L. Nelson, 1989, pp. 235–40.

such as the bakers and cooks, may have been more influential than one might expect, sometimes establishing hereditary succession to office and subscribing to charters, responsible businessmen rather than humble domestics. For business connected with the spiritual side of the bishop's office the situation is more complex and obscure. In the larger dioceses, notably in the vast Lincoln complex, archdeacons were important. It is likely that they came to exercise their authority on a territorial basis though still capable of acting centrally at the bishop's court and residence when need served. Within the Lincoln diocese the existence of seven territorial archdeaconries was, as we have seen, clearly marked out from the days of William I and Bishop Remigius. Monks as well as clerks were sometimes used as heads of administration, even referred to as dapifers or stewards. Baldwin of Bec acted as active head of Anselm's household, and another monk, Robert, was described by the archbishop as one used to look after our affairs (*res nostras custodire*).[16] Terminology is generalised. The key men are described as the bishop's clerks or chaplains and there are only very rare references to chancellors or treasurers. Service in such households opened the way to clerical preferment. The historian Henry of Huntingdon served in the elaborate household of Robert Bloet, bishop of Lincoln (1094–1123), and went on to inherit his father's archdeaconry. The closer one is permitted to look at the clerical hierarchies by surviving scattered evidence, the closer the patterns are to the situation in the secular feudal world. It is also clear that during the reign of Henry I there was a substantial body of trained literate administrators, sometimes expressly called *magistri*, capable of exercising jurisdictional power and delegated authority, and coping with the new world of refined Roman-based canon law.

One special element in the new Anglo-Norman world demanded administrative skills of a high order, and that is the day-to-day running of the cathedrals. Monastic chapters were an English peculiarity much to Norman taste. In 1066 Canterbury, Winchester, Worcester and Sherborne were monastic. Lanfranc saw to it that Rochester and Durham were also converted. Complicated moves, dependent in part on the need to unite relatively impoverished sees with wealthy abbeys, resulted by the end of the eleventh century and the early twelfth century in the creation of monastic-governed sees at Coventry, Norwich and Bath (Wells). In 1109 Ely became the centre for a new diocese administered by Benedictine monks. Towards the end of Henry I's reign the Augustinian canons took control at the new see of Carlisle. There was no further change in major diocesan structures in England for the rest of the Middle Ages. Ten were governed by monks;

---

16   Brett, *The English Church under Henry I*, p. 179; R.W. Southern, *Saint Anselm and his Biographer*, 1963, pp. 194–9.

seven remained subject to secular chapters.[17] All was not always peace and light in either group. In theory the authority of the bishop should have been enough to avert conflict, but this was not necessarily the case. Royal policy usually determined that secular bishops were called on to preside over monastic chapters, but even under monk-bishops tensions were felt. Basic questions concerning the election of canons, provision made for their sustenance, anxieties over their behaviour, particularly their sexual behaviour, were endemic. Property was involved. Prebendary stalls in a cathedral carried revenues with them and were often treated as family property. The pure form of chapters enjoying the fruits of prebends as separate incomes in their own houses appears to have been a Norman innovation. In both types of cathedral, the monastic cathedral priories and the secular prebendal, the tendency was for numbers to grow fast during the generations immediately after the Conquest, a process connected with increase in endowment and massive building programmes. In the monastic dimension the number of choir monks often exceeded 50 or 60, even reaching as many as 150 at Canterbury. Secular cathedrals were more sparing, and yet by 1135 Lincoln had 43 stalls. Canons took their share of pastoral work in the diocese, but within the cathedral exercised in rota liturgical functions. The basic governing structure evolved into the traditional four-square division of responsibility of dean, chancellor, precentor and treasurer, but at this stage such a systematic division should be regarded as an ideal to be worked towards rather than a universal practice.

In many dioceses there were further centres of episcopal influence and control in the shape of minster churches or their equivalents. York is a particularly vivid example, and the collegiate churches of Ripon, Beverley, Hexham (all former bishoprics) and Southwell illustrate the reality of ecclesiastical life. In the south also at Exeter (with former bishoprics centred at Crediton and St Germans) there is a similar pattern. The rapid increase in number of parishes, coupled with the vitality of the monastic order, diminished the importance of many of these secondary great churches, though there were still signs of their significance as centres of devotion, even places where the bishop held court or where functions connected with liturgy or finance found a convenient place, perhaps providing for the collection of Peter's Pence or for developing local cult centres, or (as in the Salisbury diocese) as sites for the collection of geld.

An undoubted greater formality in the holding of episcopal courts and in the general conduct of ecclesiastical business resulted from the Norman

---

17 Brett, *The English Church under Henry I*, p. 187: the following paragraphs depend heavily on this book.

Conquest, part of the move towards a more literate society. From the earlier days that was so. In 1070 at the Windsor Council, as we have already seen, it was laid down that bishops should ordain in their churches archdeacons and other ministers in High Orders. By the beginning of Henry I's reign there was clear proof that this ordinance had been carried out in most of the dioceses of England. Under Henry I the duties of the archdeacon's office developed as the right-hand man of the bishop in finance, administration and law. There was also a clear-cut acceleration of the use of the office as a means of obtaining preferment, especially by close kinsfolk of the bishops, but also for royal or episcopal chaplains. Their sins became notorious and matter for scandal. Expected to take the lead in enforcing clerical celibacy, they were often themselves married. Archbishop Thurstan's own nephew had at least two sons. Archdeacons who were sons or nephews or brothers of bishops were known from many dioceses, and some proved good and successful. Others proved merely successful in the worldly sense, and their abuses in office and apparent capability of independent action became regular matters of concern to ecclesiastical councils and synods.

The reign of Henry I also experienced some clarification in the position and status of rural deans. On the Continent the office developed as clearly subordinate to the archdeacon. In England the development was a little more complex and the direct dependence of rural dean on the bishop was always to be taken into account. Further complications arose naturally because of the strength of the monastic chapters in England, chapters that were normally presided over by officers called deans. Rural deans as such seem to have been essentially a Norman importation. By 1135 they had emerged as a significant and well-defined element in the ecclesiastical hierarchy, holding courts in the bishop's name, enforcing judgements, collecting episcopal revenues and even collecting fines for breaches of the king's peace when ecclesiastical or spiritual matters impinged on the royal. It is tempting to read some continuity between the rural deans and these priests who presided over minsters in late Anglo-Saxon England, but the evidence does not permit such a simple equation. Rural deans seem rather a product of Norman concentration on episcopal order and systematic financial administration exercised on a diocesan basis.[18]

Discussion so far has corresponded to available evidence from chronicles, bishops' registers, records of the activities of the highest clerics. Distressingly little has survived about the lesser clergy. Even Domesday Book figures are imperfect. Church architecture and insights from the lives of saints help, fleshing out the bare bones of disciplinary strictures and somewhat

---

18 Ibid., pp. 211–15.

idealised comments that can be teased out of the legal records of councils and synods. As we have already said, the familiar shape of medieval parishes was falling into place almost universally by the end of the eleventh century with the ideal situation realised over much of England that no Christian should be further than three miles or so from a church which would possess the rights to baptise him and to bury him. Yet there was no uniformity in the size, the status or the wealth of said churches and (as in the towns) there also existed many small shrines and chapels, some of which were only with difficulty fitted into the smooth theoretical pattern of diocese, archdeaconry and rural deanery. A prime distinction must be drawn initially by the time we reach the reign of Henry I between those who controlled the revenues and rights of churches, the rectors and parsons, and those who actually officiated in the local churches. Religious houses, especially the great abbeys, royal servants, bishops and their servants often owned many churches, and it was regarded as quite proper that this should be so. Pluralism was rife and the religious life of the community depended upon the appointment of vicars, at times poorly paid, to benefices held by wealthy institutions or busy public men, such as Roger, bishop of Salisbury, who held at least fourteen churches, some, such as Brixworth and Stanton Harcourt, of considerable importance, together with a variety of high offices, deaneries and chaplancies at various times.[19] Some of the resident clergy were prosperous, capable of making substantial bequests to religious houses. Some were of knightly class and late in Henry's reign the first of our surviving Pipe Rolls show them in 1129/30 acting as financial agents to the king and of presumably quite comfortable financial status themselves. Many, probably a very high proportion, were married, in spite of the strictures of reforming synods. Priests were freemen, even if more often than not dependent on greater lords. They might be equated with other villagers for many purposes, for holdings in the open fields or service at courts. In many instances their wealth may not have been all that much greater than the average villager's. Nevertheless in rural societies it is the little differences that count, and without making the picture too much that of Chaucer's poor parson or the lesser clergy of Victorian days, it would be wrong to deny that the parson did not exercise a strong element of leadership in many of the English villages in the mid-twelfth century.

As to his function, there one finds a difference of opinion. Some good scholars have suggested it was relatively minor and that the growth of monasteries was the key to pastoral care in the twelfth century in the same

---

19   E.J. Kealey, *Roger of Salisbury, Viceroy of England,* 1972, pp. 96–100 and *passim* for an
     indication of wealth and authority.

way as the growth of minsters in late Anglo-Saxon England. The sheer physical proliferation of parish churches in the century after the Norman Conquest would seem the chief plank in the argument against this view. Evidence, as so often, is scarce on routine duties, and yet some functions stand out as routine which could only be exercised by a resident priest operating within a territorial neighbourhood. It would be pedantic not to call such a neighbourhood a parish. Within a parish the resident priest would be expected to say mass daily and observe some at least of the canonical hours. He would baptise, and existing twelfth-century fonts in many small churches remind us of this fundamental obligation. He was expected to pray and to preach. The copying of homilies in good Anglo-Saxon well into the twelfth century reminds us of this element of pastoral care. Teaching was a duty, and the lives of some of the leading scholars of the age, such as John of Salisbury or (at an earlier period) Ordericus Vitalis, give proof of the continuity of such work in England. Both owed the grounding of their future scholarship to parish priests. Marriage, penance, administering the sacrament to the faithful at least three times a year, supervising the ordeal, were among his expected activities. He would anoint the gravely ill and the dying and officiate at the burial. As in all settled societies, Christian and other, the presence of a priest to act as intermediary and intercessor on the great occasions of birth, death, sowing, harvest, and the festivals associated with the life of the individual and the community was expected. It is distressing to the historian to find how rarely there is tangible evidence that expectations were realised, but common sense, the existence of exquisite churches such as Barfreystone in Kent, Kilpeck in Herefordshire or Kempley in Gloucestershire, warn us not to be too cynical about the priestly role. Record is always quick to point to abuse. Priests, married or not, even the time-servers, existed in large enough numbers to carry the reality of Christian worship and Christian thought through to the central Middle Ages.

A parson would be supported financially in a number of ways. Endowment with land, sometimes a ploughland, was part of the story but not necessarily the greater part. Tithes, determined by custom, were a mainstay. Tithes taken from the demesne of the lord of the manor, or indeed from any freeman, could be granted away from the village church and often in early Norman days were granted to religious houses, quite possibly a reversal of custom in later Saxon days where demesne tithes seem often to have gone to the local church and the tithes of the villeins went to support minsters. Proliferation of local churches has obscured what must have been very complicated arrangements. Certainly when new churches were founded, by the initiative either of landlords or of groups of more prosperous villagers, it would be rational to find some proportion of the tithes, sometimes all the tithes, devoted to the new church, with some financial arrangement made to compensate existing recipients. In Norman days villein tithes more often than not were paid locally, and many good judges see this division into demesne and villein tithes as the origin of the later distinction between the great tithe and the lesser. England was different from most of Western Europe in making no allowance from the tithes to the bishop as bishop.[20]

Other payments were regular and multifarious, determined by custom. Churchscot covered a number of impositions, and was at times confused with tithes themselves. Oblations were expected at the altar at fixed times throughout the year and especially at the high festivals of Easter, Whitsun and Christmas. Offerings would be made at christenings and marriages. Perhaps of greatest importance were burial fees. From early Anglo-Saxon wills we know how important the choice of burial site could be. Wealthy men and women would reward churches lavishly in expectation of burial at a favoured spot with prayers said for his or her soul. In time the custom seeped down through society in the shape of mortuary fees, which by the thirteenth century could amount to a third of a man's possessions. The notion that the second-best beast, normally an ox, should be given from the estate of the deceased to the church where he was buried begins to be found in the records by the early twelfth century. Cemetery rights by long tradition were highly prized and safeguarded.[21]

A multiplicity of complicated relationships bound together the church and the parson and the villagers, who were more and more falling into the category that we would recognise as simple parishioners. Not that even these complications, involving personal status, manorial lordships and relative wealth, begin to express the total picture. There also remained what many would consider the overriding social question of the relationship of the local church to the landlord or the patron. Increasingly patronage passed into the hands of religious houses or the newly founded monastic Orders. As many as a quarter of the parish churches of England were controlled by abbots or priors of monasteries expecting to draw revenues from their possessions. In the early days of the century this was done by granting a pension from the church to the monastery or by dividing the revenues so that the priest and the monastery would share the proceeds. Sharp distinctions between priests called rectors and priests called vicars were only embryonic. In many fields ecclesiastical rights and dues became subject to more precise legal definition, not least because of doubt sown between

---

20   Giles Constable, *Monastic Tithes from their Origins to the Twelfth Century*, 1964, especially pp. 83–98 on the policy of the Reformed Papacy.

21   Brett, *The English Church under Henry I*, pp. 127–30.

superior and lesser churches. Episcopal charters provide evidence for the struggle towards such precision. Construction of new parish churches had obvious financial consequences. Anselm in 1102 had found it necessary to forbid a bishop the right to consecrate a new church until he had found the means to supply the church and a priest with the essential resources. Such new churches and chapels could have serious impact on existing rights and in that respect the consent of a bishop was obligatory in the early twelfth century: the age when a landlord's will was enough was long past. When local churches were given to monasteries as part of their endowment, they were expressly ordered to see to it that the priests were not reduced to penury. When chapels were upgraded to parish churches, care had to be taken to safeguard the rights of the old authorities as well as the new. Exhall in Warwickshire had been a chapel dependent on its mother-church at Kineton Green. Bishop Simon of Worcester (1125–50) issued two charters in its favour, the first listing the endowments, the second amplifying the account, making specific reference to the cemetery, safeguarding the rights of the mother-church and freeing the new church from all episcopal customs and renders apart from those which it was accustomed to render.[22] Other charters tell of similar processes. Over the period 1066–1135 increased sophistication in bishops' households coupled with a sharper legal awareness resulted in the creation of a complex network of legal relationships deep within the body of the English Church.

In an age when greater respect for the written word was strongly in evidence, the Church took advantage legally of its control of literacy. Custom could quickly become law, and strong government guaranteed a degree of enforcement. Tension and dispute continued to exist within the Church and between Church and State, ready to erupt later in the century when Thomas Becket was archbishop, but by 1135 a clearer sense of permanence is to be found in the detailed institutional life of the Church.

---

22 Ibid., p. 130 for the Exhall charters.

CHAPTER SEVEN

The Reign of Stephen

By the end of Henry I's reign many of the characteristic features of the English Church of the High Middle Ages were clearly apparent. To judge from surviving enactments of church councils, there was much that needed reform, but much also was in reasonably rude health. The state of the monastic world provides a possible test for such a statement. The first half-century after the Conquest had seen a consolidation of the Benedictine and Cluniac spirit in England under vigorous Norman direction, reaching something of a climax in the work and inspiration of St Anselm. In an age characterised by ecclesiastical and spiritual turmoil, it offered stability and disciplined security. It did not offer a powerful enough outlet for many who were influenced by the new surge of religiosity manifest in the age of the Investiture Contest and the First Crusade. This outlet was provided by a number of new austere foundations, consolidated in the late eleventh and early twelfth centuries into new Orders, supremely the Cistercian. Based on the teachings of St Augustine of Hippo as well as St Benedict, these new movements, Cistercian, Carthusian, Augustinian canons, Premonstratensians, began to make impact on the English scene in the last decade of the reign of Henry I.

The Cistercians, the white monks, were in their way the most conspicuous, though not necessarily the most significant at this early stage. Patronage was fairly easy to find. Cistercian endeavour to withdraw from society and to set up their houses in the desert places, meant that landlords could make over to them painlessly relatively unimportant stretches of land, notably in the North of England. Cistercian policy also facilitated foundation. Mother-houses, once established, would colonise and supervise new groupings, and ultimately looked to Citeaux itself, where the holding of annual chapters imposed discipline in the lesser bodies. The three Continental monasteries, all brought in to the Citeaux family, of Clairvaux, L'Aumône and Savigny were very active in England. Waverley was founded from L'Aumône in 1128 and Tintern in 1131; Rievaulx and Fountains from Clairvaux by 1132. Savigny took responsibility for Furness (1123) and six other houses, including Neath (1130), Basingwerk (1131), Quarr (1132) and Buildwas (1135). By 1135 Furness had already set up itself three small daughter-houses. At this stage it would be wrong to lay too much emphasis on the size or importance of these Cistercian elements in themselves, though their potential was great and in some areas quite quickly realised. Rievaulx and Fountains provide outstanding examples. Within twenty years of her founda-tion, Rievaulx could claim eleven flourishing houses as her progeny, ranging from Sibton in Suffolk to Kinloss, not far from Inverness. In exotic range, Fountains went even further. By 1150 she had twelve daughter-houses, including Kirkstall and Woburn. She also initiated the Cistercian penetration of Norway, sending a group from York to Lysekloster on the fjord near Bergen. Another of her daughter-houses sent another group to the Oslo fjord, where they established an influential house on the island of Hovedö. But even more than by their own vitality it is as an index to the surgent spirituality of the first half of the twelfth century that they are best regarded.[1]

The foundations for all this conspicuous activity in the Church in both its secular and monastic arms was conducted in England against a background of firm and stable Norman government. The reign of Henry I had proved a time for consolidation, especially in the fields of law and finance. The so-called 'Laws of Henry I' were a private compilation, made by a learned lawyer of antiquarian tastes familiar with procedures in the Winchester circuit. The collection touched the public nerve when it stated that, over-riding the special laws of Wessex, Mercia and the Danelaw, stood the tremendous majesty of royal law itself.[2] Henry I's later reputation as a lion of justice was well deserved; and his judges, sometimes harsh and brutal, saw to it that the message was carried to every shire court in England. Royal finance was even more advanced. Under the guidance of Roger, bishop of Salisbury (1102–39), the Exchequer developed into one of the most efficient financial institutions in Western Europe. The fortunate survival of the Pipe Roll for 1129/30 testifies to the competence and relative sophistication of the royal financial officers. It has been argued that royal control had gone too far, though this is very much an *ex post facto* sentiment. And yet reaction certainly came after the death of Henry I in December 1135, and our next concern must be to examine the fortunes of the Church during the troubled

---

1 David Knowles, *The Monastic Order in England*, 1940, pp. 246–66, ch. xiv on the years of growth of the Cistercians in England, 1135–53.
2 *Leges Henrici Primi*, ed. L.J. Downer, 1972, cl. 6, p. 96.

reign of King Stephen (1135–54), sometimes dismissed by contemporaries as well as by later historians as a time of anarchy.

In a famous phrase the Peterborough Chronicler referred to the reign as a period of nineteen winters during which men said openly that Christ and his saints slept.[3] Modern scholars have shown that such a view was an exaggeration, that anarchy and resultant hoodlum violence was sporadic, fearsome in some areas, notably where local tyrants were able to set up their castles unchecked as centres of oppression. Wiltshire and parts of eastern England, including lands around Peterborough itself, suffered severely, and yet the machinery of ordered government continued to operate over much of the country much of the time. Indeed some elements of ecclesiastical life, church courts and above all monastic life, positively flourished. Such evidence counteracts the notion of permanent anarchy, and yet one must not go too far in the other direction. The general picture of Stephen's reign remains very mixed, with much dependent on local conditions. In shires where magnates and sheriffs could impose local peace either in Stephen's name or in Matilda's, life could be tolerable.

Close examination of the coinage of Stephen's reign gives potential confirmation of this picture, while also pointing to the dangers of disruption suffered by central administration.[4] At the beginning of the reign, coinage continued to be struck in orderly traditional fashion as a royal monopoly. There was modification of the policy of Henry I, possibly to the chagrin of Roger of Salisbury and the surviving hard core of Henry's financial offices. As more evidence concerning the issue of Stephen's first type of coin becomes available (and this will depend on the chance of archaeological finds) it may be possible to discover the true reasons behind the overthrow of Roger or to see the modifications as a consequence of his downfall. Henry I had effected a considerable reduction in the number of mints from some fifty-one or so to twenty-four. Stephen restored minting rights to many boroughs and their lords and created some new mints, at, for example, Rye, Dunwich, Richmond, Newcastle and Swansea. Quite naturally, as after 1139 Matilda established herself in the West Country, coins were struck in her name, sometimes bearing her imperial title, *imperatrix* or a variant, on the obverse. Further disorder in the political world, notably during the imprisonment of Stephen in 1141, led to a loss of control in many areas. Only the South-East, a symptom of the importance of London in the financial and commercial

---

3 *Anglo-Saxon Chronicle, s.a.* 1137.
4 The following paragraph draws heavily on the work of Mark Blackburn, 'Coinage and Currency', *The Anarchy of King Stephen's Reign*, ed. Edmund King, 1994, pp. 145–203. Also G.C. Boon, *Welsh Hoards 1979–81*, 1986, pp. 37–82 on the Coed-y-Wenallt hoard.

world, remained relatively firm under Stephen's control. East Anglia also was brought back into the traditional mould towards the mid-1140s. Elsewhere regional control passed profitably into the hands of great magnates, earls of the old and new dispensations, and bishops, though with effective respect for the nominal powers of kingship. Only a few men seem to have struck coins in their own names, Henry of Neubourg at Swansea, for example, or Robert III of Stuteville in Yorkshire.

For the most part the theory of the royal prerogative of control of coinage was maintained. Coins were struck in Stephen's name where the local magnates had maintained their allegiance to Stephen, and in Matilda's name (or even in the name of earlier monarchs, Henry or William) where barons or bishops had moved to active support of Matilda and the Angevin cause. Chroniclers were vociferous in expressing their dismay at the quality of the coinage, its reduction in weight standard and its decline in the hands of local magnates. Numismatic evidence, if tenuous, seems to support the general view that coinage was ultimately a matter for the king. Some elements of royal control were reimposed later in the reign, especially after the Treaty of Winchester, November 1153, paved the way for Henry II's succession; and the energetic Henry in fact proved able and willing to reimpose his authority on the coinage and to institute far-reaching reform in the late 1150s.

Coinage provides a practical, if at times enigmatic, index to disorder. If Henry of Neubourg or Robert of Stuteville had been representative of large numbers of secular lords, a truly revolutionary disruptive situation would have developed. The seeds for such disruption were there. It would be wrong to conceal the fact that many areas suffered severely. The horror stories of tyrants in castles, of torture, mayhem and savagery embedded in the Anglo-Saxon Chronicle, cannot be utterly discounted. The issue of coins in baronial names tells of the dangers that local tyranny could only too easily have been established and perpetuated over significant tracts of the kingdom. Such tyranny provided excellent copy for the pen of the monastic chronicler. Every powerful man was said to have built his castles and filled them with devils and wicked men. The wretched people, thought to have money, gold or silver, were then tortured with undesirable torments (described, it must be said, in lurid detail). Taxes were levied on villages in the form of protection money (*tenserie*). Men died of starvation, some lived as beggars who had once been wealthy, some fled the country.[5] For many inhabitants of hitherto peaceful England the reign of Stephen, and specifically the worst period of civil war between Stephen and Matilda, was a time of peril and misery.

---

5 *Anglo-Saxon Chronicle, s.a.* 1137.

As often at a time of great political uncertainty, leading churchmen emerge as figures of influence and power. This was markedly so at the beginning of Stephen's reign. Stephen's success in asserting his claim to the throne owed so much to the lavish patronage bestowed on him by his uncle, King Henry I. It also owed much in the immediate situation following Henry's death to the support given by Stephen's own brother, Henry of Blois, bishop of Winchester (1129–71). One of the most spectacular prince-bishops of the age, Henry, both monk and soldier, as the contemporary historian Henry of Huntingdon described him, rejoiced in his royal blood and exalted office.[6] He was enormously wealthy, holding the richest abbey in England at Glastonbury as well as his see at Winchester. Of the Conqueror's three legitimate grandsons of the House of Blois, he most obviously inherited William I's gifts for government and administration. From his important though secondary position as bishop of Winchester he did not, as things turned out, have the opportunity to construct or follow permanent creative policies, but he remained a force to be reckoned with throughout his long life. Disappointed of a sideways move to Canterbury when William of Corbeil died in November 1136, he received consolation in the form of a commission to act as papal legate in March 1139. For the critical period of Civil War, 1139–43, until the death of Pope Innocent II, he was a major figure in Church and State relationships, even taking precedence over the newly elected archbishop, Theobald of Bec (1138–61). But it was in December 1135 that he made his principal single contribution when he persuaded the clerical mainstays of Henry I's Old Guard, Roger of Salisbury and Roger's two nephews, Nigel, bishop of Ely, and Alexander, bishop of Lincoln, to support Stephen's candidature for the throne. He was in a position to control the castle and treasury at Winchester, key elements in the situation in 1135 as they had been in 1100. Henry I died in Normandy on 1 December. Stephen acted with somewhat uncharacteristic decisiveness. He himself was also in France, at Boulogne, but he crossed the Channel at top speed and was elected and crowned by Archbishop William with all formality by Christmas. Early in the following year the election was confirmed by Pope Innocent II.

There followed on Stephen's part a massive misjudgement from which it is arguable he never recovered. He started well, issuing a charter in 1136 by the terms of which he promised in solemn form to uphold the ancient liberties of the English Church. His definition of what constituted those

---

6   Henry, archdeacon of Huntingdon, *Historia Anglorum. The History of the English People*, ed. Diana E. Greenway, 1996, p. 611: '*qui futurus est novum quoddam monstrum ex integro et corrupto compositum, scilicet monachus et miles.*'

liberties has its interest. Some were calculable, the confirmation of privileges, customs and lands which the Church held at the death of the Conqueror, in all likelihood an oblique reference to the knowledge of the state of things in 1086–87, stored up in Domesday Book. There was also a standard obligatory reference to a rejection of simony, a limitation on the rights to be enjoyed by the king during vacancies, and a promise to redress unjust practices or exactions made by royal officials. An inquiry was promised into lands claimed by the Church to have been lost before 1087, a confirmation of land granted since that date and a specific mention of the return of land lost to the Church by Henry I's afforestation. All this might be read as commonplace, a declaration of intention on the part of a new king anxious to achieve maximum support from the Church. What is a shade unusual, and possibly an indication of the intellectual strength of some elements in the Church in the 1130s, was an emphasis on the legal separateness of the clergy. All were recognised by the charter as subject to common law and under the jurisdiction of their bishops. The hand of advanced reformers, aware of papal strictures over the integrity of the clerical order, is clearly in evidence.[7]

Such hope of reform with Church and State working in harmony was quickly dispelled. The heavy involvement of senior churchmen in government brought perils as well as advantages. In June 1139 a bitter quarrel led to the dismissal and humiliation of the great justiciar Roger, bishop of Salisbury, and of his two episcopal nephews of Lincoln and Ely. It is true that such actions need not in themselves have led to trouble. These men were not popular and were more secular governors than spiritual leaders. Other strong kings such as Henry I himself had taken against overbearing prince-bishops with success and general approval. The real fear that Roger's powerful family, representing the Old Guard of Henry's reign, might be ready to move in favour of Matilda provided Stephen with plentiful justification. Even so, the results in this instance of the personal humiliation heaped on the three bishops, and on the chancellor, Roger le Poer, the justiciar's son, had dire consequences for the ecclesiastical situation. Stephen was blamed for the handling of the crisis, and his own brother, Henry of Blois, was alienated by the affront to the episcopal order. This alienation came at a particularly bad moment. Henry, rejoicing in the authority of papal legate which had been conferred on him in March, summoned a council to Winchester on 29 August, deliberated on the matter for four days but reached no decision. Towards the end of the following month, probably on 30 September, Matilda landed in England, making her way to the West Country, where she had solid support from her illegitimate half-brother, Robert earl of Gloucester. Milo,

---

7 *EHD* ii, no. 21.

the constable of Henry I and later earl of Hereford, and Brian FitzCount, most loyal of all her followers, also strengthened the West Country following with headquarters at Bristol. It was said that Brian was induced to switch allegiance to Matilda directly on advice from Henry of Blois. By 1141, in fact, Henry himself had substantially moved back to Stephen's side, but the disruption caused by the humiliation of Roger brought weakness to the king at a critical moment. No doubt the underlying causes of the Civil War ran deep: dispute over succession to the throne, a reaction against the severity of Henry I's government, probably a malaise within the feudal order itself over legitimate succession to fiefs and to inheritance in general. Nevertheless, the events of June 1139, the trumped-up charges, the deprivation of the castles and material possessions, provoked outrage and consequent immediate withdrawal of ecclesiastical support. They constituted therefore an important subsidiary cause to the Civil War.

The war itself, though fitful, dragged on from 1139 to 1147 with a most dramatic twist to events in 1141. On 2 February of that year Stephen was captured in battle at Lincoln and imprisoned at Bristol. Later in the year, in mid-September, after the so-called 'rout of Winchester', Robert of Gloucester, commanding Matilda's forces, was in turn captured at Stockbridge. In November an exchange of prisoners was arranged, Stephen for Robert. The whole series of battles and negotiations of 1141 highlighted the disorders of a feudal society seeking to establish or re-establish a stable relationship between monarch and tenant-in-chief and to provide proper legal safeguards for hereditary tenure at all levels of the feudal hierarchy. Slowly but surely it was in working towards such stability that churchmen came to play a dominant part. In the most famous example late in the reign when the great magnates, taking advantage of weakness and uncertainty at the centre, had built up their own territorial power, two of their number, Earl Ranulf of Chester and Earl Robert of Leicester, reached an accord calculated to settle their rivalries in the Midlands. Their resulting treaty made elaborate arrangements within a feudal framework for keeping the peace and controlling castle building. The two principal agents in supervising the resulting peace were the two appropriate bishops of Coventry and of Lincoln. The threatened vacuum caused by weak central authority was averted by judicious use of the episcopate.

Who were these bishops on whom so much depended, and how were they appointed? Henry of Winchester, as we have seen, was in a special position because of his birth and also because of his contact with the Papacy. In practice, however, this contact grew less significant after the death of Pope Innocent II in 1143. By the late 1140s, Henry was working in insular interests against papal pretensions, supporting Stephen when the king forbade the primate, Theobald of Bec, together with some other bishops, to attend the Council of Rheims in 1148.[8] Henry's hostility to Theobald was scarcely concealed. Indeed he made efforts, unsuccessfully it is true, to achieve metropolitan status for his own see at Winchester with authority extending over the West and South-West.

Theobald himself was an interesting character, the third of the monks of Bec to be elevated to the archiepiscopate. Overshadowed by his predecessors, Lanfranc and Anselm, he has not always been given full credit for what was in fact a thoroughly effective period in office at a very difficult time. Initially there was full reason for that rather neutral reputation for he was also overshadowed by Henry of Blois. Only shortly after Henry ceased to be papal legate in 1143 did Theobald emerge as a significant political figure in his own right. He spent most of the first six months of 1144 on the Continent, successfully blocking Henry of Blois's attempt to have his legate's position retained. On his way home, in great honour as a senior prelate outside France, he attended one of the most spectacular religious ceremonies of the century when the reconstructed abbey of St Denis was consecrated on 11 June in the presence of the French king. The Papacy tended, though not consistently, to be pro-Angevin in sentiment, and so Theobald, clearly identified with Stephen's interests, had to steer a careful middle course. A crisis occurred in 1148. The Pope summoned a Council and ordered the English legates to attend. Stephen had always jealously guarded his right to control movement of his bishops who were also great magnates. Only five had been granted permission to attend the Lateran Council in 1139. In 1148 he confined his approval to three, excluding the archbishop. Theobald was determined to go, and crossed the Channel secretly in a small fishing boat, arriving more like a vagrant exile than an archbishop.[9] On his return he was deprived of his temporal possessions and ordered out of the country. The Pope threatened King Stephen with excommunication but was persuaded not to carry through the sentence by the pleading of Theobald himself on the king's behalf – a measure of the complexity of the situation. For although at this stage Stephen and his archbishop were often at loggerheads, their personal relationships seemed often to be amicable, a complete contrast to the violence and hatred of Henry II and Becket some twenty years later. Reconciliation was effected. Theobald returned, very sensibly not immediately to Canterbury but to Suffolk, where he was protected by the great magnate, Hubert de Burgh.

---

8   Avrom Saltman, *Theobald of Bec, Archbishop of Canterbury*, 1956.
9   John of Salisbury, *Historia Pontificalis*, ed. Marjorie Chibnall, 1986, p. 7: 'a fishing vessel that would carry no more than a dozen men and lacked even the most essential equipment. And so he crossed the Channel more like a survivor from shipwreck than in a ship.'

For the last five years of Stephen's reign, Theobald emerged as a power in the land. At some point, probably early 1150, he obtained legatine authority. He played a central role in bringing Stephen and the Angevins together, refusing, under papal instruction, to consecrate Stephen's elder son, Eustace, as heir to England, and working towards a universal recognition of the young Duke Henry as the legal successor to the throne as Henry II.

Henry of Blois, bishop of Winchester, and Theobald of Bec, archbishop of Canterbury, were the outstanding figures in the episcopate; and, indeed, men of that calibre would have been likely to achieve prominence in any period. They did not stand alone. The unrest and occasional outbreak of savagery and destruction which characterised the Civil War threw great responsibility on the shoulders of all the bishops. Most lived up to that responsibility to the best of their abilities. By and large the Church emerged from the struggles of Stephen's reign in a strong position. Appointment to the office of bishop was as always a matter shot through with political implications. Both Stephen himself and the Angevin party favourable to Matilda took pains to ensure that suitable candidates were considered for high and lucrative office when bishoprics or other prominent positions in the Church became available. Even so, the overall position, regarded in retrospect from the end of the reign, was quite surprisingly favourable to the principles of the reformers.

Let us take first the question of free election to the office of bishop. The interest of contemporary chronicles is naturally aroused when disputes occur, sometimes mirroring the political divisions between King Stephen and Matilda's Angevin supporters, sometimes the religious divisions between what are loosely called the Cluniacs and the new blood of the Cistercians. In the early years of the reign there was much justification for such interest. From 1139 to 1143, politics were fully in play, especially in relation to the archiepiscopal see at York. Archbishop Thurstan (1114–40), venerated for, among other things, the dramatic part he played in the defeat of the Scots at the Battle of the Standard in 1138, had attempted to resign his see in favour of his brother, Audoen, bishop of Evreux. The attempt failed and opened the way for a succession of legal disputes. After Thurstan's death, King Stephen more or less intruded his candidate, William Fitzherbert, who was consecrated by Henry of Blois as papal legate, not by Theobald of Bec, archbishop of Canterbury. In 1147, under strong pressure from St Bernard of Clairvaux, William was deprived of office and the Cistercian abbot of Fountains, Henry Murdoc, elected in his place. There is a final twist to the story which is worth exploring, even if slightly out of chronological sequence. In October 1153, after Henry Murdoc's death, William Fitzherbert was restored, only to die on 8 June 1154, under the strong suspicion that he had been poisoned by his own archdeacon. A folk-cult sprang up around him (there is a wall painting representing him far south in St Albans Abbey), and he was ultimately canonised in the early thirteenth century. The fact remains that Theobald, representing a reformist element, was initially ineffective in the matter of York. In the early stages he was successful in pressing for free election only at Rochester and probably the Welsh sees of Bangor and Llandaff. After 1143, however, the situation slowly changed, and of the fourteen elections held between 1143 and 1154, at least six were scrupulously correct in reflecting the free choice of the chapter (Norwich, Lincoln, London, Coventry, Worcester, Durham). At York in 1147 and at Chichester papal pressure was decisive, while Theobald's own influence proved powerful at Rochester, Hereford, St David's, Llandaff and in the second election of 1154 at York. The archbishop's own brother, Walter, was elected to Rochester in 1148 to enjoy a long term of office until his death in 1182. Hereford was a special case, passing under the ministration of Gilbert Foliot (1148–63), who afterwards moved to London (1163–87), where he became the archenemy of Thomas Becket. Trained at Cluny, Gilbert had been appointed abbot of Gloucester in 1139 and had followed his patron, Milo, in support of Matilda and the Angevins. His election as such was straightforward and yet politics made it necessary for him to seek consecration in 1148 from Theobald in Flanders, on condition that he would perform fealty to Henry of Anjou, Matilda's son. In practice, and very sensibly, he sought out Stephen on his return to England and proved a critical figure in the last years of the reign, with public allegiance to Stephen, yet support for the succession of Henry. On the matter of election the principles of canon law were better understood and the practice of canon law better implemented under the guidance of Archbishop Theobald and his household.[10]

The result of the elections also suggests a certain degree of fairness in ranging across the various possible categories of bishop. Of the thirty-four bishops who held office during the reign, no fewer than nineteen were secular clerks who had worked their way up through the hierarchies surrounding bishops, deans and diocesan offices. Only six were specifically from the royal household. There were twelve monks, all Benedictine, except the Cistercian Murdoc at York. Three of the Benedictines had been Cluniac-trained.[11] Elements of stability and continuity within the episcopate stood out from the dangerous disruption of central authority in the secular world.

---

10 An element by example and reaction in the Angevin leap forward under Henry II:
    D.M. Stenton, *English Justice between the Norman Conquest and the Great Charter, 1066–1215*, 1965.
11 Christopher Holdsworth, 'The Church', *The Anarchy of King Stephen's Reign*, ed.
    Edmund King, 1994, pp. 212–13.

Elections of bishoprics represent on balance an element of ecclesiastical probity during this troubled period. The Church was also active in the matter of holding councils at which basic teaching concerning moral law could be stated. Evidence for the holding of specific councils has survived relating to meetings at London (1140, 1143, 1145, 1151, 1152 and 1154) and at Winchester (1139 and 1143). Alberic of Ostia had been papal legate in 1138–39, and the Winchester Council of 1143 was also legatine, presided over by Henry of Blois. By 1151, Archbishop Theobald was legate, and his council at London had legatine status. The canons issued at it reflect the spirit of the whole reign. Maledictions were hurled against unjust exactions, *tenseries* and tallages inflicted on the Church or the possessions of the Church, although the king was not refused his just rights. Indeed the canons of the councils, in seeking out new remedies for old afflictions, showed a marked tendency to favour co-operation with the king. Illegal baronial exactions aroused fury and churchmen were expressly forbidden to answer to the barons in respect of pleas of the Crown. An excommunicant who remained contumacious for a year was to lose his legal rights and to be disinherited by the king. An interdict was invoked where robbery of church property was involved; and officiants in chapels were to cease performing divine office at the same time as the mother-church. Credentials of priests and others in Holy Orders were to be closely checked. Baronial abuse in the form of illegal tolls was heavily condemned.[12]

Reforming impulses therefore continued to be felt and expressed through the decrees of councils, though a degree of scepticism is inevitable when placed side by side with the woeful stories of oppression and misrule put forward by contemporary historians and chroniclers. The Peterborough Chronicler told how if two or three men came riding to a village, the villagers would all flee because they feared they would be robbers; and he added caustically that bishops and learned men were always excommunicating them but to no avail for they were all accursed and perjured and doomed to perdition.[13] Yet some features emerge from close study of the reign which speak of better things and warn us not to interpret the reign as a whole as merely a miserable negative interlude between two periods of growth in monarchical institutions and therefore in progress, given twelfth-century conditions, towards a more rational society.

To begin with, there is the persistent attitude of respect towards properly constituted monarchy, even among those in array against the individual

---

12 Saltman, generally favourable to Theobald, reminds us that theoretical penalties could be ineffective: Theobald's interdict of 1148 is described as a complete fiasco, *Theobald of Bec*, p. 29.

13 *Anglo-Saxon Chronicle*, s.a. 1137.

monarch. Stephen had been elected and crowned. Matilda, even in her moments of political triumph in 1141, remained lady of the English or of England, *domina Angliae*, and would have needed that extra touch of brutality – the killing of Stephen – and the support of the higher clergy and Rome in order to achieve the status of queen regnant. To be ex-empress as the widow of Henry V, to have her young son, Henry of Anjou, Henry Plantagenet, referred to as fitz-empress, was all well and good, but coronation and the reservoir of authority that went with the hallowing eluded her. This attitude towards the sanctity of Christian monarchy was firmly implanted in the thinking of the Papacy. Some popes might favour the Angevins, but the consistent motive of papal policy towards England aimed at stability. Bishops, even in the areas most subject to Angevin control, had to live in the knowledge that Rome recognised Stephen as the rightful King of England.

All this was high theory, and practice could be different, involving the misery of civil war, uncertainty over succession, and the settlement of disputes by warlords who at times employed mercenaries, notoriously Flemish soldiers of fortune only too prone to acts of savagery. In such circumstances the Church and individual churchmen came to exercise a special role, sometimes to prevent violence, often to pick up the pieces after violence. There was a long history on the Continent of attempts to contain feudal disorder by means of devices which developed into highly regulated institutions supervised by churchmen, the Peace of God or the Truce of God. Such development was alien to England.[14] Royal authority had become under strong Norman leadership the principal means of imposing peace. One has only to read through the pages of the best historians, William of Poitiers, Eadmer, Ordericus Vitalis or William of Malmesbury, to see how what was truly the central Roman imperial model had been taken over by the Normans: to impose the custom of peace was the ideal, to spare the subject and to suppress the proud-hearted. With civil war and the breakdown of traditional order in some localities, the Church, no matter how inadequately, attempted to fill the breach.

We have already referred in passing to the most famous case. Ranulf, earl of Chester, most powerful among the magnates, had taken advantage of political turbulence and disorder to build up his territorial strength in a swathe of country stretching eastwards from Chester to Lincoln. He was compelled to give up some of his gains in 1146 after confrontation in rivalry with the formidable Beaumont twin, Robert of Meulan, earl of Leicester. Later in Stephen's reign the two earls drew up an agreement, setting out

---

14   H.E.J. Cowdrey, 'The Peace and Truce of God in the Eleventh Century', *Past and Present* 46, 1970, pp. 42–67.

formal feudal rules that were to be followed before entering conflict and significantly establishing a neutral area within which both pledged themselves not to build castles. The pledges, held in case the agreement were broken, were held by two bishops, Walter Durdant, bishop of Coventry, on behalf of the earl of Chester, and Robert de Chesney, bishop of Lincoln, for the earl of Leicester. Both bishops were new to their sees (Walter in 1149, Robert in 1148) but prestigious, well-connected and young. They operated at a high level in what was threatening to become established practice. Close investigation by modern historians of chronicles and charters has revealed the existence of more than twenty of such agreements, or *conventiones*, some it is true of short duration, that were reached in the course of Stephen's reign.[15] Most occurred out of range of Stephen's own royal authority. Nevertheless, the principle emerges quite clearly. The search for peace, essential to ordered Christian life, involved increasingly the practical involvement of higher-ranking churchmen, carrying with them spiritual authority, personal prestige and a solid awareness, too, of papal overlordship vested in the successors to Peter, the bishops of Rome.

Two further special phenomena deserve discussion in relation to this important phase in English ecclesiastical history, that is to say, contact with Rome coupled with intensified notions of Roman law, and independently a positive and unexpected flourishing of monasticism. Neither represents the popular picture of the reign of Stephen, but both have left powerful evidence of their existence. Contact with Rome was continuous, significant, and very much a two-way traffic. As we have seen, Henry of Blois enjoyed legatine authority from 1139 to 1143, and Theobald of Bec from 1151, possibly late 1150. An edge was given to the councils they summoned during these periods, the decrees bearing indirectly some of the authority of the Pope himself. There were also visitations by special envoys from Rome. Alberic of Ostia held a legatine council in 1138 at which the general reforms promised by Stephen at his accession were fleshed out in the form of seventeen specific canons. Popes, in line with general Hildebrandine principles, fostered contacts with English bishops. Stephen, anxious to preserve some at least of the ancient customs which favoured the monarchy, was hesitant in giving them permission to leave the kingdom. He allowed only five to attend Innocent II's great Lateran Council of 1139 and only three to be present at Eugenius's Council at Rheims in 1148, the latter becoming something of a *cause célèbre*, precipitating as we have seen, a major dispute between the king and Archbishop Theobald. But nothing could

---

15   Edward King, 'Dispute Settlement in Anglo-Norman England', *Anglo-Norman Studies* xiv, 1992, pp. 115–30.

prevent the flow of ideas and men in these vigorously active intellectual decades. The revival of the study of Roman law, initiated in the late eleventh century, was reaching a new peak. Gratian's masterpiece, his *Concordance of Discordant Canons*, made its appearance in the early 1140s. In England the scholar Vacarius began to earn a reputation as a teacher of the advanced methods and contents of civil law in the mid-forties.[16] Theobald had been responsible for bringing him to England, and it was during these years that the archbishop built up his household at Canterbury so that it became a recognised centre for the training of young men in law and theology. These young trained scholars of the stamp of Thomas Becket and Roger of Pont l'Evêque, later archbishop of York (1154–81), were far from isolated and were firmly in touch with Continental scholars from their Canterbury base. They were known as the *Cantuarienses*, and their reputation was such that one of the greatest scholars of the age, John of Salisbury, left papal service in 1154 in order to join them.

Direct personal contact with Rome itself was also strong. Appeals were made to Rome on the great matter of the throne itself, and it is possible that we have underestimated the impact of this example on attitudes to the process of appeal. The Empress Matilda had her case pleaded at the Lateran Council of 1139. The Pope, Innocent II, upheld his earlier support for Stephen but Matilda's case was heard and papal claims to be the supreme arbiter reinforced. After Innocent's death in 1143 there was a tendency for the Papacy to favour the Angevins, but not to the point where support was withdrawn from Stephen. He was a crowned, anointed king, and stability was of prime importance. Succession to Stephen was quite another matter, and relationships grew very strained late in the reign as Stephen attempted to ensure the succession of Eustace, his elder son. Pope Eugenius III, 1145–53, a Cistercian and friend to St Bernard of Clairvaux, expressly forbade Archbishop Theobald to crown Eustace. Cross-currents within the Papacy and within the Church at large between the Cistercian and Cluniac interests make it difficult to isolate consistent personal trends but one political strand is clear. The Papacy was anxious to build up its position and prestige as arbiter and to emerge as the natural source of authority in deciding what was or was not legitimate.

At the same time the influence of clerics who were either English or deeply involved in English affairs reached a peak. Most prominent among

---

16 Francis de Zulueta and Peter Stein, *The Teaching of Roman Law in England around 1200*, Selden Society, 1990, pp. xxii and *passim*. R.W. Southern, 'Master Vacarius and the Beginning of an English Academic Tradition', *Medieval Learning and Literature: Essays for R.W. Hunt*, ed. J.J.G. Alexander and M.T. Gibson, 1976.

them were Robert Pullen, cardinal and chancellor of the Roman Church (1144–46); Hilary, canon lawyer and a worker in the papal chancery before his translation to the bishopric of Chichester (1146–69); Boso, a cardinal and chamberlain in the late 1140s; and above all Nicholas Breakspear. Nicholas was already a cardinal in 1149, poised to make a great reputation as reformer of the Scandinavian Church and virtual creator of the archbishopric of Nidaros (Trondheim). Nicholas became the only English Pope as Adrian IV, 1154–59. Awareness of the contribution of these scholars and administrators, including John of Salisbury, must lighten the deep gloom that often falls on any attempt to describe the state of England in the reign of Stephen.

The same must be said when we turn to reflect on the extraordinary growth of monasticism which characterised the period. In a startling short appendix to his magisterial work on the monastic order, Dom David Knowles gave a rough estimate of the number of religious houses active in England and Wales between 1100 and 1175. At the death of Henry I in 1135, he calculated the number to be 193, at Stephen's death in 1154 no fewer than 307, and in 1175, 340; that is to say, a third of all the religious houses (114) owed their origins to the reign of Stephen. Many of these (36) belonged to the new Cistercian groupings and an equal number to canons living to a Rule (36). The Empress Matilda was also a patron, known to favour in particular the Augustinian canons. The brand new Gilbertines accounted for another ten or so houses. Later scholars, notably Christopher Holdsworth, have shown that Knowles's figures were an underestimate and that the true figure could be as high as 175 (171 in England, 4 in Wales).[17] Many were small houses with only a relatively primitive set of structures, but many were not and include, for example, Melrose, Revesby, Sibton, Kirkstead, Woburn and Kirkstall in England and Margam, Cwmhir and Abbey Dore in Wales. Heavy building work was also in progress in some of the older foundations such as Ely, Norwich, Lincoln and St Albans. Vigorous lay activity inevitably accompanied the institutional expression of the monastic impulse.

A special word should be said about the Gilbertines. The Order has always received attention because of its specific English quality, strong in Lincolnshire and the eastern counties, and also because of its bringing together of so many different strands in monastic thought and observance, ranging from memories of double houses in Anglo-Saxon England and the

---

17 Knowles, *The Monastic Order in England*, p. 711, appendix xiii; Holdsworth, 'The Church', has discovered some 171 foundations over 17 English dioceses, an average of 10 per diocese, though with great variations. Lincolnshire and Yorkshire are particularly rich in new houses, naturally so in contrast to the more settled South, and especially the South-East.

pages of Bede, to current practice at Fontevrault and Citeaux. Its creation has not perhaps been emphasised sufficiently as a pointer to the spirituality of the age and the capacity for expression of new ideas in the more peaceful parts of England even during the troubles of Stephen's reign. The impetus came from the work of one extraordinary man, Gilbert[18] of Sempringham, born in the early 1080s and living to a great and well-authenticated old age until 1189. He was the son of a prosperous Norman knight of the first generation after the Conquest and lived most of his life at Sempringham in Lincolnshire where he was the parish priest. In the later years of Henry I, *c.*1131, he established himself as a spiritual director to a number of dedic-ated women of good family, a phenomenon by no means unusual but not normally institutionalised. In a turbulent world, widows and spinsters of a spiritual turn of mind found communal living outside the main Orders often to their taste. Gilbert was influenced by the example of Fontevrault, a double monastery founded at the very beginning of the twelfth century by the Breton hermit Robert of Arbrissel, much favoured later by the Plantagenets. Further advice came from the Cistercian abbot of Rievaulx. Gilbert brought in lay brothers and sisters after the Cistercian model, and attempted to have his establishment accepted as part of the Cistercian Order. He failed in this but, guided by Pope Eugenius III, himself a Cistercian, he introduced secular canons as chaplains and set up in 1147 a new Order, the Gilbertines, which quickly became popular in England. By the time of his death, the movement had spread vigorously in a limited field with a dozen or so monasteries and also leper houses and orphanages under Gilbertine direction. His nuns followed the Rule of St Benedict, his chaplains the Augustinian. The lay folk conformed to Cistercian usage. The Gilbertines became famed, especially in eastern England, as a leading Order for women, serving as a reminder of the creative elements in religious life persisting through the reign of Stephen in continuous and unbroken succession from Cluniac and Cistercian inspiration of an earlier generation.

There was also continuity, substantially unbroken, in manuscript pro-duction and craftsmanship in centres such as Canterbury, Winchester, York and St Albans. Under one of its great abbots, Geoffrey de Gorron (1119–46), St Albans became a noted cultural centre, so selective in its intake that it is reputed to have refused admission to Nicholas Breakspear himself, born at nearby King's Langley. One of the best-known anchorites of the day, Christina of Markyate, flourished in proximity to the abbey. Other hermits and holy women abounded, and it is likely that the number of such men and women who testified to their faith through reclusive lives has in the past

---

18   *The Book of St Gilbert*, ed. Raymonde Foreville and Gillian Keir, 1986.

been seriously underestimated. It is, for example, only the fortunate survival of a life of Christina that enables us to glimpse others such as Roger, a hermit and former monk of St Albans, or the recluse Sigar of Northaw. Christina herself had a great influence, considered by some contemporaries as excessive, on Abbot Geoffrey at St Albans. When Geoffrey's successor, Abbot Robert, visited Pope Adrian IV at Rome in 1155, he took with him some sandals of exquisite workmanship made by Christina herself, a gift which the Pope was graciously pleased to receive.[19]

Vitality as well as misery can therefore be found in the history of the Church during the reign of Stephen. With secular government and the instruments of local secular administration in disarray, zealous and energetic churchmen took on more responsibility and built up traditions based on revived church law that led to sometimes excessive claims over jurisdiction. Some of the seeds of conflict between Church and State that erupted in the 1160s between Henry II and Becket were well and truly sown in the 1140s. There is no sign of abatement in church building and in church ornamentation. Wall paintings of the richness now existing only in comparatively few places such as Kempley in Gloucestershire provide one example of what must have been a creative period in architecture and art. The names of Geoffrey of Monmouth, William of Malmesbury and Henry of Huntingdon are enough to signal the existence of creative minds, writing and disseminating literary and historical work of enduring influence. Many men and women, too, found a role for themselves, not to be lightly dismissed as negative, in monasteries and nunneries. At the highest religious level it is possible to see conflict between the traditional Benedictine and Cluniac spirit exemplified in the life of the grandee Henry of Blois, and the new intense Cistercian attitude to personal discipline and attitude to government. The greatest of the Cistercians, St Bernard of Clairvaux, had a profound influence, directly and through his pupils and followers, on events in England, often expressed, especially later in the reign, in hostility or cautious scepticism towards King Stephen. Only at the parish level, where civil war raged, were there signs of ecclesiastical retrogression. Elsewhere there is conspicuous advance. The English Church was firmly integrated as part of the Western European Hildebrandine Church, though it retained some private peculiarities. Under the guiding hand of the young Angevin prince and heir, Henry II, the somewhat old-fashioned partnership of Church and State was poised for further direction along a reforming path.

---

19 Christopher Holdsworth, 'Christina of Markyate', *Medieval Women*, ed. Derek Baker, 1978, pp. 185–204.

CHAPTER EIGHT

Doctrine, Belief and Ritual

To this point we have dealt mainly with the external life of the Church, and it is arguable that we are too ambitious if we attempt to go further. Records deal with such external phenomena, the lawyer's view of clerical duties, the appointment of bishops and abbots, their endowment in land and revenues, their duties and their relationship to kings and secular magnates, contacts with Rome and the weight that should be given to such contacts. What of the inner life of the Church, the acceptance of forms of belief and worship, the questioning that could lead to social action? Was there significant identifiable development in these two centuries on matters of doctrine and social discipline that had effect on the religious and everyday life of the people of England?

There are subtleties to be considered on matters of doctrine. The eleventh century is often described as a revolutionary century in the history of the Church, comparable in some respects to the sixteenth and the Protestant Reformation. In matters of church organisation and the authority of the Pope *vis-à-vis* the Emperor and other crowned kings of Western Europe, this is true. The so-called 'Investiture Contest' ravaged the existing political and ecclesiastical structures of much of Western Europe. Yet the consequent upheavals, notably in Germany and in Italy, were not accompanied by major doctrinal disputes. For all of our two centuries, Western Europe persisted solidly orthodox in basic doctrine, Trinitarian, its beliefs firmly planted in the works of the Early Fathers, especially St Augustine of Hippo and Pope Gregory the Great. Reformation in the eyes of groups such as the Patarines in Milan was directed towards closer study of the Scriptures, a haunting desire for reversion to the simplicity of the early Church of the Gospels and some elements of millenary thought in looking forward to the kingdom of God and the life to come after death.

This is not to say that there were no disputes in detail over fundamental articles of faith. To take a telling example which had a bearing on the English scene, Lanfranc in his earlier days won his reputation as a scholar for the vigour with which he defended the orthodox view of the real presence in the Eucharist against the new and ultimately unsuccessful theories of Berengar of Tours.[1] William of Malmesbury devoted three chapters of his 'History of the Kings' to it, giving space to the long eulogy of the reformed Berengar in the poem by Hildebert, though tempering it with mention of the damage done by Berengar's earlier heresy, which was rife at one stage throughout Gaul. Berengar denied that after priestly consecration the elements of the communion, bread and wine, were truly and in substance the body of the Lord, as the Holy Church asserted. William of Malmesbury recognised that this view was refuted at papal councils and answered in books both by Lanfranc and by Guitmund of Aversa (the most eloquent man of his time). Berengar's ideas were indeed, according to the thought of the age, truly heretical, but no significant party rallied around them. Elsewhere accusations of heresy were freely made, though rarely defined with any accuracy; and the violence of theological debate implied in the pamphleteers during the struggle between Pope Gregory VII (1073–85) and the Emperor Henry IV (1056–1106) reached astounding heights. However, accusations were more often than not directed against relatively prosaic matters such as the sale of clerical offices rather than fundamental belief. Indeed the phrase 'simoniacal heresy' was one that came most trippingly off the pen of the protagonists. The sin of Simon Magus, the sale of clerical office, was the most conspicuous abuse manifest to contemporaries.

Acceptance of the central tenets of the Christian faith was, therefore, if we read the record accurately, a major characteristic of our period in Western Europe. These tenets were, as expressed by all involved in teaching and preaching, a belief in the Trinity and the Creeds, a submission to the rituals of the Church, above all to the rules governing baptism and the reception of Holy Communion, and an acknowledgement of the authority of the Scriptures. All folk, no matter how humble, were expected to know the Ten Commandments and the Nicene Creed. That basic framework remained solid, but outside it much was questioned and in flux. Intellectually the age produced giants such as St Anselm and St Bernard of Clairvaux. Their finer theological speculations might be conducted in an atmosphere remote from ordinary life, and yet their immediate influence on, for example, matters concerning colour and ornament in church ritual could be powerful.

---

1 William of Malmesbury, *Gesta Regum Anglorum*, vol. i, ed. and trans. R.A.B. Mynors, R.M. Thomson and M. Winterbottom, 1998, chs 284–6, pp. 512–20.

Experience shows how seemingly abstract thought can impinge with devastating effect on secular society. Both the Byzantine and the Muslim worlds suffered such trauma. Even now within Western Christian communities differences between Catholics and Protestants can erupt with disproportionate violence. But in the eleventh and early twelfth centuries no powerful political parties developed to exploit such differences. Western Europe remained universally orthodox.

This general orthodoxy is a phenomenon that invites attention. Pressure from outside may account for it in part. With the Crusades, certainly after 1095, awareness of the Byzantine world and of the Muslim would grow sharper and helped to stiffen native Western orthodoxy. In England itself the situation was more complicated and at an earlier stage. It must not be forgotten that in the 940s and early 950s a great part of England, more than half its area, was controlled by Scandinavian settlers and soldiers, most of whom were only recently converted to Christianity and many of whom were still pagan. Evidence of pagan belief or at least interest in pagan belief is to be found in literature and especially in the sculpture of the Viking Age. Great controversy surrounds discussion of the date at which the epic poem *Beowulf* was composed, and on balance the eighth century still seems the most likely date. But the unique manuscript in which it has survived was written in the late tenth century. Dealing as it does with distant struggles within Scandinavia against a background of conflict and alliances between Danes, Swedes and Geats, its epic sentiments reveal much of the age at which it was copied as well as the age of its first composition. Loyalty to a secular lord is a dominant theme, and yet the Christian overtones, the reserved might of the Creator, are unmistakable. J.R.R. Tolkien, in the most influential critical comment of the twentieth century, taught us to see Beowulf's struggle against the monsters, Grendel, Grendel's mother and the dragon guarding the treasure-hoard in an ancient mound, as allegoric echoes of man's struggle against evil.[2] Even more evocative is the evidence from sculpture. We tread with great caution in this field. There were no stone crosses in Scandinavia until the late tenth century, and the bulk of surviving Anglo-Scandinavian sculpture dealt in a tradition that was pre-Viking, embracing elements common to both the Celtic and the Anglo-Saxon worlds. Some of the memorial stones, such as the most famous of the Middleton crosses in the Vale of Pickering, need to be interpreted as offerings to a new dominant Scandinavian landlord class rather than as purely religious symbols. The relative proliferation of stylised animal ornament

---

2   J.R.R. Tolkien, 'Beowulf: The Monsters and the Critics', *Proc. Brit. Acad.* 22, 1936, pp. 245-95.

that is Viking-influenced, the grave-slabs at York or the circle-headed crosses of Cumbria, indicate a use of native sculptural traditions in the interest of new lords, Danish or Norwegian in origin, and conscious of their own artistic backgrounds. Monastic patrons had controlled the pre-Viking sculptors, but they were now replaced by a new ruling élite. We must therefore tread warily before we ascribe Scandinavian elements in sculpture to pagan religious survival.[3] And yet the impact on the religious life of the Danelaw should not be neglected. Parallels were found between paganism and Christianity. At Nunburnholme in Yorkshire a panel from a Christian cross appears to represent the great pagan hero Sigurd feasting; and the panel is recarved over a Eucharistic scene. The most telling and dramatic example comes from the Gosforth Cross in Cumbria. On the east face of the high cross in the churchyard is a portrayal of the Crucifixion, but above it is vividly carved a scene from the Ragnarök, the vengeance of Vidar, son of Odin, on the Great Wolf. To read this as a conscious representation of the triumph of Christianity over paganism is going too far. The Gosforth Cross nevertheless provides the clearest possible evidence for the awareness of Scandinavian religion and legend among the population of later Anglo-Saxon England.[4]

We are right to talk of Scandinavian religion in those terms. An elaborate and developing cosmology among the Scandinavian peoples involved the existence of a great company of gods, Odin, Thor and Freyr the most prominent; and also some set forms of worship and ritual. Looking back through the centuries, there is close correspondence to the common Germanic gods and beliefs of the Migration Ages when the Anglo-Saxons moved into Britain during the fifth and sixth centuries. Looking forward we find the full formulation of Scandinavian myth and legend achieved by the Icelandic writers in prose and verse during the twelfth and thirteenth. And yet within Anglo-Scandinavian England itself there is astonishingly little evidence that, as an alternative religion to Christianity, it achieved any significant success at all. There are few accredited Viking burials even in areas of heaviest Danish settlement. Only in the special Hiberno-Norse context of the Isle of Man are to be found substantial evidence of ship-burial, the use of runes, and other characteristics that suggest serious survival of organised paganism. We have already suggested some of the obvious reasons for such a phenomenon. The intrinsic merits of the Christian faith,

---

3 D.M. Wilson, 'The Scandinavians in England', *The Archaeology of Anglo-Saxon England*, 1976, pp. 393–403. The volumes of the *Corpus of Anglo-Saxon Stone Sculpture in England*, published by the British Academy, gen. ed. Rosemary Cramp (1986ff.), add essential detailed information, now covering most of northern England.
4 *The Anglo-Saxons*, ed. James Campbell, 1982, p. 163: elements of the Borre style in the Gosforth Cross.

literate and rooted in the traditions of the deeply literate culture of the Mediterranean world, Hebrew, Greek and Roman, must be taken into account. Some aspects of Scandinavian belief could be quickly assimilated into the Christian world. Baldur the beautiful, for example, could be equated with a Christ-like figure. But Scandinavian religious experience seemed inadequate for a settled agrarian people when set side by side with the Christian. To the homilists and to the chroniclers, especially during the wars of Ethelred the Unready's reign, there was constant reminder of the dangers that came from the heathen. Yet these specifically heathen beliefs appear to have been overwhelmed once the peoples had settled. The rapidity of conversion to Christianity stands out as a major element in the history of Anglo-Scandinavian England.

Even so, it must be recognised that, while exact knowledge of the pagan gods might be scanty and ill transmitted, fear of heathendom was great. The works of the Devil against which the Christian was offered defence at baptism were directly equated with the worship of false gods. Homilists constructed powerful sermons against their worship. The Classical Gods, Jove, Juno, Saturn, Minerva, Venus, Mars and Mercury, were dismissed contemptuously as folk memories of ancient heroes or villains who had over time been allotted God-like qualities. They were in turn aligned to the Germanic Gods, Jove with Thor, Mercury with Odin, Mars sometimes with Tyr, at other times with Seaxneat or Saxnot of early Anglo-Saxon and Old Saxon genealogy and legend. No matter what the detail, paganism as such and especially Scandinavian paganism was to be taken seriously.[5]

Mohammedanism was a rather different matter and came to present a different set of problems. There does not appear to have been a deep awareness of the Mohammedan world among the Anglo-Saxons. It was known that the Muslims governed Jerusalem and the Holy Land. Their control of the greater part of Spain was also familiar. Routes to Rome were well known to Anglo-Saxon clerics, pilgrims and merchants; and for at least a century (c.870–973) such routes were subject to regular raids by Muslims from their stronghold at Fréjus (Le Freinet), not far from Marseilles. Brigands operating over the Alpine passes could often be Muslim. There were other, more peaceful contacts that involved an element of knowledge of the mysterious non-Christian world. Arab gold coins were known and it is generally assumed that most references to gold coins were either to Byzantine coins (bezants) or to Muslim. The latter were sometimes called mancuses, though the term in late Anglo-Saxon England was commonly used as an

---

5   Richard North, *Heathen Gods in Old English Literature*, 1998; *Wulfstan's Homilies*, xii, 'De Falsis Deis', pp. 221–4.

equivalent of thirty silver pence. It used to be thought that the very word 'mancus' was derived from an Arabic term, though it is now regarded as more likely to have been a derivative of a Low Latin word cognate with the modern French *manqué*, signifying an imperfect version of a standard heavy *solidus*.

The great arc of country, the southern half of the Fertile Crescent, stretching from the Pyrenees through North Africa even to Sind in India, was under Mohammedan control from the eighth century; but to Anglo-Saxons it was substantially unknown territory. When they wrote of the marvels of the East or the so-called 'letter of Alexander to Aristotle' their concern was with the world of fantasy, stories of strange creatures living in remote lands. The Orient vaguely might be regarded as a source of learning and love in esoteric fields, but there was no hint of any precise knowledge of Mohammedan belief nor of the Koran. Charlemagne and his paladins, including Roland at Roncevalles, might have been fighting against a group of nature worshippers as far as the Anglo-Saxon records are concerned. The venom of the homilists and Christian apologists against the forces of evil outside was reserved for Viking heathens and pagans and those who, still in their wilful ignorance, worshipped streams and lakes and holy groves and other holy places, remains and memories often of very ancient natural worship. To associate strangeness or beauty in nature with the supernatural is a basic element in human religious sentiment. Admonitions against the dangers of such aberrations abound in the law codes and homilies, but of Mahomet himself there is no hint.

It was not until after the Norman Conquest that the inner meanings of the other great Western universal religion based on the teachings of Mahomet impinged fully on English consciousness, and even then only fitfully. Tall stories concerning the worship of idols, rampant sexuality and the innate violence of the creed swirled around the undercurrents of travellers' tales to emerge full-blown at the time of the early Crusades as false but only too acceptable fact by the writers of the Christian West. Poets and chroniclers in the late eleventh and early twelfth century began to transmit some more accurate, if distorted, information about Mahomet. Hugh of Fleury, abbot of St Augustine's, Canterbury (*c.*1091–1124), described the marriage of the Prophet to Khadija, lady of Corozan, as a move both social and political.[6] As knowledge of Arabic through Spanish sources grew more common, some shape was given to the picture of Mahomet. He was at best represented as a magician. The *chansons de gestes* seized on the themes of sexuality and idol-worship. There was little, if any, recognition that Muslims were monotheistic, that they recognised the sequence of Old Testament and the

---

6 Norman Daniel, *The Arabs and Medieval Europe*, 2nd edn, 1979, pp. 235–7.

Prophets, including Jesus, and that they embraced a literate religion, relying on the Koran as the final resolution of the religious experience of the Semitic peoples of the Near East. Nevertheless the preaching of the First Crusade brought the presence, if not always the nature, of Mohammedanism fully home to England. Accompanying it and to some measure preceding it were the links with the Carolingian past and so with Charlemagne himself and his ventures against the Muslims in Spain. The *Song of Roland* may well mark as important an element in the pricking of English consciousness in its generation as the dissemination of *Beowulf* had in relation to Germanic heathendom in pre-Conquest times. The earliest version of the *Song of Roland* appears in an Anglo-Norman manuscript and is probably of Norman provenance. It consists of nearly 4000 lines of assonant decasyllables, with the main themes treating the heroic death of Roland at Roncevalles and the consequent vengeance inflicted on the Saracens by the Christians.[7] Even there, however, there is no hint of the true theological divide. The Muslims, Saracens of Spain or of the Holy Land, were treated negatively. They embody the forces outside the Christian fortress, instruments of evil, helpmeets of Antichrist. In the first half of the twelfth century the floodgates were opened to Muslim learning, notably through Spain and Sicily. An English monk, Adelard of Bath (1090–1150), scientist and mathematician, translated into Latin some of the best work of Islamic mathematicians. His version of Euclid, based on an Arabic text, became a standard introduction to geometry in the Latin West. He is also believed to have introduced knowledge of the astrolabe, one of the many Greek achievements better preserved by Muslims than Christians, back into the Western medieval world. But of a corresponding serious study of Muslim theology there is little sign.[8]

There remains one other important religious group to consider before we look again at the reality of religion as experienced by the bulk of the population in England. The Christian religion was deeply rooted in Jewish life and thought; and yet there was virtually no contact between Jewish communities and the Anglo-Saxons, except perhaps among the slave-traders of the day. Aelfric assumed there were no Jews in England for, when he reflected on the sack of the Temple in 70 AD, he found it necessary to tell his readers that great numbers of Jews were still to be found widely elsewhere.[9] Frankish penitentials referring to the Jews were copied in England; but that provides no proof of the physical presence of Jews in the country. It is

---

7   D.R.R. Owen, *The Song of Roland* (Eng. verse trans.), 1972; also for great detail Rita Lejeune and Jacques Stiennon, *The Legend of Roland in the Middle Ages*, 2 vols, 1972, (Eng. trans.).

8   Louise Cockrane, *Adelard of Bath: The First English Scientist*, 1994.

9   Cecil Roth, *A History of the Jews in England*, 3rd edn, 1964.

highly probable that William the Conqueror was responsible for their introduction, though there is an outside chance that some may have been in
London during the reign of the Confessor. One can easily associate them
with the financing of great building projects, first at Westminster and
Waltham in the Confessor's reign and then during the Norman period, but
there is no hard evidence to support such an assumption.

It is Eadmer, the biographer of St Anselm, who tells us explicitly that
a Jewish community was set up in London.[10] As an example of William
Rufus's irreligion, the king is said to have summoned a company of Christian
bishops and Jewish rabbis to dispute and to have been willing to accept the
creed of the better disputants. Eadmer even says that he was willing to convert back a Jewish youth who had forsaken his synagogue. More significant, because reliant on fact and not malicious gossip, is the nature of the
great Anselm's work on the Atonement. As Richard Southern has rightly
said, the Jews were the only learned and uncompromising opponents of
the very idea of the Incarnation within Anselm's experience.[11] While it is
true that he would have met such Jewish scholars in Normandy and at
Lyons during his exile, it is likely that some contact was also achieved at
Canterbury and at London when the basic thought behind *Cur Deus Homo*
was germinating. Gilbert Crispin, correspondent and friend of Anselm, was
grappling with similar problems in the 1090s, and Gilbert tells us clearly
that his opponent was a Jew from Mainz lately settled in London. The idea
of God's incarnation was a deep affront to Jewish belief in the transcend-
ental majesty of the Creator and indeed proved the likely spur to Anselm's
thought that the Incarnation was necessary, the only logical means of man's
redemption. We have probably been blind to the presence of an influential,
intellectual and yet discreet group of Jewish settlers and scholars in the
Anglo-Norman world as one of the most potent factors in the religious life
of the English community after 1066. Such a presence may also have contributed, as we have already suggested, to the success of the extravagant
building projects, castles, cathedrals, abbeys, local churches, that characterised the first Norman generations, and even to the evolution of the most
advanced financial institution in Western Europe in the shape of the English
Exchequer. International links must have helped, and the Jews could provide international mobility. From the purely religious point of view, they
could provide an exotic element from within, different yet mainly tolerated,
in what was otherwise a somewhat monolithic structure.

---

10   Eadmer, *Historia Novorum in Anglia*, ed. Martin Rule, Rolls Series, 1884, pp. 99–101.
11   R.W. Southern, *Saint Anselm and his Biographer*, 1963, pp. 88 and 90–1, for discussion of the
     Jew from Mainz.

Yet to describe the English Church, 1066–1154, even more so 940–1154, as monolithic can be misleading unless the epithet is strictly qualified. During the two centuries that concern us here, the shape of the Western Church was never seriously questioned. The authority of the Bible and of the Early Fathers was universally accepted. Differences in emphasis naturally abound. The person of the Pope could be questioned and schism result. But the basic theological belief on both sides of the schism, even during the venomous dispute over Investitures, remained solidly Trinitarian with no heretical groupings around the nature of the Godhead such as created permanent divisions among the Christians in earlier centuries and resulted in the creation of Monophysite and Nestorian Churches in the Near East. The one exception was the separation of the Byzantine Church over the *filioque* clause in the Creed; and modern scholarship is inclined to regard this as more political than religious, more associated with the position of the Pope in the hierarchy, indeed more a drifting apart than a dramatic permanent split caused by the politics of Constantinople in 1054 and the tensions of the Crusades.[12] Within the Western Church ritual was subject to regional change in both the secular and the monastic fields, though the basic form of the mass and teachings on other sacraments remained constant. Considering the richness of the period in its detailed growth of intellectual and artistic life, the strength of the elements of stability and continuity in the inner life of the Church remains altogether remarkable.

For, in many respects, as we have already seen, this was one of the truly formative periods in the intellectual life of Western Europe, the movement from Epic to Romance, a movement away from emphasis on the oral and unwritten, from memory, to the more literate world of reliance on the written word. In law, theology, art, architecture, poetry and sentiment changes came about that were as influential in moulding civilised life as any that occurred later in the crises of fifteenth-century Renaissance thought. Yet no Protestant Revolution followed the twelfth-century Renaissance; and it was not until the latter half of the twelfth century that the ferment and agitation of thought produced conditions in the south of France and parts of northern Italy that led to truly heretical Manichaean ideas or to the divisive elements in the beliefs of the Waldensians and other gathered groups.

Basic stability is one thing. Change and development is quite another. On one major tenet of Christian belief it was Anselm, operating within the English Church, who contributed the most important single element to Christian theology during this whole period in his teaching on the Incarnation, a

---

12   Steven Runciman, *A History of the Crusades*, vol. i, 1951, pp. 96–7. On 1054 Runciman
       comments that there was no difference at all, except that bitterness was aroused.

contribution so profound that it has remained a matter for serious consideration in theological discussion up to the present century. The heart of his teaching lay in its logical insistence on the necessity that God should become Man in order to effect redemption. Man's willing disobedience to God could not be redeemed by his own fallen nature. Therefore the mystery of a God who became Man was the only solution, an exercise of God's mercy that would not infringe the rational justice of the universe. To an older generation, brought up on the teachings of St Augustine, heavily conscious of the power of the Devil, this was a subtle and unhelpful line of thought. In England Aelfric had expressed the older view in a set of homely images. Man by sin had yielded himself to the Devil. The death of Christ, the perfect man without sin, had tricked the Devil, who had, by bringing it about, acted against the rational justice of Creation and so forfeited his power over Man. Even as the unwary fish had swallowed the angler's bait, so had the Devil, seizing the bait of a human soul but failing to recognise the hook of Christ's divinity. Elements of this belief persisted, and Anselm's *Cur Deus Homo* was respected but not greatly favoured by the schoolmen of the twelfth century and the later medieval age. Yet the depth of his analysis of the torment of deciding between principles of justice and mercy and also of freedom and obedience made permanent impact on Western theological and political thought.[13]

The Incarnation was the chief and most important theological theme in which thinkers from the English Church played a major part, but it was not the only one. We have already mentioned Lanfranc's opposition to the ideas of Berengar of Tours, and now is the time to look at this controversy more closely. Berengar (*c*.1000–88) had followed a line of argument which led to a belief that in the central mystery of the mass, transubstantiation occured not in the elements themselves but in the sentiments of the believers. Lanfranc refuted such an approach, using his grasp of Aristotelian logic and force of rhetoric to great effect. He succeeded in having Berengar's teaching condemned in a great council at the Lateran in April 1059. The assertion of orthodoxy, while not stifling discussion, helped to ensure continuity in the Western institutional Church.[14]

The agitations over the Incarnation and transubstantiation were matters of high theory affecting only the few. The same might be said of such basic questions as the nature of grace and the hope of salvation. Considered statements on these matters, often dependent on interpretation of the work

---

13 Southern, *Saint Anselm and his Biographer*, pp. 77–121, provides far and away the best introduction in English to the *Cur Deus Homo*.

14 Ibid., pp. 20–5.

of St Augustine, would and did ultimately result in action, modification to liturgy or alteration in emphasis on aspects of pastoral care, but by and large they were matters for the small minority of the learned, mostly monastic scholars. It might be useful now to consider briefly, as far as the evidence allows, what happened during our centuries to the basic teaching and practice of the Church insofar as it affected the ordinary Christian of the day from cradle to grave.

We can start with baptism. Every parish priest was expected to have access to a handbook on baptism. In the early Church adult baptism conflated with what later became confirmation was commonplace, but in the Western Church from the fifth century onwards infant baptism was normal, and indeed heavy penalties were invoked on parents who failed to bring infants to the font. Even so, there was a degree of flexibility in procedures. Baptism by bishops of specially holy reputation was much regarded. We hear, for example, of many children baptised by bishop Wulfstan of Worcester on his travels around his large diocese in the later eleventh century, especially at the high festivals of Easter and Whitsun. Baptisms by aspersion, the signing of the cross on the forehead of the infants and the anointment with the holy oil, the chrism, were a universal practice. Rights over baptism, the provision of the chrism, were jealously guarded. The naming of the infant also appears to have been universally the practice and the provision of godparents, who then occupied a special legal relationship to the child in the eyes of the lawyers, ecclesiastical and lay.

Great care was taken by the Reformers in tenth-century England to provide proper instruction for priests in the administration of baptism. Drawing heavily on the writings of the Carolingian reformers who had faced similar problems in the preceding century, they set out a formal procedure which allowed for both infant and adult baptisms. The two essentials leading to baptism were the renunciation of the Devil and all his works, and the confession of faith in God. Sponsors took the necessary oaths for infants not yet able to speak for themselves. The ritual before baptism, sometimes referred to as the christening, involved a succession of symbolic acts, the signing of the cross on the head, the placing of salt on the tongue (possibly connected with exorcism), of saliva on the ears and nostrils (to hear and smell the advent of the Holy Spirit), the anointing with oil, and at times, at least in the tenth and early eleventh centuries, an immersion in purifying water. The baptised would be clothed in white as a symbol of their purified state.[15]

Confirmation is a more complex problem. We tend to think of it as a solemn affirmation of faith at the age of reason, interpreted by some as

---

15 *Wulfstan's Homilies*, viiia, 'Incipit de Baptismo', pp. 169–71.

seven or nine or puberty, and there is reason to believe that some confusion existed within the Church itself. In the early days, confirmation was at times subsumed in the act of baptism, but this was clearly not so in our centuries. Uncertainty exists over the formality needed to give the young Christian access to the communion, for that is the essential of confirmation. Our best evidence, as so often, comes from the Life of Wulfstan II, who is credited with confirming as many as 3000 in a single day. It was the bishop's duty to confirm, though how scrupulously this duty was performed it is hard to say. To have received baptism was sufficient for a Christian to receive the viaticum *in extremis*, and there must have been many priests in out-of-the-way rural parishes who did not ask questions if the faithful men and women attended mass.[16]

Baptism, confirmation and the Eucharist were the three sacraments of the Church which eventually passed down through the crisis of the Protestant Reformation as deemed necessary for salvation in the English Church. By the tenth century, sacramental status, in the sense that the rite served as an outward and visible sign of an inward grace divinely instituted, was also accorded Penance, Extreme Unction and (with more hesitation in a world where celibacy was the religious ideal) marriage. There was much deep interest in penance. If the Church were to be effective at all in helping to establish a moral order in society, some means of imposing discipline on sinners had to be established. The most extreme punishment of all, of course, was excommunication. In a world where both rationality and superstition were exercised with the afterlife and the penalties of Hell and Purgatory, to be cut off from the faithful and the hope of salvation was indeed a fearsome punishment. Only the most hardened, such as William Rufus, could mock such things; and he was brought to heel quickly enough, agreeing despairingly, as we have seen, to the appointment of Anselm to Canterbury, when threatened by apparently mortal illness.[17] For most offences, penalties far short of excommunication could be imposed, and indeed increasingly we are aware that composition in terms of hard cash could often alleviate the severe legal impositions laid on penitent sinners. The most famous example of a corporate penance in our period occurred immediately after the Norman Conquest. During the visit of the papal legate Ermenfrid of Sitten to England in 1070, he issued a penitentiary that was to apply to all who fought under William's command at Hastings. A careful scale was built up: one year's penance for each man killed, forty days for each

---

16   Emma Mason, *St Wulfstan of Worcester c.1008–1095*, 1990, pp. 169–70; also *Vita Wulfstani*, ed. R.R. Darlington, Camden Society, 1928, p. 51.

17   Frank Barlow, *William Rufus*, 1983, pp. 299ff.

wounding and, if number unknown, one day a week for life at the discretion of the bishop or – a significant alternative – a perpetual alms, or by building or endowing a church. Special attention was paid to the clerks, who were forbidden by the canons to do battle, and to the monks, subject to their Rule and the discipline of their abbots. Penance was possible for them, but a nice distinction was drawn between those who fought merely for gain, who owed penance as for homicide, and those who fought in a public war, for whom a penance of three years had been allotted by their bishops out of mercy. Archers were a special case, necessarily ignorant of the damage they had done: penance for three Lents was regarded as appropriate. Further distinctions were made between those who killed in battle and those who killed while foraging or plundering, especially if such offence took place after the coronation of the king. A touch of full reality comes with strictures against those who committed adulteries or rapes or fornications and against violations of the church. Looting from churches was to be restored, if possible, and, if not possible, to some other church. If the looter would not restore it, then the bishops deemed that he should not sell it, nor could anyone buy it. We wonder how effective such rulings were, but at least on the question of penance it is as clear a sign as possible that the notion of appropriate penance after evil acts such as killing fellow Christians (even in a public war) was deeply embedded in the social consciousness of the age.[18]

This was as true, as we have already seen, of Anglo-Saxon England as of Anglo-Norman. A vast accumulation of penitential literature, much of it based on Carolingian material but some representing a native Anglo-Celtic tradition, has survived from the tenth and eleventh centuries. In England virtually all penance, which mostly involved fasting, had been private and the local priest at minster or manorial church was the normal confessor. This tradition persisted, though, under the influence of the Benedictine Reformation, a greater uniformity was aimed at with more advanced Carolingian custom. Archbishop Theodore's comparative laxity over marriage law, for example, appears to have been modified or rejected. An element of public confession and penitence came to be regarded as desirable under the control of the bishop and in extreme cases leading to exile and penitential pilgrimage to Rome. In a society accustomed to the payment of compensation as an amend to offence, it is natural that similar principles should be applied to offences considered proper to ecclesiastical discipline, mostly sexual and connected with marriage law. The most conscientious of the bishops took pains to lay down principles for confession. In Cnut's legislation, the work of Archbishop Wulfstan, there are echoes of the teaching

---

18   *EHD* ii, ch. 81, pp. 606–7.

of Gregory the Great when we read that for religious penance as well as for secular judgement many things had to be taken into account, including the age or youth of the offender, his status, whether wealthy or poor, or free or slave, and his intention, whether prompted by necessity. In a more elaborate statement, Wulfstan carried this idea further:

> When anyone comes to his confessor for the sake of telling him his needs and confessing his sins, then ought the confessor earnestly to ask him about those things which he confesses to him, how they were done, whether intentionally or unintentionally, and whether suddenly or in a premeditated way: and let him then for every misdeed prescribe the remedy according as the deed had been done. Very unlike is the man who, defending himself, slays another to him who seeks out another to slay him: so it is, both in adulteries and in every misdeed.[19]

One consequence of the tenth-century reformation was an increased awareness of the use of public penance and a desire on the part of the more conscientious bishops to use this weapon. Wulfstan himself held firmly to the view that there were occasions when this should be done and ranked it among the duties of the bishops. In a sermon to penitents, he tells how it is right that they should be excluded from church on Ash Wednesday and then readmitted after due penitence on Maundy Thursday. With fine rhetoric in their own Anglo-Saxon tongue, he preached the orthodox doctrine that just as Adam was driven from Paradise because of his sin, so was the sinner now driven from the Church. And just as Adam, redeemed by the sweat of his brow and penitence and the blood of our lord Jesus Christ, was readmitted into Paradise, so were the repentant sinners readmitted to the Church. But no bishop could readmit them unless by their own penitence they had become worthy of readmission. Alms-giving as well as fasting were openly praised as means of redemption.[20] The secrets of the confessional then as now remained hidden and private. There are only rare indications of the offence or the motive for confession. Bishop Aethelric of Dorchester imposed a public penance on a witch guilty of making a love-potion and also of being involved in the murder of a child.[21] The nature of the record suggests that public penance was somewhat unusual and that private confession and private penance remained the more common ecclesiastical reaction to

---

19 *EHD* i, Laws of Cnut, Secular, cl. 68. It is significant that the clause appears in the secular section (Cnut II) not the ecclesiastical.

20 *Wulfstan's Homilies*, App. 1, 'Sermo in Cena Domini ad Penitentes', pp. 367–73: texts in Latin and Anglo-Saxon.

21 Frank Barlow, *The English Church, 1000–1066*, 1963, p. 271.

offence at least until the twelfth century, when seepage from the great revival of canon law from Italy and the Continent entered fully into the English system. Yet St Wulfstan at Worcester, acting as a dominant figure carrying Anglo-Saxon custom through to the brave new Anglo-Norman world, following the example of his namesake from early in the eleventh century, reconciled penitents on Maundy Thursday. Sadly his biographer fails to give details of the ritual and merely contents himself with describing the graciousness with which Wulfstan treated the penitents. That they were likely to be of a certain class and prosperity in winning the privilege of confession to so holy a man is suggested strongly by the information that Wulfstan, after the cleansing, took it upon himself to dine with them.[22]

Baptism, confirmation, mass and the communion represent three great stages in the progress of the life of the Christian. There remains the question of vast importance, psychologically and socially, the approach to death and to burial. For man throughout the ages this was one of the principal moments when religious belief reached its most intense expression. Boat burials, still in use during our period on rare occasions among the pagan element in the Isle of Man, represent a most extravagant pagan way of honouring the dead, and literary memories persist of the burning of the body of dead heroes with burial mounds erected over the remains. The physical presence of ancient memorials, mounds, henges, barrows, brought constant reminders of pre-Christian practice and ceremony. But for the overwhelming majority in England burial by the tenth century meant interments in God's acre, simply with the minimum of grave-goods, the orientation normally towards the east, waiting the dawn of resurrection. Burial procedures were simple and quick after death. Burial rights were jealously safeguarded by parish churches and minster churches. A burial in a deep grave with no memorial stone was the most that could be expected for the ordinary person, though there was thereinafter a great range of possibility, some dictated by regional custom, virtually all dependent on wealth and social status. The range, as archaeologists have discovered, was vast, from no coffin to light unadorned wooden coffin to stone coffin with fine carved grave-lids. Great concern was shown by the wealthy to have themselves buried at some special place, preferably within a church and near the shrine of some saint or sacred person. Gifts would be made by will to the church to which the deceased should be brought. Aethelgifu, the prosperous Hertfordshire aristocratic widow who died in the 980s or early 990s, made substantial bequests to St Albans so that her burial could take place in the

---

22 *Vita Wulfstani*, ed. Darlington, pp. 49–50.

revived and newly endowed abbey.[23] At the royal level Edward the Confessor's patronage of the great new church at Westminster was directly connected with its planned place of burial; and so too, in a curious way, may well have been Harold's Waltham Abbey.[24] Certainly the canons and later the monks of Waltham made every effort to keep his memory green and to ensure that later generations believed that Harold intended Waltham as his burial place and that his body was brought there, mutilated but properly identified, after Hastings. Disputes over burial rights were common and sometimes reached macabre proportions. Martin Brett brought to our attention one *cause célèbre* that has special interest because it led to a judgement at Whitsun 1108 that all men might be buried where they wished. Following the death of Ralph fitz Ansketill, a benefactor of a dependency of Gloucester Abbey in Herefordshire, the abbot of Gloucester took his body for burial at Gloucester Abbey in the diocese of Worcester. This act was hotly disputed by the new bishop of Hereford, who had the body dug up and transported back to Hereford. It was at King Henry I's court that judgement was made. The bishop's plea that Ralph was his parishioner and therefore should be buried in Hereford was rejected.[25] Similar cases occurred sporadically throughout the centuries. For the ordinary peasant or other humble inhabitant of England there was no question. Burial and with it all the rites that made possible entry into another and better world was matter for the local priest and the local church. The multiplication of churches as estates were consolidated into manorial complexes was associated with the need for burial grounds at a convenient distance; and the diverse and various arrangements between minster and old established churches and new territorial foundations were made essential as the patterns of settlement underwent slow but certain change.

Churches, as normally the single most substantial building in a community outside the lord's *aula* or manor-house, were also the place where meetings were held outside the routine of baptism, funeral and the round of customary services. Great festivals seem to have fallen universally into the agreed set pattern of Easter, Whitsun and Christmas. Pagan elements had further been incorporated into the Church's calendar, notably Harvest Festival and celebrations of the coming of summer at Walpurgis night and of winter on All Saints' Day. Local saints were also honoured and a whole regular litany was created in Anglo-Saxon days ranging from St Alban, protomartyr, to the saints of the tenth-century reformation, Dunstan,

---

23   *The Will of Aethelgifu*, trans. Dorothy Whitelock, ed. Lord Rennell of Rodd, Roxburghe Club, 1968, pp. 21–2.

24   *The Waltham Chronicle*, ed. and trans. Leslie Watkiss and Marjorie Chibnall, 1994, pp. 52–3.

25   Martin Brett, *The English Church under Henry I*, 1975, p. 98.

Aethelwald and Oswald. Cults grew around Christian martyrs, attracting local loyalties. St Edmund in East Anglia is a conspicuous example, but by 1066 virtually every shire or local district possessed some local saint specially honoured. The influence of Bede's 'Ecclesiastical History' was powerful, and the allegiance of Durham to the memory of St Cuthbert or York to St Wilfred was tenacious. Some of the local saints were obscure in the extreme, local boy princes regarded as martyrs or hermits whose lives were otherwise unknown. At Hereford the cathedral was dedicated to St Ethelbert, king of the East Angles, murdered in the 790s at Sutton Walls just four miles from Hereford, apparently at the instigation of Offa or his queen, Cynethryth. Relics also became increasingly venerated, serving as focal points for worship – and profit – at local churches.[26]

The Normans, with a certain Latin, one might almost say Roman, logic, felt that the whole business had gone too far and took effective steps to prune the official ecclesiastical calendar, as we have already seen. Control of the inner beliefs and customs of local communities was beyond their power, and there is a natural survival and persistence of local cults through the trauma of Conquest. Indeed in the generations after the Conquest there was a further tendency for local sentiment to accrete around the examples of lives of holy men and women, hermits and anchorites who demonstrated their faith by fasting and austerities; and the examples of Christina of Markyate, with her contacts with St Albans, already discussed above, and Godric of Haslemere, were no more than indications of a widespread phenomenon.

To see the structure of a theocracy in place in the tenth, eleventh and early twelfth centuries is to interpret at least some of the legal and theoretical evidence accurately enough. Practice can be very different, however, and the violence of both the Anglo-Saxon world and the Anglo-Norman fits very uneasily into the picture. We deal with an overwhelmingly agrarian society, it is true. Perhaps at most one in ten of the inhabitants of England, a percentage which rose slowly in the Anglo-Norman period, dwelt in towns or incipient towns where not all the men and women depended directly on the farming base. Such a society made for stability and was receptive to Christian teaching. We have good evidence of the type of teaching that was given in local churches throughout the kingdom. The language of instruction was Old English, Anglo-Saxon, modified towards the end of our period into early Middle English. Manuscript evidence paints an intelligible picture of the framework of instruction which would be delivered by priests to the populace. The great accumulation of homilies that have survived,

---

26   R.C. Finucane, *Miracles and Pilgrims: Popular Beliefs in Medieval England*, 1977.

notably those attached to the names of Aelfric and Wulfstan, indicate the substance of the teaching. It would be grotesque to think that the little parish priest would deliver his message in the polished prose of Aelfric or the ringing rhetoric of Wulfstan, but the homilies could provide the matter for a whole series of simple instructional talks; and such must have been the regular fare served up in all the local churches of England. Those who have had practical experience of missionary work in Africa or the Caribbean in more recent times probably have some idea of how the Christian message could have been conveyed in the central Middle Ages. Indeed Wulfstan, in one of his most impressive homilies, condenses the essentials of Christianity into one short tract that illustrates perfectly the force of Christianity as an element in establishing peace and social discipline. Drawing his material directly from his favoured sources, notably Atto of Vercelli and Pirmin of Reichenau, he compresses into some 200 lines most of the basic doctrine needful for the ordinary Christian to know: the Ten Commandments, respect for the Church and church property, the Eight Deadly Sins (at considerable length and countered by the need for penitence), corresponding Christian virtues, a simple comment on the Trinity, the need for good works and the exercise of Christian virtues (including loyalty to one's secular lord), with a final invocation to the fear of Doomsday and the Last Judgement. Into the logical framework provided by the story of Adam and Eve, the fall from grace and the expulsion from Paradise, a coherent picture, dependent on the Augustinian view of original sin, could be provided by the Church through the pulpit and through the conscientious exercise of the confessional.[27] In theory, indeed, we have the makings of a theocratic world; in practice, a world where serious philosophical thought concerning Man and his place in Creation was moulded by priests and deacons preaching rigorously a moral code based on the certainties of accepted Christian cosmology and doctrine.

---

27 *Wulfstan's Homilies*, xc, pp. 200–10.

BIBLIOGRAPHY

Excellent bibliographies to dates of publication are given in the two relevant volumes of *English Historical Documents* (*EHD* i to 1979, *EHD* ii to 1981). For Anglo-Saxon England, thorough up-to-date information is provided year by year in the regular publication *Anglo-Saxon England*, Cambridge, 1972 onwards. Simon Keynes provides a valuable selective bibliography, third revised edition, *Old English News-letter: Subsidia*, vol. 13, Western Michigan University, 1998. There is a vast literature on the Norman Conquest, Domesday Book and Anglo-Norman England. The annual volumes of *Anglo-Norman Studies*, Baydell Press, successors to the *Proceedings of the Battle Abbey Conference*, offer the best way of keeping in touch. Established periodicals, notably *English Historical Review* and *Speculum*, regularly contain material of importance to the subject matter of this book.

The following bibliography contains references, mostly to books, of work that was of direct value to the preparation of the present volume.

Abels, R.P., *Lordship and Military Obligation in Anglo-Saxon England*, 1988.

Aelfric, *Catholic Homilies*, ed. and trans. B. Thorpe, 2 vols, 1843–46: text of first series, ed. P. Clemoes, EETS, 1997; of second series, ed. M. Godden, EETS, 1979.

Aelfric, *Lives of Saints*, ed. W. Skeat, EETS, 1881–85.

Aelfric, *Homilies of Aelfric. A Supplementary Collection*, ed. J.C. Pope, EETS, 1967–68.

Aelfric, *Colloquy*, ed. G.N. Garmonsway, rev. edn, 1978 (trans. M. Swanton, *Anglo-Saxon Prose*, 1975, rev. edn, 1993).

Alexander, J.J.G., and Gibson, M.T., eds, *Medieval Learning and Literature: Essays for R.W. Hunt*, 1976.

Anglo-Saxon Chronicle, see Whitelock, D.

Backhouse, J., Turner, D.H., and Webster, L., eds, *The Golden Age of Anglo-Saxon Art, 966–1066*, 1984.

Bailey, R.N., *Viking Age Sculpture in Northern England*, 1980.

Baker, D., ed., *Medieval Women*, 1978.

Barlow, F., ed., *Vita Aedwardi Regis*, 1962, 2nd edn, 1992.

Barlow, F., *The English Church, 1000–1066*, 1963, 2nd edn, 1979.

Barlow, F., *The English Church, 1066–1154*, 1979.

Barlow, F., *Edward the Confessor*, 1970.

Barlow, F., *William Rufus*, 1983.

Bately, J., ed., *Anglo-Saxon Chronicle, MS. A*, 1978.

Bates, D., 'The Land Pleas of William I's Reign: Penenden Heath Revisited', *BIHR* 51, 1978, pp. 1–19.

Bates, D., *Normandy Before 1066*, 1982.

Bates, D., *William the Conqueror*, 1989.

Bates, D., *Bishop Remigius of Lincoln, 1067–1092*, Lincoln, 1992.

Bates, D., and Curry, A., eds, *England and Normandy in the Middle Ages*, 1994.

Bethurum, D., ed., *The Homilies of Wulfstan*, 1957.

Biddle, M., ed., *Winchester in the Early Middle Ages, Winchester Studies* i, 1976.

Biddle, M., ed., *The Anglo-Saxon Minsters at Winchester, Winchester Studies* iv, forthcoming, 2000.

Blair, J., 'Secular Minster Churches in Domesday Book', *Domesday Book: A Reassessment*, ed. P.H. Sawyer, 1985, pp. 104–42.

Blair, J., 'Local Churches in Domesday Book and Before', *Domesday Studies*, ed. J.C. Holt, 1987, pp. 265–78.

Blair, J., ed., *Minsters and Parish Churches: The Local Church in Transition 950–1200*, 1988.

Blair, J., and Sharpe, R., eds, *Pastoral Care before the Parish*, 1992.

Blair, P.H., *An Introduction to Anglo-Saxon England*, 1956, 2nd edn, 1977, revised with up-to-date bibliography, 1995; reset with introduction by Simon Keynes, Folio Society, 1997.

Blake, E.D., ed., *Liber Eliensis*, Camden Society, 1962.

Bonner, G., Rollason, D., and Standiffe, C., eds, *St Cuthbert. His Cult and his Community to AD 1200*, 1989.

Boon, G.C., *Welsh Hoards, 1979–81*, 1986.

Bradbury, J., 'The Early Years of the Reign of Stephen', *England in the Twelfth Century*, ed. D. Williams, 1990, pp. 17–30.

Bradshaw, H., The Henry Bradshaw Society provides access to several useful volumes concerning liturgy such as *The Winchcombe Sacramentary*, ed. A. Davril, 1994.

Brett, M., *The English Church Under Henry I*, 1975.

Brooke, C.N.L., 'The Archdeacon at the Norman Conquest', *Tradition and Change*, ed. D.E. Greenway C. Holdsworth and J. Sayers, 1985.

Brooke, C.N.L., *The Medieval Idea of Marriage*, 1989.

Brooke, C.N.L., with Keir, G., *London, 800–1216: The Shaping of a City*, 1975.

Brooke, Z.N., *The English Church and the Papacy*, 1931.

Brooks, N.P., *The Early History of the Church of Canterbury*, Leicester, 1984.

Burton, J., *Monasteries and Religious Orders in Britain, 1000–1300*, 1994.

Butler, H.E., ed., *The Chronicle of Jocelyn of Brakeland*, 1949.

Campbell, A., ed., *Encomium Emmae Reginae*, 1949, reprint with introduction by Simon Keynes, 1998.

Campbell, A., ed., *Frithegodi Monachi Breviloquium Vitae Wilfredi et Wulfstani Cantoris Narratio Metrica de Sancto Swithuno*, Zurich, 1950.

Campbell, A., ed., *Charters of Rochester*, 1973.

Campbell, J., ed., *The Anglo-Saxons*, 1982.

Cantor, N.F., *Church, Kingship and Lay Investiture in England, 1089–1135*, 1958.

Chibnall, M., ed., *Ordericus Vitalis, Ecclesiastical History*, 6 vols, 1969–81.

Chibnall, M., *The World of Ordericus Vitalis*, 1982.

Chibnall, M., ed., *John of Salisbury: Historia Pontificalis*, 1986.

Chibnall, M., *The Empress Matilda*, 1991.

Clark, C., ed., *The Peterborough Chronicle, 1070–1154*, 1958, 2nd edn, 1970.

Clemoes, P., and Hughes, K., eds, *England before the Conquest*, 1971.

Clover, H., and Gibson, M., eds, *Letters of Lanfranc*, 1979.

Cockrane, L., *Adelard of Bath: The First English Scientist*, 1994.

Constable, G., *Monastic Tithes from their Origins to the Twelfth Century*, 1964.

Corbett, W.J., 'The Development of the Duchy of Normandy and the Norman Conquest of England', *Cambridge Medieval History*, vol. v, 1926, pp. 481–520.

Cowdrey, H.E.J., 'The Peace and the Truce of God in the Eleventh Century', *Past and Present* 46, 1970, pp. 42–67.

Cowdrey, H.E.J., 'Pope Gregory VII and the Anglo-Norman Church and Kingdom', *Studi Gregoriani* ix, 1972, pp. 77–114.

Cowdrey, H.E.J., *Popes, Monks and Crusaders*, 1984.

Cramer, P., *Baptism and Change in the Early Middle Ages, c.200–c.1150*, 1993.

Cramp, R., gen. ed., *Corpus of Anglo-Saxon Sculpture in England*, Brit. Acad., in progress, 1986ff.

Cronne, H.A., *Reign of Stephen*, 1970.

Crook, J.M., ed., *Winchester Cathedral: Nine Hundred Years, 1093–1993*, 1993.

Crosby, E.U., *Bishop and Chapter in Twelfth-Century England: A Study of the Mensa Episcopalis*, 1994.

Dales, D., *Dunstan, Saint and Statesman*, 1988.

Daniel, N., *The Arabs and Medieval Europe*, 1975, 2nd edn, 1979.

Darby, H.C., *Domesday England*, 1977.

Darlington, R.R., ed., *Vita Wulfstani*, Camden Society, 1928.

Darlington, R.R., 'Aethelwig, Abbot of Evesham', *EHR* xlviii, 1933, pp. 1–22, 177–98.

Darlington, R.R., 'Ecclesiastical Reform in the Late Old English Period', *EHR* li, 1936, pp. 385–428.

Davis, R.H.C., *King Stephen, 1135–54*, 1967.

Dawtry, A., 'The Benedictine Revival in the North: The Last Bulwark of Anglo-Saxon Monasteries', *Religion and National Identity*, ed. S. Mews, 1982, pp. 87–98.

Dickinson, J.C., *The Origin of the Austin Canons and their Introduction into England*, 1950.

Dolley, R.H.M., ed., *Anglo-Saxon Coins*, 1961.

Domesday Book, see Morris, J.

Dornier, A., ed., *Mercian Studies*, 1977.

Douglas, D.C., ed., *The Domesday Monachorum of Christ Church, Canterbury*, Royal Historical Society, 1944.

Douglas, D.C., ed., *English Historical Documents, c.1042–1189*, 1953, 2nd edn, 1981.

Downer, L.J., ed., *Leges Henrici Primi*, 1972.

Eadmer, *Historia Novorum*, see Rule, M.

Eadmer, *The Life of St Anselm*, see Southern, R.W.

Eales, R., and Sharpe, R., *Canterbury and the Norman Conquest*, 1995.

Finucane, R.C., *Miracles and Pilgrims: Popular Beliefs in Medieval England*, 1977.

Florence of Worcester (John of Worcester), *Chronicon ex chronicis*, ed. B. Thorpe, 2 vols, 1848–49: *The Chronicle of John of Worcester II*, (text and trans. to 1066), ed. R.R. Darlington and P. McGurk, 1995.

Foreville, R., and Keir, G., eds, *The Book of St Gilbert*, 1986.

Fröhlich, W., trans. and ann., *The Letters of St Anselm of Canterbury*, 3 vols, 1990–94.

Gameson, R., *The Role of Art in the Late Anglo-Saxon Church*, 1995.

Gibson, M., *Lanfranc of Bec*, 1978.

Giles, J.A., ed., *Lanfranci Opera*, 1844.

Graham, R., *English Ecclesiastical Studies*, 1929.

Gransden, A., 'The Legends and Traditions Concerning the Origins of the Abbey of Bury St Edmunds', *EHR* c, 1985, pp. 1–24.

Greenway, D.E., *Le Neve: Fasti Ecclesiae Anglicanae, 1066–1300*, vol. iii, Lincoln, 1977.

Greenway, D.E., Holdsworth, C., and Sayers, J., eds, *Tradition and Change*, 1985.

Gwara, S., and Porter, D.W., *Anglo-Saxon Conversations: The Colloquies of Aelfric Bata*, 1997.

Hall, R., *Viking Age York*, 1994.

Harmer, F.E., ed., *Select English Historical Documents of the Ninth and Tenth Centuries*, 1914.

Harmer, F.E., ed., *Anglo-Saxon Writs*, 1952.

Harper-Bill, C., *The Anglo-Norman Church*, Bangor, 1992.

Harper-Bill, C., Holdsworth, C.J., and Nelson, J.L., eds, *Studies in Medieval History Presented to R. Allen Brown*, 1989.

Harvey, B., *Westminster Abbey and its Estates in the Middle Ages*, 1977.

Henry, archdeacon of Huntingdon, *Historia Anglorum. The History of the English People*, ed. D.E. Greenway, 1996.

Hicks, C., ed., *England in the Eleventh Century*, 1992.

Hill, D., ed., *Ethelred the Unready: Papers from the Millenary Conference*, *BAR* 59, 1978.

Hill, D., *An Atlas of Anglo-Saxon England*, Oxford, 1981.

Hoey, L., 'New Studies in Canterbury Cathedral', *Avista Forum* 9, 1995, pp. 6–9.

Holdsworth, C., 'War and Peace in the Twelfth Century: The Reign of Stephen Reconsidered', *War and Peace in the Middle Ages*, ed. B.P. McGuire, 1987, pp. 67–93.

Holdsworth, C., 'The Church', *The Anarchy of King Stephen's Reign*, ed. E. King, 1994.

Holt, J.C., ed., *Domesday Studies*, Woodbridge, 1987.

Holtzmann, W., *Papsturkunden in England*, Berlin and Göttingen, 1932–52.

Hunt, R.W., Pantin, W.A., and Southern, R.W., eds, *Studies in Medieval History Presented to F.M. Powicke*, 1948.

John of Salisbury, *Historia Pontificalis*, see Chibnall, M.

Kealey, E.J., *Roger of Salisbury, Viceroy of England*, 1972.

Ker, N.R., *Catalogue of Manuscripts Containing Anglo-Saxon*, 1957.

Keynes, S.D., *The Diplomas of King Ethelred 'the Unready', 978–1016*, 1980.

Keynes, S., ed., *The Liber Vitae of the New Minster and Hyde Abbey, Winchester*, EETF, Copenhagen, 1996.

King, E., 'The Anarchy of King Stephen's Reign', *TRHS* (5th Series), 34, 1984, pp. 133–53.

King, E., ed., *The Anarchy of King Stephen's Reign*, 1994.

Kirby, D.P., *The Making of Early England*, 1967.

Knowles, Dom. D., *The Monastic Order in England*, 1940.

Knowles, Dom. D., *The Monastic Customs of Lanfranc*, 1951.

Knowles, Dom. D., and Brooke, C.N.L., *The Heads of Religious Houses in England and Wales, 940–1216*, 1972.

Korhammer, M., ed., *Words, Texts and MSS: Studies in Anglo-Saxon Culture Presented to Helmut Gneuss*, 1992.

Lapidge, M., *Anglo-Latin Literature, 900–1066*, 1996.

Lawson, M.K., *Cnut: The Danes in England in the Early Eleventh Century*, 1993.

Lejeune, R., and Stiennon, J., *The Legend of Roland in the Middle Ages*, 2 vols, 1972.

Lemaguen, S., and Manneville, P., eds, *Chapitres et cathédrales en Normandie*, 1997.

Lennard, R., *Rural England, 1086–1135*, 1959.

Liebermann, F., *Die Gesetze der Angelsachsen*, 3 vols, Halle, 1903–16.

Liuzza, R.M., *The Old English Version of the Gospels*, EETS, 1994.

Love, R., *Three Eleventh-Century Anglo-Latin Saints' Lives*, 1996.

Loyn, H.R., *Anglo-Saxon England and the Norman Conquest*, 1962, 3rd edn, 1991.

Loyn, H.R., *The Governance of Anglo-Saxon England, c.500–1087*, 1984.

Loyn, H.R., 'Peter's Pence', *Lambeth Palace Library Annual Report*, 1984, pp. 10–20.

Lunt, W.E., *Financial Relations of the Papacy with England to 1327*, 1939.

McC. Gatch, M., *Preaching and Theology in Anglo-Saxon England: Aelfric and Wulfstan*, 1977.

MacDonald, A.J.M., *Lanfranc*, 1926.

Marx, J., ed., *Chronicle of William of Jumièges*, 1914.

Mason, E., *St Wulfstan of Worcester, c.1008–1095*, 1990.

Matthew, D.J.A., *The Norman Monasteries and their English Possessions*, 1962.

Miller, E., *The Abbey and Bishopric of Ely*, 1951.

Moray, A., and Brooke, C.N.L., *Gilbert Foliot and his Letters*, 1965.

Morris, C., 'William I and the Church Courts', *EHR* lxxxii, 1967, pp. 449–63.

Morris, C., *The Papal Monarchy: The Western Church from 1050 to 1250*, 1989.

Morris, J., gen. ed., *Domesday Book*, vols i and ii, Phillimore edition, 1975–86 (from 1977 under the supervision of John Dodgson and Alison Hawkins).

Napier, A.S., ed., *The Old English Version of the Enlarged Rule of Chrodegang Together with the Latin Original*, EETS 150, 1916.

Needham, G.I., ed., *Aelfric: Lives of Three English Saints*, 1976.

Nicholl, D., *Thurstan, Archbishop of York*, York, 1964.

North, R., *Heathen Gods in Old English Literature*, 1998.

O'Donovan, M.A., *Charters of Sherborne*, 1988.

Ordericus Vitalis, see Chibnall, M.

Ortenberg, V., *The English Church and the Continent in the Tenth and Eleventh Centuries*, 1992.

Owen, D.R.R., trans., *The Song of Roland*, 1972.

Parsons, D., ed., *Tenth-Century Studies*, 1975.

Pfaff, R.W., ed., *The Liturgical Books of Anglo-Saxon England*, Old English Newsletter (Subsidia 23), 1995.

Plummer, C., *Two of the Saxon Chronicles Parallel*, Oxford, 1892–99.

Poole, A.L., *From Domesday Book to Magna Carta*, 1951.

Raine, J., ed., *Vita Oswaldi archiepiscopi Eboracensis*, in *The Historians of the Church of York and its Archbishops*, vol. i, Rolls Series 71, 1879.

Ramsay, N., Sparks, M., and Tatton-Brown, T., eds, *St Dunstan: His Life, Times and Cult*, 1992.

Rees, D., ed., *The Benedictines in England from Augustine to the Present Day*, 1997.

Ridyard, S., *The Royal Saints of Anglo-Saxon England*, 1988.

Riley, H.T., ed., *Gesta abbatum Sancti Albani*, Rolls Series, 3 vols, 1867–69.

Robertson, A.J., ed. *The Laws of the Kings of England from Edmund to Henry I*, 1925.

Robertson, A.J., ed., *Anglo-Saxon Charters*, 1939, 2nd edn, 1956.

Robinson, J.A., *The Times of St Dunstan*, 1923.

Rollason, D.W., *Saints and Relics in Anglo-Saxon England*, 1989.

Roth, C., *A History of the Jews in England*, 1941, 3rd edn, 1964.

Rule, M., ed., Eadmer: *Historia Novorum in Anglia*, Rolls Series, 1884.

Rumble, A.R., ed., *The Reign of Cnut*, Leicester, 1994.

Runciman, S., *A History of the Crusades*, 3 vols, 1951.

Saltman, A., *Theobald of Bec, Archbishop of Canterbury*, 1956.

Sawyer, P.H., *Anglo-Saxon Charters: An Annotated List and Bibliography*, Royal Historical Society, 1968.

Sawyer, P.H., *Charters of Burton Abbey*, 1979.

Sawyer, P.H., ed., *Domesday Book: A Reassessment*, 1985.

Searle, E., *Lordship and Community: Battle Abbey and its Banlieu, 1066–1538*, 1974.

Searle, E., ed., *The Chronicle of Battle Abbey*, 1980.

Smyth, A.P., *Scandinavian York and Dublin*, 2 vols, 1975–79.

Southern, R.W., 'Ranulf Flambard and Early Anglo-Norman Administration', *TRHS* xvi, 1933, pp. 95–128 and reprinted in *Medieval Humanism*, 1970.

Southern, R.W., ed., Eadmer: *The Life of St Anselm, Archbishop of Canterbury*, 1962.

Southern, R.W., *Western Views of Islam in the Middle Ages*, 1962.

Southern, R.W., *Saint Anselm and his Biographer*, 1963.

Southern, R.W., *Medieval Humanism*, 1970.

Stafford, P.A., *The East Midlands in the Early Middle Ages*, 1985.

Stafford, P.A., *Unification and Conquest: A Political and Social History of England in the Tenth and Eleventh Centuries*, 1989.

Stanley, E.G., ed., *Continuations and Beginnings*, 1966.

Stenton, D.M., *English Justice between the Norman Conquest and the Great Charter, 1066–1215*, 1965.

Stenton, F.M., *The Early History of the Abbey of Abingdon*, 1913.

Stenton, F.M., *The First Century of English Feudalism*, 1932.

Stenton, F.M., *Anglo-Saxon England*, 1943, 3rd edn, 1971.

Stubbs, W., ed., *Memorials of St Dunstan*, Rolls Series, 1874.

Sullivan, D., *The Westminster Corridor*, 1994.

Symons, Dom. T., ed., *Regularis Concordia*, 1953.

Taylor, H.M. and J., *Anglo-Saxon Architecture*, 3 vols, 1965–78.

Temple, E., *Anglo-Saxon Manuscripts 900–1066*, 1976.

Thompson, S., *Women Religious: The Founding of English Nunneries after the Norman Conquest*, 1991.

Thomson, R.M., ed., *The Life of Gundulf, Bishop of Rochester*, 1977.

Thomson, R.M., 'The Norman Conquest and English Libraries', *The Role of the Book in Medieval Culture II*, ed. P. Ganz, 1986, pp. 27–40.

Treharne, R.F., *The Glastonbury Legends*, 1967.

Ure. J., ed., *The Benedictine Office: An Old English Text*, 1957.

Van Caenegem, R.C., *Royal Writs in England from the Conquest to Glanvill*, Selden Society, 1959.

Von Zupitza, J., ed., *Aelfrics Grammatik und Glossar*, Berlin, 1880.

Warren, W.L., *The Governance of Norman and Angevin England, 1066–1272*, 1987.

Watkiss, L., and Chibnall, M., eds, and trans., *The Waltham Chronicle*, 1994.

Whitelock, D., ed., *Anglo-Saxon Wills*, 1930.

Whitelock, D., 'The Conversion of the Eastern Danelaw', *Saga-Book of the Viking Society*, 12, 1941, pp. 159–76.

Whitelock, D., 'Archbishop Wulfstan, Homilist and Statesman', TRHS 1942, pp. 25–45.

Whitelock, D., *The Beginnings of English Society*, 1952.

Whitelock, D., ed. and trans., *Anglo-Saxon Chronicle*, 1961.

Whitelock, D., ed., *Sermo Lupi ad Anglos*, 1939, 3rd edn, 1963.

Whitelock, D., trans., *The Will of Aethelgifu*, ed. Lord Rennell of Rodd, Roxburghe Club, 1968.

Whitelock, D., *English Historical Documents, c.500–1042*, 1955, 2nd edn, 1979.

Whitelock, D., Brett, M., and Brooke, C.N.L., *Councils and Synods with Other Documents Relating to the English Church, AD 871–1204*, 1981.

William of Malmesbury, *Gesta Regum Anglorum*, 2 vols, ed. and trans. R.A.B. Mynors, R.M. Thomson and M. Winterbottom, 1998–99.

Wilson, D.M., *The Archaeology of Anglo-Saxon England*, 1976.

Wilson, D.M., ed., *The Bayeux Tapestry*, 1985.

Winterbottom, M., ed., *Three Lives of English Saints*, 1972.

Wood, I.N., and Lund. N., eds., *People and Places in Northern Europe 500–1600*, Woodbridge, 1991.

Wormald, C.P., ed., *Ideal and Reality in Frankish and Anglo-Saxon Society*, 1983.

Wormald, C.P., *The Making of English Law: King Alfred to the Twelfth Century*, vol. i, 1999.

Wormald, F., *English Kalendars before 1100*, 1934.

Wormald, F., *English Drawings of the Tenth and Eleventh Centuries*, 1952.

Wormald, F., *The Benedictional of St Aethelwold*, 1959.

Wulfstan, *Die 'Institutes of Polity, Civil and Ecclesiastical': ein Werk Erzbischof Wulfstans von York*, ed. K. Jost, 2 vols, Bern, 1959.

Wulfstan, *Sermo Lupi ad Anglos*, see Whitelock, D.

Yorke, B., ed., *Bishop Aethelwold: His Career and Influence*, Woodbridge, 1988.

Zarnecki, G., Gem, R., and Brooke, C.N.L., *English Romanesque Art 1066–1200*, 1984.

Zulueta, F. de, and Stein, P., *The Teaching of Roman Law in England around 1200*, Selden Society, 1990.

INDEX

Abbey Dore, 135
abbots, 15–17, 20, 22, 28, 50, 58, 64, 67,
   69, 70, 76–82, 91, 95, 101, 104–12,
   119, 130, 135, 150, 153
Abbotsbury, 43
Abingdon, 12, 18–21, 26, 35, 40, 49, 59,
   77, 83, 95, 108
Adela of Blois, 106
Adelard of Bath, monk, 144
Adrian IV, pope (Nicholas Breakspear),
   135, 137
adultery, 27, 150, 151
Aelfgifu, Lady, 36
Aelfgifu of Northampton, 52
Aelfheah, b. of Winchester, archb. of
   Canterbury, St, 8, 11, 12, 36
Aelfhere, ealdorman, 17
Aelfric, abbot of Eynsham, homilist, 25, 26,
   28, 47, 48, 65, 144, 147, 155
Aelfric, abbot of St Albans, b. of Ramsbury,
   archb. of Canterbury, 18n17, 19
Aelfric Puttoc, archb. of York, 50, 50n2,
   54, 55, 59
Aelfric, br. of Odda, 40
Aelfsige, b. of Winchester, archb. elect of
   Canterbury, 5
Aelfsige, abbot of Ramsey, 76
Aelfthryth, queen, 21
Aelfweard, abbot of Evesham, b. of
   London, 49
Aelfwig, monk, 81
Aelfwine, b. of Winchester, 49
Aelfwold, thegn, 17
Aethelgar, abbot of New Minster, 14
Aethelgifu, 152
Aethelhelm, b. of Wells, archb. of
   Canterbury, 11
Aethelmaer of Benington Lordship, 94
Aethelmaer, b. of Elmham, 60, 61, 69
Aethelnoth, archb. of Canterbury, 49, 54
Aethelric, b. of Selsey, b. of Chichester, 69,
   99

Aethelric, b. of Dorchester, 151
Aethelthryth, abbess of Nunnaminster, 14
Aethelweard, chronicler, 53
Aethelwig, abbot of Evesham, 77, 80, 100
Aethelwine, b. of Durham, 69
Aethelwold, St, abbot of Abingdon, b. of
   Winchester, 1, 9, 10, 12–21, 26, 28, 77,
   154
Aethelwulf (Aldulf), b. of Carlisle, 112
Ailsworth, 20
Alberic of Ostia, 131, 133
Aldenham, 100
Aldulf, abbot, b. of Worcester, archb. of
   York, 20
Aldwin, prior of Winchcombe, 81
Alexander II, pope, 69, 71, 75, 98
Alexander, b. of Lincoln, 125, 126
Alfred, k., 1, 2, 9, 24, 29, 48
Alfred, s. of k. Ethelred, 52
alms, 8, 27, 150, 151
Alsace, 81
Alwine, merchant, 80
Amalarius of Metz, 13
Ambrose, St, 41
Amesbury, 21
Amiens, 107
anarchy, 123
Andover, 129
Angevins, 124, 128–30, 130n10, 132, 134,
   137
Anglo-Saxon Chronicle, 13, 24, 52, 64, 85,
   105, 107, 108, 118, 124
Anglo-Saxon(s) (*see also* vernacular), 14, 35,
   39, 41, 43, 62, 68, 71, 76–82, 88, 90,
   93, 96, 97, 107, 116, 118, 119, 135,
   140–4, 150–4: myth and legend, 73, 82,
   142
Anschil of Ware, 94
Anselm, abbot of Bec, archb. of
   Canterbury, 68, 86, 103–8, 112, 114,
   120, 121, 128, 139, 145–7, 149
archaeology, 14, 35, 37, 39, 50, 123, 152